Henry Drummond:
AN ANTHOLOGY

From a photograph by Lafayette Ltd.

HENRY DRUMMOND AT THE AGE OF THIRTY-SEVEN

"The distinctive and commanding feature of his face were his eyes. No photograph could do them justice and very often photographs had done them injustice, by giving the idea of staringness. His eyes were not bold or fierce; they were tender and merciful. But they had a power and hold which were little else than irresistible and almost supernatural. When you talked with Drummond, he did not look at you and out of the window alternately, as is the usual manner; he never moved his eyes, and gradually their penetrating gaze seemed to reach and encompass your soul. No man could be double, or base, or mean, or impure before those eyes."—JOHN WATSON

Henry Drummond:

AN ANTHOLOGY

Edited, and with the story of his life by

JAMES W. KENNEDY

INTRODUCTION BY SAMUEL M. SHOEMAKER

Harper & Brothers · *Publishers* · *New York*

Library of Congress catalog card number: 52-10673

To My Mother

❦

In the Words of St. Paul—II Corinthians 5:17, 19:

> Therefore if any man be in Christ,
> he is a new creature. . . . God was in
> Christ, reconciling the world unto
> himself, not imputing their trespasses
> unto them; and hath committed unto
> us the word of reconciliation.

Contents

PART III. HIS METHODS

Introduction

THE tens of thousands of readers of *The Greatest Thing in the World*, which is Henry Drummond's best-known writing, must often ask themselves who this man was, with his clear insights and his delicate pen and his winning method of presenting the truth. Others, like myself, who have been profoundly moved and influenced by some of his other writings also, have often wished that the best of his thought might be made available for present-day readers. Many of his writings are now out of print, and I have waited for months to to get hold of a copy of *The New Evangelism*.

It fell to the happy lot of my good friend James W. Kennedy to undertake the assembling of those writings which represent the heart of Henry Drummond's thought, cut them down to essentials, add to them some explanatory material, and give them to the world inside the covers of one book. To my mind, he has done an excellent piece of work, and one which will put many in his debt for long years to come.

Henry Drummond reached out in two important directions. He had a mind steeped and trained in the scientific approach and method, which must come at religion in an empirical and experimental fashion—this makes him kin to nearly all educated men and women today. He also had a spirit attuned to God and to life's higher harmonies, and a great capacity to make spiritual things clear, reasonable and attractive—and this ought to make him kin to all in any age who would pierce behind phenomena to meanings. He stood on a border, between the lands of science and of religion. There has been much war across that border—some of it perhaps inevitable when either side claimed too much. Henry Drummond stood on that

9

border, not as a storm-center, but as a reconciler, as a peace-maker. He felt the two lands were different, but not enemies. He felt called to interpret one to the other. In seeing for himself, and helping to effect for others, this reconciliation between science and religion, seeing them as two sides of God's Creation, he was helped by the clarity of his mind and by the humility of his intellectual temper. Some of the controversies then raging have passed into history; but the insights with which he "waged peace" between the two are ageless and abiding. Some of the thought and some of the sentences in this book are so timeless that they might have been written yesterday. I would commend this volume, therefore, to all who need or want help in their thinking about the whole subject of science and religion.

I would commend the book, also, very especially to those who are seeking effective ways by which to commend the Christian Gospel to men's minds and hearts and wills. No man ever knew better the inner nature and quality of true, intelligent, heart-warming evangelism than did Henry Drummond. His was not the talent of his great friend and collaborator, Dwight L. Moody, to sway and move thousands in vast assemblies; but to speak in smaller companies, and still more often with one individual, about Christ and His message for man. A young Christian minister today, if he would have spiritual power both in his preaching and in personal dealing, could do no better than to master the innermost thoughts and perceptions of Henry Drummond. No man perhaps ever knew the human heart better than he. It is astonishing, I think, with what comprehension this man could observe some fact of nature, and then some turn of human nature, understanding them both with sympathy and insight. He knew the human heart as à Kempis and Fénelon and Pascal knew it. Indeed I have sometimes thought of him as a kind of Protestant Pascal.

So great was his contribution to "placing the study of the soul on a scientific basis" that a distinguished psychiatrist once told me he had been one of the influential pioneers in the whole field of psychotherapy.

As I go on in the ministry, I find his insight and phrases coming back to me again and again. He had the thought I need, and it could not be said better. The knowledge of the human heart contained in *Spiritual Diagnosis*, written—mind you—when he was only twenty-two, has never, I believe, been superseded. Henry Drummond is a "must" for men who would deal with human souls in the light of the accumulated wisdom of the new science of psychology, but with the purpose of leading them into the unfading Light of the everlasting Christ.

May this book find the mind and heart of many who want to come out at the destination of faith in God and in His revelation of Himself in Jesus Christ, but who must take a scientific and reasonable approach to arrive there. I think that would be Henry Drummond's own wish for the book, were he here to express it.

SAMUEL M. SHOEMAKER

Foreword

A YOUNG professor of natural science in Free Church College, Glasgow, Scotland, who was trained for the ministry, on whom the theologians frowned and whom the scientists ignored, changed the spiritual climate of his half-century.

Henry Drummond lived when the theories of Darwin were hot in men's minds, when the first stirrings of Biblical criticism were reaching the people, when the voices of Moody and Sankey were still heard in the land. Drummond spoke in this time of ferment with words fashioned to fit the doubts, fears and confusions of religious people.

But are not the words and days of that era totally dispossessed by our advanced scientific knowledge and our "modern" theological positions? Drummond reached the ears of his generation, but will not his words fall on ears deafened to these issues today?

I feel that the answer is "No" to both questions.

Just as the confusion of his day centered in the tensions between theology and science, so today the Christian religion must speak to a scientific age and, as Einstein said, convince it that "religion without science is blind; [that] science without religion is lame." There is no date line on the theme that God's laws govern both the material and the spiritual, that His kingdom is not divided.

The intelligent man, once he begins to think about religion and life, comes to the same questions: Does the Bible, God's word to man, have the final answers to the fundamental problems of existence? Does it tell us where we came from, why we are here, and where we are going?

The feeble and futile efforts of man on his own to change the world

13

are still apparent and need the voice of a Drummond to awaken and release the full potential power of man's spirit which comes when God through Christ is encountered. And yet neither Drummond's science nor his theology, both mainly intuitive and poetical, fits perfectly the needs of this generation. Both *Natural Law in the Spiritual World*, published in 1883 (the most widely read religious book in the world in its day), and *The Ascent of Man*, published in 1894, can be left in forgotten corners of libraries or dingy booksellers' shops—even though they both contain metaphors and analogies, still valid, which give fresh insight into many aspects of the Christian religion.

What is it, then, that makes Henry Drummond—what he did and wrote and was—of importance to this modern age, so far removed from the last quarter of the nineteenth century? Primarily, his vital and practical grasp of the Spirit of the living Christ as immediately possessible for men's lives. Christ, whom men saw in him and caught through him, is still the answer to the almost incredible spiritual hunger and longing in the hearts and minds of men today. Drummond made available a working reality of the Christian faith in the everyday lives of men, and helped to banish doubt and to straighten out twisted thinking and twisted relationships.

The process of Redemption is the same now as then and neither science nor theology can help much in the *initial* stages of man's struggle within himself to find a solid piece of ground on which to stand securely. Henry Drummond profoundly influenced the lives of countless thousands in his day by introducing them to Christ; he saved them from the dry rot of futile assent to the lifeless bones of doctrines which did little to affect their lives, and from succumbing to doubts engendered by Darwin's theories. He helped them throw out the bath water without also casting out the baby.

From a privileged background Drummond went into the slums of Edinburgh Cowgate and Cannongate and into the luxurious homes of lords and dukes; and he was equally effective and loved in both atmospheres. Remarkably free from sin in its grosser forms, he heard the confessed sins of thousands and led them to new life. That was ever his theme, *life*, man's God-given treasure which many wasted and tossed lightly aside. His major passion was for men's lives to be given over to the direction of the only One who could really master them and lead them into their destined fulfillment, even Jesus Christ.

One hundred and one years ago he was born. Over fifty years ago he died, still so young. And yet on a recent pilgrimage to Scotland I felt his presence in the Oddfellows Hall on Forrest Road, the Henry Drummond Parish Church in Possilpark, Glasgow, the old classroom and museum at Trinity College (the Free Church College, Glasgow, where he taught). I sought the remains of Henry Drummond in dusty books and yellowed papers, in buildings and monuments. I traced down his old lodgings and his places of public utterance. I handled the neat pages of script written in his own hand—the carefully penciled notes and rough drafts of talks and addresses, the meticulously corrected manuscripts and galleys; letters from the jungles of Africa, from beside the rapidly flowing salmon streams of Canada, from the university town of Tübingen, Germany, from the graveyard at Yale University, from the hospitable guest places of Haddo House and Dollis Hill, from his own homes at Glenelm Lodge and 3 Park Circus, and from hotel rooms. I have "watched" his mind create and revise sermons and meditations and handled the first rough drafts of what later became books. I have reread his jottings in the Bible he used during the Moody mission days and the Possilpark years. But I found Henry Drummond elusive. He was everywhere I went, not in the books or the places or the writings, but primarily in memories of the few who remain who knew him during the last days of his rare life—like Lord Aberdeen and members of the second and third generations of his family and dear friends who remember and feel his presence and influence still—who handed down the precious tales told and who passed on the printed testimonies. He is not forgotten. His spirit still pervades the atmosphere of Haddo House, Possilpark, and a thousand other places and persons touched by him and his word. A niece wrote that her Uncle Henry's life was "the full flowering of several generations of people to whom Christ and God were much more important than anything else."

I read where Drummond died in Tunbridge Wells on March 11, 1897, and yet I found that his bright life, so rudely cut short, remains.

I went in pursuit of the man and found him, and discovered the richness of his testimony left to any generation that dares to remember. I discovered that life but how hard it is to contain a man like Henry Drummond within the pages of a book. He cannot be contained in a book, but as one reads about him and absorbs his life and message, one begins to feel why those who knew him best could say that he was the most Christlike man they had ever known. He has left us the pattern and content for the successful approach of one Christian to another, both of which lie ready for anyone who would use them for penetrating the blindness and stubbornness of men's wills, or men's ignorance, or men's helplessness and honest doubt.

Henry Drummond speaks again to those who listen to his voice and try to live by the message he spoke and exemplified.

JAMES W. KENNEDY

Henry Drummond:
AN ANTHOLOGY

Part I

A GLIMPSE OF THE MAN

1

1851-1873—Preparation for Growing

HENRY DRUMMOND was born one hundred years ago in Stirling, Scotland. King's Park lay directly in front of his home; and across the green fields, perched high upon its mighty rock, the historic castle surveyed the countryside for miles around. Soon after Henry's birth his father built a large new house next door to the old one on Park Place and named it Glenelm Lodge. Here Henry's boyhood was spent.

From a small tower in his new home he could look over the rock ridge, which blocked off the view lower down, across the wild wide expanse of the Park to the dim outline of the old castle. He could dream to life the bloody battles of Scotland's past fought out in that very place, within the castle walls, on the field of Bannockburn where Wallace and Bruce asserted the freedom of the Scottish nation.

When the day was free of mist he could see Ben Lomond, Ben Ledi and the hills around the Trossachs, blue in the distance.

His vivid imagination thrived in this environment. He was constantly exploring the caves and woods and sand wreaths in the remote parts of King's Park. Nature in all its glory lay at his very doorstep and his observant eye grew keen as he investigated rocks and streams and growing things; and he learned to love the out-of-doors, especially this part of his native land, "with its thick lichen growth of history." He excelled in almost every kind of sport from cricket to angling—the latter his special hobby.

Henry's entire life was influenced by these early years surrounded as they were with the evidences of God's handiwork in nature and the romantic atmosphere of Scotland's history. In addition he was set in the midst of a happy and affectionate home life. His two brothers and two sisters helped to keep things moving. His father and mother, who were deeply religious yet never pious, guided their relationships. Family life was never a solemn affair for the Drummonds but one filled with games, devices and notions of all sorts, and often they went "gipsying" into the woods on family picnics.

Henry's father was a seedsman and he tended carefully the "seedlings" he had planted in his own "garden," nourishing his children on love and a wholesome concern for the kingdom of God. From his father, who conducted the Sunday school at the little community of· Cambusbarron about half a mile down the lane from Glenelm Lodge, he learned to respect religious truth. From his Uncle Peter Drummond, who printed and distributed religious tracts, young Henry learned to respect religious work. From his Uncle James Blackwood of Gillsburn his eager mind learned some of the vocabulary and paraphernalia of science. Very early indeed, Henry stored up a love for both religion and science which grew to full maturity through the years, preparing the way for his great contribution to his age.

Henry's school days were spent first at Morison's Academy in Crieff, not far away in the lovely Perthshire hills, then at Stirling High School on Spittal Street, half way up the Rock toward the Castle. His bright and merry disposition made his presence a joy to both his family and his school companions. Only one slight shadow crossed these boyhood years—he was a small lad and feared he would never grow very much taller. Even at age fifteen, when he matriculated at the University of Edinburgh, Henry was still slight and boyish, much too youthful looking for a "college man."

School subjects never did stir Henry quite so much as living people and intimate contacts with nature; nor did the usual college curriculum he found at the University excite him. Academically he was an average student. Only one course brought forth more than routine interest—Natural Philosophy. This subject struck fire and inspired him, and he fed this newly awakened zeal for science with much extra reading. But his most interesting hours were spent in extracurricular activities.

His membership in the Philomathic Debating Society, which Society still flourishes, helped develop his latent powers for writing and speaking. He also developed a passion for reading general literature, beyond the requirements of the classroom. He read far more than any of his fellow students. Robert Louis Stevenson was one of these fellow students and he, like Drummond, was undistinguished in his college career, and he too rebelled against the traditional and the commonplace. However, their paths apparently never crossed then or later.

One can imagine Drummond browsing at the open air Book Hunter's stall of John Grant's on George IV Bridge backing on Candlemaker Row, picking up second hand some of the miscellaneous volumes of his first library. His book rack gradually filled and became crowded with such diverse authors as Ruskin (who taught him to see with his eyes), Emerson (who taught him to see with his mind), George Eliot (who opened his eyes to the meaning of life), Channing (who taught him reverence and to believe in God as a moral being), Robertson of Brighton (who gave him his first glimpse of liberty in the intellectual life), and many others, from Browning and Lamb to Lowell and Twain. All of them in some way influenced his thinking and his writing. Drummond once noted trenchantly, "The thing sought is not what you will get in an author, but what the author will enable you to find in yourself."

Henry had few intimate friends during his four years at the University, although those who knew him best testified to his extraordinary faculty for putting himself *en rapport* with others, gaining their confidence and quickly drawing them out of themselves. Everyone liked him but very few knew him well.

Contrary to his expectations, Henry "shot up into a tall man, graceful when at rest, and moving with a litheness and a spring that were all his own." He also developed a carefulness in dress to the point of fastidiousness, which earned him the title, "The Prince."

Henry Drummond finished his University course in the spring of 1870 with no definite plans for the future. His father wanted him to enter the ministry of the Free Church of Scotland. This meant entering New College in the fall. Drummond felt within himself a real though vague "call" to the direct service of God, even though God had not yet made it clear what form that "call" should take. On his nineteenth birthday, while reflecting seriously on what he could render God for His great gifts to him (he does not enumerate them), he experienced a religious crisis as near a "conversion" as anything recorded in his life. He notes his experience in his diary, the climax of which was that he was "led" to enter New College and prepare for the ministry. So, after a good vacation, with a study of Hebrew on his own, he passed the ordeal of entrance examinations before the stern-faced Presbytery and matriculated as a regular divinity student on November 17, 1870.

New College, like the University, failed to arouse his zeal over the normal pursuits of the academic side of the theological student's life. But still, as usual, Henry did sufficiently well in his studies: Hebrew, Apologetics, the Old Testament—the lectures on Higher Criticism of the Pentateuch giving him his first taste of the battle to be fought over "Revelation"; New Testament, Exegesis, Systematic Theology and Church History. His greatest interest, however, was manifested in the Natural Science course at the College and the extra work he took in the same field at the University. He could not leave science alone. At this point the dual role he was to play began taking shape—pursuing science and religion side by side, finally harnessing the power and appeal of both to serve his generation. When the Chair of Geology was founded at the University in 1871, Drummond was the first enrolled student of its first professor, Archibald Geikie. He won the class medal in this subject and "Geikie found in him not merely an apt pupil but a geologist of rare talent that just fell short of genius." He also won first prize in Natural Science at the College. The papers written for his courses show his interest in and knowledge of Darwin's theory of evolution and indicate the trend of his thinking toward the full acceptance of it.

In addition to his courses, both at the College and at the University, Henry worked under the College Missionary Society. He taught a Sabbath-school class in the neighborhood of Cowgate—both geographically and socially the very lowest part of old Edinburgh— and visited the poor families in Covenant Close. He also participated in the meetings of the Theological Society and contributed his share of papers.

So for three years Drummond spent his time preparing for the ministry and pursuing scientific knowledge, not at all sure just what his true "call" was.

In the spring of 1873 Drummond decided to spend a summer term at the ancient University of Tübingen, Germany, which was quite the thing for the divinity students of his day to do. After the chill of a Scottish winter the warmth of this southern clime had an immense appeal. Henry apparently enjoyed the good fellowship of the student life more than he benefited from the scholarly lectures; he impressed the students far more than he did the professors. But he was still uncertain about the future and during his stay abroad he resolved to postpone his fourth and final year at New College and to give a year or two to the more earnest study of Natural Science and to some regular mission work. His brief experience in Cowgate stimulated this latter desire and Geikie's influence undoubtedly led to the former.

Upon his return to Edinburgh Drummond took charge of the humble Riego Street Mission Hall, located in a dog-leg alley. Free St. Cuthbert's Church, not far away under Castle Rock, had established this mission in 1862. Here, before a dozen people, Henry began his first halting words as an evangelist.

His plans for study did not materialize, for he was soon caught up to a higher platform, much more exciting than routine study or work in a small mission, which gave him the first real proof of his extraordinary influence and power among men.

At the first meeting of the Theological Society in November (1873) Drummond, who had retained the presidency, read an essay on "Spiritual Diagnosis—an argument for Placing the Study of the Soul on a Scientific Basis." The excellence of the paper showed how long he had been thinking on its contents and how deeply convinced he was of this lack in the Church's life. He had barely begun his tentative experimenting with "spiritual science" in his little mission, so his startling proposal was almost entirely theoretical.

It was a remarkable coincidence that at almost the same time Samuel Butler, in the shabby seclusion of Clifford's Inn (London), was writing The Way of All Flesh and expressing the same conclusions through one of his characters: "You know, my dear Pontifex, it is all very well to quarrel with Rome, but Rome has reduced the treatment of the human soul to a science, while our own Church [the Church of England], though so much purer in many respects, has no organized system either of diagnosis or pathology—I mean, of course, spiritual diagnosis and spiritual pathology. . . . The history of the ages has shown . . . that as men cannot cure the bodies of their patients if they have not been properly trained in hospitals under skilled teachers, so neither can souls be cured of their hidden ailments without the help of men who are skilled in soul craft. . . ."[1]

The "Great Mission" of Moody and Sankey to Scotland opened in Edinburgh on Sunday, November 23, 1873. Through it, Henry Drummond, barely twenty-two years of age, with practically no experience of religious work among adults, had the opportunity of taking his remarkable presentation of a theoretical technique of personal evangelism and testing it thoroughly under the most rigorous conditions. Moody won him to this work by his sincere and practical concern for translating sermonic utterance into living reality. From the cloistered life of the student Henry Drummond was thrust into the arena where he was forced to deal at first hand with the rude, raw conditions of

[1] Donald Carswell, Brother Scots (London: Constable and Company, Ltd., 1927), p. 10.

sinful life. His theory stood up and became his guide thereafter for personal dealing with men. Under the pressure of the Great Mission he crowded a lifetime of practical religious work into two short years. Henry grew up, found the full measure of his talent, and heard the first unmistakable sound of his "call."

2

1873-1877—Experience with Life

THE Moody and Sankey "invasion" of Scotland began quietly and inauspiciously in the Barclay Free Church, Edinburgh. Though interest was slow in coming, by Christmas the tide of popularity had risen sharply and all the leading churches were co-operating, including the Episcopalians. On all sides the fire of revival spread and began to consume the sins of Scotland. Hundreds were converted and added to the churches. Thousands of dormant church members were led to a renewal of their Christian faith. For twenty months those two Americans—Moody and Sankey—won Scotsmen for Christ. Henry Drummond was with them through it all.

The success of Moody and Sankey was not accidental. The atmosphere of Scotland had always been heavily charged with religion and this was especially true in the middle of the last half of the nineteenth century. But the people were bottled up in their religious life by stuffy, heavy, theological discourses, which dulled the life-giving spirit of the Gospel of Christ. Moody's simple, sincere, practical religious insights reached into men's hearts and stirred them. There was no sensationalism nor rabble-rousing, so typical of lesser revivals, but the sane, inescapable reality of Christ's words.

The churches of Scotland were ripe for an a wakening.[1] Moody and

---

[1] This awakening was especially needed by the Free Church of Scotland to which Henry Drummond belonged. In 1843 the Free Church had "disrupted" the Established Church (Presbyterian) by breaking away, chiefly because of what some considered the interference of the state in the appointment of local

Sankey arrived at exactly the right moment and moved rapidly to the forefront to win both the ordinary Scotsman and the intellectual, the careless and formal church members as well as those who never went to church.

Moody's sincerity, practical wisdom and effective dealing with people appealed to the eager young Drummond, who recognized him as a man with a purpose, whose life was utterly consecrated and Christ-centered, and who was practicing the very things Drummond himself had advocated in "Spiritual Diagnosis."

During these arduous yet extremely stimulating days Drummond ripened into spiritual maturity and became one of Moody's most effective workers. He was especially good in the "inquiry room," which Moody provided after every meeting for those who wished to discuss religion further and to take steps toward living a new life in Christ. Drummond was also Moody's chief aid in conducting follow-up meetings for young men as an aftermath to the great evangelist's visit to a town or city. In Moody's school of life Drummond found his theories worked. In this new spiritual adventure he learned to deal with people of all kinds, presenting the facts of Christianity to them and leading them from the muok of their former existence to the solid reality of a new faith in Christ. Adept at fly-fishing from boyhood, he

---

ministers to congregations and other "spiritual" (rather than temporal) matters. They believed in the "spirituality and freedom of the Church under the sole headship of the Lord Jesus Christ." This was a courageous act for it meant leaving the security of settled "livings" for the clergy and handsome church buildings for the people. But the decision was made and almost every congregation was split, with the "free" group moving out and building costly churches as close to the "state" churches as possible. They also established colleges for educating their own clergy, academically as well as theologically. New College, Edinburgh, for example, was built by the Free Church in 1846. The established church maintained their training centers within the framework of the universities. The first few years were filled with enthusiasm and power under such great leaders as Chalmers and Cunningham, Brewster and Miller. But gradually these early years of stimulation and zeal passed, leaving the preachers stranded on the barren shore of Calvinistic discourse spiced with the abuse of Establishmentarianism. The Free Church was ready for a spiritual revival and literally "grabbed" at the fresh message of Moody for bringing life back into her congregations. She co-operated wholeheartedly with the "Great Mission," furnishing many of the meeting places, much of the machinery and a large supply of man power, especially young men from her colleges.

found "fishing for men" the most satisfying experience of his life, and he became as expert in the one as he had been in the other. He chose the appropriate bait, plied his line with infinite skill and resourceful ingenuity, and seldom failed to catch his man. "The fish, ancient symbol of mystery and divinity, dweller in that element that is at once life and death, shining, swift and subtle, that was Drummond's image of the soul." While Moody swayed masses, Drummond won individuals. Moody was a wonderful teacher and one of the most potent and lasting influences on Henry's life. It was not until later, however, that Drummond began to develop the style that was peculiarly his own—a rare combination of Moody's inquiry-room technique combined with the reasonable, sensible atmosphere of the scientific classroom.

During this interlude of itinerant evangelizing, from one end of Scotland to the other, Drummond composed for platform delivery the first drafts of most of the discourses which made him famous in later years, and found the poised and calm assurance which marked all his public appearances.

One mystery remains: how Drummond could ever have been happy in the large bare "Halls" so often used by Moody, when his own personal tastes were satisfied with only the finest, as evidenced by his careful selection of gifts on special occasions. The only answer which fits: the reality of Moody's presentation of the Gospel overcame Drummond's need for visible beauty.

Since the Bible was the textbook in Moody's school and the source-book for the Gospel he taught, a great deal of time was spent in Bible reading and study. In a letter to his father, June 23, 1875, Henry wrote: "Am to have the privilege of joining Moody and three others in a series of Bible studies every morning for a full two hours. You must know how much I stand in need of teaching, with so much preoccupation, and so much attempt to teach others." Moody opened to Drummond the riches of the Bible and made him expert in its use.

The Bible he used all through the Great Mission and for several years after, contains many marginal notes, terse comments on meanings of texts, outlines for addresses, quotations from favorite authors suggested by the passage, and underscorings of the part which struck him at the moment. Often single words were outlined in ink which called attention at once to the significant word or phrase. The Psalms, Ecclesiastes, Isaiah and Jeremiah were the most extensively marked books in the Old Testament; while John's Gospel was the most used book in the New Testament. Clues to almost all the ideas hammered home in his later writings can be found etched in the wide margins of this Bible, although strangely enough, the insights into chapter thirteen of I Corinthians, which appear in his best-known writing, are not indicated.

The Great Mission ran its flaming course and finally came to an end. Moody wanted Drummond to go to America with him as a permanent member of his "team." Drummond was tempted, for his "call" seemed strongly in this direction. He had found joy and success in firsthand contact with people and in seeing them begin to live again; and he felt much more could be accomplished with Moody than in any other type of ministry. However, an incident changed the direction of his going.

"Barbour Land," in the north of Perthshire among the lovely Highland hills, was one of the great centers of evangelism, philanthropy and missions in Scotland for more than a generation. George Freeland Barbour had made a fortune in cotton in Manchester and retired at thirty-five to Bonskeid House in the Valley of Tummel, which was the focal point of life on the large estate. Henry Drummond met Robert, one of the brilliant Barbour sons, in the early days of the Moody Mission and they became inseparable friends.

One Sunday morning, while visiting at Bonskeid House, Henry sat on the front steps with Mrs. Barbour and talked of his future. The River Tummel rushed below them; the Lower Grampians rose in front of them. Henry, so alive in every fiber to nature in her multitudinous forms, was also aware of Mrs. Barbour's words as she warned him against the dangers of becoming a professional evangelist and urged him to finish school.

Later, on the same visit, he stumbled over a stone and wrenched his knee as he walked under the shelter of the silver birch trees from Bonskeid House to the road fork where Glen Fincastle began. He had time to think over Mrs. Barbour's advice during the two weeks' enforced rest while recovering from his accident. The uncertainty about his future course was resolved and the decision made to give up the idea of a professional evangelist's career and to return to New College. He wrote his friend Robert Barbour about it. "I should rather like to make a pilgrimage to that stone at Bonskeid. Sometimes I think I owe more to it than I know. Perhaps if it had not been for that stone I should not be at college this winter. That stone! I wish it had been anything else but a stone. A wheelbarrow would almost have been as poetical."

So, on November 16, 1875, Henry Drummond matriculated at New College for his fourth and last year. But he did not forget his experiences with Moody nor did he grow rusty in his newly learned techniques of evangelism. In order to keep them fresh he, along with the other men in New College who had worked with Moody, rented the small Gaiety Theater on lower Chambers Street across from the old quadrangle of the University. They held meetings every Sunday evening for the purpose of training their fellow students in the art of showing another person the way to a new Christian life. This small hall of entertainment on week nights became a busy meeting place for worship on Sundays. Those who labored together that winter organized the "Gaiety Club" which met once a year thereafter.[2]

The year went quickly. Drummond completed his theological course and passed his exit examinations. He spent the summer partly on holiday and partly in short courses of evangelistic work. But he was not happy. Indeed he was "most miserable"—not yet seeing what definite work he could do to earn his bread and yet get time to preach the kingdom. He was still not sure of his "call" to the full-time ministry.

Toward the end of the year (1876) he accepted an assistantship at the Barclay Free Church, so closely associated with his Moody experi-

[2] Composed of James Stalker, Alexander Skene, James Brown, John Watson (Ian MacLaren), David Morison Ross, Frank Gordon (Ralph Connor), George Adam Smith, John F. Ewing, Robert W. Barbour and Henry Drummond.

ence, where he spent the rest of the winter. He lived at 6 Lonsdale Terrace, close to his work and facing the beautiful park—"The Meadows"—which skirted the university campus. The majority of the addresses given during his brief stay at Barclay Church were published later in *The Ideal Life*. One of these, "On the Will of God," was personally significant. The chains of indecision were about to drop off forever, and he was soon to know God's will for his own life. However, an entire summer of uncertainty lay ahead, which he spent restlessly in spurts of mission work here and there, and a trip to Norway with Robert Barbour. At summer's end he was more or less resigned to the work of the regular ministry and returned, ready to be examined for his license to preach. Almost by chance he noticed the vacancy in the lectureship on Natural Science at the Free Church College in Glasgow. He applied on sudden inspiration and got the job, mainly, he thought, on the strength of Professor Geikie's recommendation.

This lectureship was "founded to take the sting out of science, and, if need be, of fighting it in the name of religion." Drummond gave a broad interpretation to the outline laid down for his course. From the beginning he taught his students at least not to fear science, and if they could not get a complete reconciliation, meanwhile, they must work with broad, flexible hypotheses, which would keep their minds from narrowing and hardening. He helped to answer the many vexed questions of the interrelation of science and religion; but best of all for Drummond, he had found his life work. The "call" had sounded clear and loud at last, like one stroke of a giant bell.

3

1877-1883—The Settling Down Process

THE new lecturer in Natural Science took up his work with enthusiasm born of assurance. All the first-year men were in his class, and a bond of sympathy between teacher and pupils was evident from the beginning. The roll was called every day, but there was little need for it, as attendance was almost perfect. It was customary for all classes at the College to open each session with prayer. Drummond observed this practice on the first day of the term only, probably for fear the students would think it overly pious ("cant") to do so at each time of meeting.

His addresses were always on science with but infrequent allusions to the Bible. Fine good humor pervaded his classroom and he often made puns on current events. His famous "stupidity examination," given at the beginning of each year, revealed to the student how little he really knew about the most commonplace realities of God's world, and also how unusual this teacher and course were going to be.

During the year the students gained certain information about geology, botany and zoology. But more important than this, they also acquired the scientific bent, and learned that science "is knowledge in its relations," that "science stretches the imagination and helps put the world in its place in the cosmos." He was more anxious to secure for his students an enlargement of their horizon than to have them learn difficult names of strata or orders.

Occasionally, to vary his classroom procedure, he read from some classic, or from a new author to test the quality of his book. He made frequent use of the blackboard and was skilled in drawing large, almost perfect circles at one stroke of the crayon—this special display would often bring forth a burst of applause from the class. At the end of the term he gave fine books as awards to the two making the highest marks on the final examination. A few of the old benches from his lecture room are still in use and bear the scars of the years. But no carving will be found dating back to Drummond's time—his classes were never boring. His lectures were enlivened by demonstrations and exhibits in his museum, the contents of which only one very shabby crocodile remains today.

At the end of his "trial" year Drummond was appointed for another session of the lectureship by the General Assembly meeting that year (1878) in Glasgow.

The most important, disturbing, and far-reaching business brought before that Assembly, however, was the consideration of the "relevancy" of the charges of "heresy" brought against Professor W. Robertson Smith, one of the leading scholars of his day and professor of Old Testament at the Free Church College in Aberdeen. His statement on the non-Mosaic authorship of Deuteronomy had just been published in the *Encyclopedia Britannica*. The new Biblical scholarship had been presented frequently and openly for several years in theological classrooms and societies, but now the subject was brought into the open arena for the world to inspect and "judge."

The determined orthodox position of the Free Church, which had been encased in an iron shroud of dogma, contrary to its name, was beginning to yield. The bitter struggle between orthodoxy—meaning then the literal inspiration and divine revelation of the Scriptures—and Biblical criticism—that is, the scientific study of the Bible under the stimulus of Darwin's recently published theory of evolution (1859)—had begun.

The Free Church was hopelessly out of harmony with the growing liberalism of the age. She was undergoing a process of intellectual starvation, and her days of influence were waning. The acceptance of the "literal inspiration" of Holy Scripture left no room for the critical appraisal of many parts of the Bible which some scholars had long suspected were quite human in production; and many had been pursuing "dangerous thoughts" to account for these fallacies and contradictions. Smith was the first one to air his views publicly. The airing of this controversy, bringing all the facts out in the open, prepared the general public for the new view of the Bible more quickly than could have been foreseen. Although Smith's views were voted down by the Assembly, they gave form and a new discrimination to inquiring minds, so that many puzzling difficulties were removed, especially from the Old Testament.

Drummond's thinking was affected by this trial, and while, at the time, he had not gone as far as Smith, his mind was set free for the fuller appreciation of the divine content of the Old Testament. The core of this early controversy was the doctrine of creation—the version in Genesis against Darwin's theory of evolutionary development. "Drummond's scientific training had given him a sense of facts, an appreciation of evidence; while his strong and cheerful faith in God saved him from the confusion into which so complete a revolution in his views of the methods of inspiration must otherwise be cast."[1]

During the first year of his lectureship Drummond was too busy preparing his lectures and keeping one jump ahead of his students to take on any outside work, although only four lectures a week for five months were required. The thoroughness with which Drummond prepared for his work nevertheless made the winter a strenuous and confining one for him. He was glad to take charge of the Free Church preaching station at Malta as chaplain when school was out. He had a restful summer and made his first acquaintance with the sunny Mediterranean.

At the beginning of the second year at the College, with his status more secure and with his lectures well in hand, Drummond took over a full-time mission congregation in Possilpark, a suburb of Glasgow. As this new settlement among the mines and foundries grew, a mission of the Free Church had been opened in August, 1877, with meetings held in a hired shop. On May 19, 1878, the congregation

[1] George Adam Smith, *The Life of Henry Drummond*, (New York: Doubleday and McClure Co., 1898), p. 141.

moved into a new metal hut in Allendar Street at the center of the housing development, across from its present location. The mission was placed under the Renfield Free Church of Glasgow, Dr. Marcus Dods, pastor, and Drummond was called there June 20, 1878 upon Dr. Dods' recommendation.

With his science lectureship well established and his mission work in full swing Drummond was busy, happy, and at home. He gave all his time to these two tasks. He held both his students and his parishioners by sharing with them the absorbing adventure of making the two great fields of science and religion more at harmony with each other. He appealed equally to the intellectual and the average man, for he had answers which gave some semblance of order and security to a generation stirred and shaken by the threats and possibilities of Darwin's theory. Drummond was beginning to see the resemblances between the laws of nature and those of the spiritual world and to discern the hand of God in both. He was making clear that truth is of God and will never lead man astray no matter how far it advances from any "present" set of beliefs.

His father was sometimes afraid that the versatility which characterized his son was not compatible with perseverance and doing some one thing well. But he soon found out that Henry could do a solid, consistent, continuous piece of work, demonstrated by the growth of the Possilpark mission.

Several important developments took place in Drummond's life in these four years of combined teaching and missionary activity.

For one thing Marcus Dods came into his life as another mighty influence, alongside Geikie, Moody and the Barbours. Dr. Dods, the pastor of the Renfield Church and under whom Drummond worked, helped repair the defects in his young assistant's education. Dods' wealth of knowledge of literature and his excellent grasp of philosophy helped to mold Drummond's thinking, especially in the field of Biblical criticism and the application of the hypothesis of evolution to the interpretation of religion. Hardly a Saturday passed when they did not take a long walk together, usually in the country, talking as they walked. Henry probably owed more to him than to any other man. As a member of Renfield Church, as an associate worker, as a friend, Drummond sought Dods as his constant intimate. Drummond said, "Dr. Dods discovered me . . . he is a friend and older brother . . . the greatest influence in many directions that has come across my life."

Another major event of the Possilpark years was his first trip to America. In the summer of 1879 he went with Professor Archibald Geikie on a geological expedition to the Rocky Mountains. Geikie never lost track of his first student and one of his best in geology. His recommendation had clinched matters for Drummond's lectureship. Geikie's influence helped keep Drummond balanced. Living and "geologizing" with Geikie these months increased his working capital of science and gave both a stimulus and a set to his ideas on the relationship between science and religion which jelled as he gave them forth upon his return, both in the classroom and from the pulpit at Possilpark.

One incident on this trip is worth recording. As he prepared to sail from Boston on his return crossing, he found he had five days before sailing time. What should he do with them? He had the opportunity to meet Holmes and Longfellow. But some eight hundred miles off were two men who were more to him than philosopher or poet. He said, "I am one of those that think that the world is not dying for poets so much as for preachers." So off he went to Cleveland to see his old friends Moody and Sankey. Even so the choice must have been a difficult one, for he had looked forward to meeting Holmes and Longfellow whose writings he knew so well. George Adam Smith, who relates this incident, asks, in conclusion, "And yet, and yet, O Henry, why didn't you dine with Longfellow and Holmes?"

Drummond's mission had soon outgrown the hut and was forced to provide larger quarters. With the aid of the Renfield Church the building program was carried to a swift conclusion. The first service was held in the new church building at Possilpark on January 2, 1881. Drummond stayed as pastor until another minister was called on August 29, 1882, to take over the work of the full-fledged church which had grown out of the mission. Through four years Drummond

had labored among these people doing all the work of a regularly or-
dained minister, although he was only licensed to preach. During
these years he lived in an old house near the mission and was never
too busy to minister to his people's needs, which were many, especially during the winter of 1879 when the Bank of Glasgow failed.
He was listed as an elder from March 15, 1883, to October 3, 1886,
and his name was carried on the church roll. He stayed long enough
to see a flourishing, independent, harmonious congregation emerge
from a small mission. Before he left, Moody preached from his
pulpit, and Drummond was able to free himself in time for participation in the first part of the second evangelistic trip of Moody and
Sankey to Scotland and England.

Looking back on these formative and creative years Drummond
declared, "It has been my privilege for some years to address regularly
two very different audiences on two very different themes. On week
days I have lectured to a class of students on the Natural Sciences,
and on Sundays to an audience consisting for the most part of working men on subjects of a moral and religious character." He felt, at
first, that the two departments must be kept entirely by themselves.
"They lay at opposite poles of thought; and for a time I succeeded in
keeping Science and Religion shut off from one another in two
separate compartments of my mind. But gradually the wall of parti-
tion showed symptoms of giving way. The two fountains of knowledge also slowly began to overflow, and finally their waters met and
mingled. The great change was in the compartment which held the
Religion. It was not that the well there was dried; still less that the
fermenting waters were washed away by the flood of Science. The
actual contents remained the same. But the crystals of former doctrine were dissolved; and as they precipitated themselves once more
in definite forms, I observed that the Crystalline System was changed.
New channels also for outward expression opened, and some of the
old closed up; and I found the truth running out to my audience on
the Sundays by the weekday outlets. In other words, the subject
matter Religion had taken on the method of expression of Science,
and I discovered myself enunciating Spiritual Law in the exact terms
of Biology and Physics.

"Now this was not simply a scientific coloring given to Religion, the mere freshening of the theological air with natural facts and illustrations. It was an entire re-casting of truth. And when I came seriously to consider what it involved, I saw, or seemed to see, that it meant essentially the introduction of Natural Law into the Spiritual World."[2]

As each one of these Sunday addresses was finished he consigned it to his growing stack of neatly penciled notes in a desk drawer. Very often a single theme would be continued for several Sundays in a row. Many of his manuscript outlines are marked "same subject continued." One of them was fished out of the drawer and published in The Clerical World. Another was requested by an orphanage and printed as a pamphlet. The encouraging letters which came in response, indicating the papers had helped, prompted Drummond to gather the addresses together for publication in book form. Two publishers turned them down. Once again they were dropped in the desk drawer and forgotten.

A happenstance meeting one day on Paternoster Row,[3] London, however, with Mr. H. M. Hodder of the book publishing firm of Hodder & Stoughton, led to a quick resurrection and polishing of the papers and their final publication under the title Natural Law in the Spiritual World.

Drummond saw the manuscript through the page-proof stage but before the first edition of one thousand copies rolled from the press he was on his way to East Central Africa.

[2] From the "Preface" to Natural Law.

[3] That fateful narrow lane, named after a prayer and dedicated for so many years to books, is just off St. Paul's Church-yard at the top of Ludgate Hill. It is really a projection of Amen Court from Stationer's Hall, at right angles to and intersecting with Ave Maria Lane. In honor of that providential meeting and its subsequent effects I sought the spot on a recent trip to England. But there is nothing left since that flaming night of the blitz in 1940 when so much of the City of London was destroyed. Only the pavement and the walkway, the rubble and holes and blackened buildings remain. But still St. Paul's Cathedral bell rings out the hours and its dome reigns over the City, and Hodder & Stoughton, book publishers, still do business a short step away from their former location on Paternoster Row in St. Paul's House, Warwick Square.

4

1883-1884—Deepening Maturity

MR. JAMES STEVENSON, f.r.g.s., of Largs, Ayrshire, sent
Henry Drummond to Africa in 1883 to investigate and report
upon the natural resources of Nyassaland and surrounding counties
in East Central Africa. Mr. Stevenson, and other gentlemen from
Glasgow, had invested a considerable fortune in a trading company
operating around Lake Tanganyika, Lake Nyassa, Lake Shirwa, the
Shire and the Zambezi Rivers. This same Mr. Stevenson, before
Drummond left in June, gave £6,000 to endow a Chair of Natural
Science at the Free Church College and the gift was accepted by the
General Assembly.

Drummond fulfilled painstakingly the scientific assignments and
in addition discovered a fossil fish unknown before. But his trip was
notable principally for his first-hand investigation of the value of
Christian missions. He was impressed with the heroic assaults of
Christianity upon the heathendom of the Dark Continent, and was
deeply affected by the sacrifices and suffering which seemed inseparable from such work. He recorded the impressions of this trip in a
diary of his months in Africa, which was published under the title
Tropical Africa; one reviewer said, "It is almost the only book of
travels that left any ideas in my mind."

The natives called Drummond by a name which meant "he who
looks" or "gazes," probably both for his close scrutiny of minerals and
insects, and the keenness of his eyes when looking at them. His

friend John Watson said of Drummond, "Nobody could be double
or base or mean or impure before those eyes."

During Drummond's absence from Scotland, his book *Natural
Law in the Spiritual World* had caught the public fancy, chiefly because of the favorable review in *The Spectator*, which influenced a
tremendous number to buy and read it. "No book of our time . . . has
showed such a power of relating the moral and practical truths of
religion, so as to make them take fresh hold of the mind and vividly
impress the imagination." His family sent this review on to him in
Africa. But he was not conscious of the tremendous impact of the
book until his return almost a year later.

The universal acclaim *Natural Law* received was due primarily to
its practical presentation of Christianity. It was fresh and vital, and
gave one of the best pictures ever presented of real Christian life over
against lukewarm Christianity. All through its chapters the same
principles enunciated in "Spiritual Diagnosis" are held to and enlarged, especially the principle of "buttonholing" the reader. Drummond summarizes in this volume the essence of what it means to be a
Christian and illuminates his points richly from the discoveries of
science.

Drummond's aim was to show the thinking Christian of his day
that the doctrine of evolution, so clearly discerned in nature, was
not contradictory to the doctrine of development as conceived in
spiritual terms. He believed God's plan and purpose, as well as His
law, were clearly revealed in the process of evolution. He tried to
show that if God is God He is the God of both the natural and the
spiritual. This process of evolution meant simply that in the beginning God dealt with inorganic matter, then at the next level up with
organic, and at last, after the firm foundation was made, man's turn
came. Further, man's life began to unfold and grow, realizing the
potential inherent from the beginning of life. In other words,
Natural Law made it evident that a man could be at the same time a
thoroughgoing evolutionist, and a thoroughgoing Christian.

James Y. Simpson, one of Drummond's biographers, said that in
his "mind there was no sharp distinction of things as secular and
sacred. Life itself was too divine in its opportunities to suffer such

cleavage. He sought the underlying unity of the natural and the spiritual and believed that truth is a unity, which may be regarded from different sides; but it is impossible that two bodies of true thought can remain in permanent antagonism."

The storm of criticism, which also came along with the praise, centered mainly on the thesis in the "Introduction" that natural laws and spiritual laws are not only analogous, which few would have quarreled over, but identical, with which practically no one agreed. Philosophically, perhaps, and scientifically Drummond was on shaky ground, but from the viewpoint of value for Christian living his arguments were valid and sound. Drummond was an intuitive thinker who, according to his friend Stalker, "saw single points in isolation with extraordinary clearness, and could describe his visions with unrivalled skill; but he had not the logical and systematic faculty which makes contradictory things intolerable."

His book went into several editions and sold to hungry and confused people in many lands. Henry Drummond followed his search for God's truth with relentless scientific thoroughness, and wherever he felt this truth led he was unafraid to go. He miscalculated the seriousness of the tension between literal inspiration and the scientific approach to religious truth and did not foresee that the same battle would have to be refought and won afresh in succeeding generations, in almost every mind.

Natural Law restored men's faith, saved them from atheism, and helped them make the transition from fundamentalism to modernism. To thousands Drummond was a "savior from confusion," and he satisfied in part the hunger of his generation for religion and the spiritual life.

By the time Henry Drummond returned from Africa in 1884 he was a famous man, but the mark of his second scientific journey was upon him, for his reddish hair was streaked with gray, evidence of the almost constant exposure to suffering and death, and of his witnessing the "cost" of Christian missions.

Immediately after his ship docked in England he went to join Moody and Sankey in the final weeks of their mission to London.

The plunge into the busy, exciting work of the mission helped cleanse his soul of much that haunted him from his African travels. No contrast could have been greater—from the solemn quiet of the Dark Continent to the roar of mass humanity in Piccadilly.

On May 31, Drummond was unanimously elected to the new chair endowed by Mr. Stevenson and on November 4 he received the simple rite of ordination and induction, the full orders of the Presbyterian Church, and delivered his inaugural address on "The Contribution of Science to Christianity." The title, "Professor," he used from that day on in preference to "Reverend," for he believed that too often the "clerical manner" blocked men off from Christ. He preferred to think of himself as a "lay evangelist."

5

1884-1894—Full Fruit and Flower

THE decade from 1884 to 1894 was the richest period of Drummond's life and was filled with a host of important events. But overshadowing all the rest and preferred above them was his work among students, especially at Edinburgh University, which he considered the best and most important contribution of his life.

In April, 1884, the University celebrated its Tercentenary. This event brought together distinguished scientists and literary figures from many places. Such men as Louis Pasteur from France, Hermann von Helmholtz from Germany, Emile de Laveleye from England, and many others, gave expression not only to their devotion to learning, but to their religious faith. Much to everyone's surprise, the emphasis was spiritual. De Laveleye, for example, in his address, pointed to the teaching of Jesus as the one hope for the future of mankind. These distinguished visitors made a deep and lasting impression on guests, faculty and students alike, and opened the way for a great spiritual movement in the University.

A few months after the University's Tercentenary celebration the Principal, Sir Alexander Grant, in his inaugural address at the opening of a new session, called upon the students to recognize and sustain the distinctly Christian character of the University.

The students took him seriously and the already well-organized Medical Students' Christian Association prepared a follow-up program for the winter session. One of their first meetings was arranged

43

to hear two Cambridge athletes. They were C. T. Studd, the famous cricket star, and Stanley P. Smith, the equally famous "stroke oar," who had volunteered for Christian missionary work in China. Before leaving for their mission station they made a farewell tour of the colleges and universities telling the story of their "call." When they spoke at the University of Edinburgh on December 10, 1884, in the Free Church Assembly Hall, New College, a capacity crowd was present. The students wanted to hear what these famous athletes had to say about religion. These two serious young men captured the imagination and won the admiration of their audience. Those who heard them were convinced that since these stalwart he-men were giving their lives to the furtherance of the Christian religion it was no weak or unmanly thing to be associated with it. The students were stirred by the frank and forthright challenge to lead a more Christian life. Studd and Smith were invited back for three more meetings in January by popular demand. This time even the United Presbyterian Synod Hall, the largest assembly place available, was not big enough to hold those who wanted to hear. But these two men were "off for China" and could not return again before sailing. The Medical Students' Association felt the meetings should be continued. But who could draw the same crowds and make the same impression? Someone came up with Henry Drummond's name. He had spoken recently to the Association on "The Contribution of Science to Christianity" and had made a reputation through his book *Natural Law*. He spoke a tongue they understood. No one could think of a better person to carry on the inspiration and motivation of the Christian religion engendered by the Tercentenary celebration and the two Cambridge speakers.

Drummond accepted for one meeting, provided it was held in some neutral place, not associated with either the University or the Church. The Oddfellows Hall was chosen, and on Sunday evening, January 25, 1885, he began what became "a series of addresses, prolonged through ten years, which is the most famous series of a religious character which has ever been delivered anywhere to university men. Drummond captured his audience from the first, taking as his opening subject, 'Seek ye first the kingdom of God....' "—the same theme used by de Laveleye at the Tercentenary celebration.

Principal William Muir was appointed to the University in February, 1885, and on the day following spoke these prophetic words at the Oddfellows Hall meeting: "This work has enormous possibilities of blessing . . . it will radiate spiritual influence both near and far." And it did. Sunday after Sunday Drummond returned. For nine winters afterward the Oddfellows Hall was taken, tickets were printed and the meetings were arranged for by a "secret" committee.[1] As regular as the clock the good Principal's note came in November asking if Professor Drummond could be engaged and offering help

[1] The "secret" committee was chiefly A. R. Simpson of the Medical Faculty and Alexander Whyte, minister of Free St. George's, with A. H. F. Barbour, Marcus Dods, Professor Calderwood, William Muir and Professor Charteris doing their share. They collectively supported the meetings by taking financial responsibility and by winning continuing faculty support and providing someone to act as chairman for each meeting. Here we have further evidence of the Barbour influence. Both Simpson and Whyte married Barbour girls. The Simpson home at 52 Queens Street, the Whyte home at 7 St. George's Square and A. H. F. Barbour's home at 4 St. George's Square formed a small "Barbour community" which became the town headquarters for Drummond's student work. In the early days of the Moody Mission and at the very beginning of his friendship with Robert Barbour, Henry began to frequent the Simpson home. Mrs Simpson often invited young people in. During the Great Mission the purpose of these gatherings was to practice hymns, and Sankey was there occasionally to teach them. Robert brought Henry, "with his always welcome tenor voice," and the Simpson home became a haven for Henry ever after. During the days of his student work in Edinburgh these homes, with Queens Street just a "nip" around and down in a jiffy from St. George's Square, were open at all times for student gatherings—prayer meetings, Bible study and parties, especially on Saturday nights. Drummond had many wonderful times in these homes, especially the Simpsons' where he was like a member of the family. He had a latch-key and came and went as he pleased in the hospitable Simpson home. There was also a room at the Whytes' at his disposal, where he might meet students who wanted to talk, or where he might stop for the night. It was sometimes two in the morning before he returned from the streets which he had paced with anxious inquirers after the Oddfellows Hall meeting, to warm the cocoa left by the fire. The Barbours not only provided for the students in Edinburgh but Bonskeid House was always open for a few days of conference in the fall and spring and longer times in the summer. Many gatherings were held there during the ten years of the meetings. The trip from Edinburgh to Pitlochry took about three hours, with another forty-five minutes for the drive to Bonskeid. But what a wonderful spot for making a retreat. Long walks by day, up the path to the cross-roads, forking to Glen Fincastle and to Killiecrankie, with the spring at the head of the path and the private Barbour chapel near by. Long talks in front of the fire in the evening with serious themes to the fore. Walks and talks filled up these happy excursions to "Barbour Land."

for any expenses. Drummond always accepted, and no preacher of his day had a larger congregation nor presented it with finer issues.

Out from the Oddfellows Hall streamed hundreds of men who heard Henry Drummond and had their minds and hearts opened to a larger and stronger faith in Christ. And some of these men went to the far corners of the earth to bear witness (Gordon went to Canada, Ewing to Australia). In him they found "a religious teacher utterly free from conventionalism, ardent and enthusiastic as any of themselves, fearless of facts, loyal to the intellectual methods of the age, but still with an unshaken faith in God and in the reality of spiritual experience," and they told the world.

From Edinburgh and Scotland the work spread to England, to Wales, to America, to Germany, to Australia and to Japan. Even Russia was on the list. Deputations of students, recruited from the Oddfellows Hall meetings, went to the universities of Scotland, England, Wales and Ireland, and their work became the nucleus for the organization of university Christian associations wherever they went. Holiday Missions were sent forth to many important centers of population, ("Henry's Colts") again recruited from the Oddfellows Hall meetings, seeking to carry the Gospel message to other youth. Both Deputations and Holiday Missions gave many young men a chance to bear witness to their new-found faith.

The fruits of these ten years of labor on Drummond's part were many fold: the firm planting of the student Christian movement in the major universities of the world; the tremendous impetus given to missionary work through student volunteers; the development of a consecrated and trained laity, especially among medical men; and the arousal of a practical concern over social conditions—evidenced in Edinburgh by the establishing of the Chalmers University Settlement, near the coal wharf terminus and the slaughterhouse, which was run by the men recruited from the Oddfellows Hall meetings.

Henry Drummond was busy with a variety of other work and engagements during this golden decade of his life, in addition to the Edinburgh student work and his regular teaching in Glasgow. A few of the more important events should be sketched to fill in and complete the picture of his life.

In the fall of 1885 he had moved from Possilpark to 3 Park Circus in the new residential section just one block from the Free Church College. His large and beautiful house was one of the continuous circle of identical houses on the Circus, opening on one side into West End Park and on the other into Park Place, the street leading to the College. Here Drummond had everything he desired and needed for comfort and his work. The most used part of the house was the study on the second floor, which was spacious, and in quiet and exquisite taste.

Since this section of the city was situated on a small knoll Drummond could see out of his back windows, over the chimney pots, the low-lying Campsie Hills. All of his writing was done in a chair with his back to the light, and a large blotter on his knee, chiefly in the late morning before his lecture at noon, and early evening right after tea. Surrounded by books old and new, solid furniture, a few pictures —Millet's *The Angelus*, a Turner, and several portraits of friends— in the quiet of this study Drummond did his literary work. There were, however, countless interruptions day and night—by those in spiritual distress, by politicians, by freaks and fanatics, by students, and by friends.

In the same year he gave three addresses at Grosvenor House, London, through the invitation and sponsorship of Lord and Lady Aberdeen. They had met him the year before during their stay at Holyrood House in Lord Aberdeen's capacity as High Commissioner for the General Assembly of 1884. They had heard him during the Great Mission. They had read *Natural Law*. They felt he had a message for the socially elite.

Grosvenor House was the palatial town residence of the Duke of Westminster, which fronted on Hyde Park. Drummond agreed to give three addresses in the grand ballroom of this house on the last Sunday in April and the first two Sundays in May, 1885. He did so reluctantly because of the demands of his Edinburgh work. But he undoubtedly realized the great opportunity to reach this influential group which was not often touched vitally by the Christian Church.

The following advertisement appeared in the society columns of the London *Morning Post* on April 25, 1885:

Professor Henry Drummond (author of *Natural Law in the Spiritual World*), will, by request, give addresses at Grosvenor House, by kind permission of the Duke and Duchess of Westminster, on Sundays April 26 (tomorrow), May 3 and 10. Admission can be had by ticket, which can be obtained on application to Mr. R. Thompson, 37 Grosvenor Square (Lord and Lady Aberdeen's town house).

Over five hundred came that first Sunday, expecting, no doubt, to hear a scientific lecture; but instead they heard a simple evangelistic address on "Conversion—the Difference between Believing in Christianity and Christ." There was no service—only a short closing prayer. All of the meetings were crowded with the class of people for whom they were intended. All the addresses were strictly religious, for Henry assumed they also "wanted a religion."

The impression he made is indicated in an article which appeared after the series on May 27, 1885, in the London *World*, in which the writer said:

"Professor Drummond . . . has struck out [on] a completely new line of his own, in which there is nothing that is not dignified, nothing that is not telling. . . . He applies the principle of evolution . . . to spiritual existence. He does not consign to perdition all who fail to lead a highly spiritual life here. He only reminds them that they are not qualifying for the life to come. . . . And [those who heard] . . . departed profoundly impressed by the words of wisdom and solemnity issuing from the lips of a graceful young man with a good manner, a not ill-favored face, a broad Scottish accent, clad in a remarkably well-fitting frock-coat, and reciting . . . [a prayer] in a tone of devout humility remarkable for the professors of the period. . . . He has caused society to talk, not only about himself, but about the subjects which he expounds."

There were many lasting proofs of the value of these meetings, with both individual and social implications and applications of religious truth. One, in particular, was the organization of the Associated Workers League for young women of leisure from the West End who met for continued religious study and inspiration under the impetus of Drummond's addresses. They also, as a natural consequence, engaged in philanthropic and missionary work, especially in the less privileged East End. The group sought to unite their members in definite Christian and social effort.

Three years later, on June 3, 10, and 17, 1888, Drummond gave a second series of addresses at Grosvenor House, this time for men only, chiefly because of the limited size of the ballroom. Once again he dealt in turn, simply but graphically, with the fundamental tests of Christianity, both in relation to human society—*The Program of Christianity*—and in relation to the individual. Once again he drew a distinguished audience. "The great square room . . . was densely crowded by an interested and representative gathering—politicians, clergymen, authors, artists, critics, soldiers and barristers; with a large sprinkling of smart young men whose appearance would scarcely have suggested a vivid interest in serious concerns."

At the address that brought the series to a close, the great ballroom was crowded to the point of suffocation, and many had to hear him from adjacent corridors. Drummond had proven he was equally at home and effective with the flower of the aristocracy in London as he was with the shepherds and gillies of Aberdeen and the schoolboys and students of Edinburgh. "There was a kind of witchery in his personality which drew the intellectual as well as moral best out of a man."

Another result of this second visit was the formation of a second young women's club to enlarge the work begun in 1885. They called themselves the Eighty-Eight Club, with this motto: "I undertake and I persevere." This excellent work, which gave a Christian contact between the classes, persisted until almost the end of the century.

There were also a number of indirect fruits of these Grosvenor House meetings in London. His friendship with Lord and Lady Aberdeen, who arranged the meetings, deepened into intimacy, and was followed through the years by frequent visits of Drummond to Dollis Hill, the Aberdeen London country estate, to Haddo House, their ancestral estate in Aberdeenshire, to Dublin Castle while Aberdeen was Viceroy of Ireland, and to The Citadel while Aberdeen was Governor General of Canada. At Dollis Hill he met William E. Gladstone and was involved briefly in politics.

A mere mention of other items of importance during these ten fruitful years must suffice. He refused to run for Parliament from the district of Lanarkshire, outside of Glasgow, because he felt his work lay elsewhere. But he did stump the district for Gladstone and the Home Rule Party. He turned down the offer of the secretaryship of the Shipping Commission, again because he felt it was not his given task. He was always interested in labor relations and acted more than once as an arbitrator in labor-management disputes. Lord Aberdeen offered him an appointment to his Vicegeral staff in Dublin, but again he declined, although his visits to the Aberdeens were frequent, wherever they were, and their warm friendship for each other grew through the years. Drummond was fortunate in that his decisions concerning his work and his friends both led to a greater measure of fulfillment in his major task of evangelism.

During this busy decade Drummond made several trips, most of them in the interest of student Christian work. Wherever he went the story was the same—"men stirred and won" by the hundreds; an ethical and spiritual uplift as well as an impulse for social betterment; and a zeal for evangelism.

In the summer of 1887 he went to America. Moody got him to Northfield at last to give that talk on "Love." He gave a number of addresses for Moody, visited Lord and Lady Aberdeen at Niagara, took part in two Chautauqua summer gatherings, and at last made a tour of the principal American universities on a "Student's Holiday Mission" of his own. Several of his Edinburgh workers joined him for this swing around Williams, Dartmouth, Amherst, Princeton, Yale, Harvard, Wellesley, Philadelphia (University of Pennsylvania) and winding up with New York medical students from Columbia and New York universities. He was very busy. In one of his letters home he wrote. "My life is roaring along like a cataract. . . . I write in the Yale graveyard—the only uninhabited spot I can find."

This visit quickened the spiritual life of the universities and gave a boost to the Student Volunteer Movement. Follow-up meetings were held in the "Edinburgh manner" of Oddfellow's Hall—a series, for example, began in New York in Dockstader's Theater the evening after Drummond sailed for Scotland the last of October.

Dr. Peabody of Harvard declared his visit "was as though a comet had flashed upon the view and had left a trail of light as it sank below the horizon." All agreed he was the most effective university speaker on religion they had ever heard. William Lyon Phelps said of his visit to Yale: "I have never seen so deep an impression made on students, by any speaker on any subject."

In 1890 Drummond responded to a signed appeal from two hundred and thirty students at Melbourne University for him to visit Australia. He arrived the last of April and stayed with his old friend and fellow Gaiety Club member John Ewing. But Ewing contracted typhoid fever and died within a week.

It was Drummond's sad duty to make all final arrangements, break the news to his wife who was on a visit to Scotland, and deliver a memorial address. This address gave an insight into Drummond's feeling about the shortness of life, especially the following brief passages:

"There are two ways in which a workman regards his work—as his own and as his Master's. If it is his own, then to leave it in his prime is a catastrophe, if not a cruel and unfathomable wrong. But if it is his Master's, one looks not backwards, but before, putting by the well-worn tools without a sigh, and expecting elsewhere better work to do.

"For one man to do too much for the world is in one sense the whole world's loss. So it may be that God withdraws His workers even when their hands are fullest and their souls most ripe: to fill the vacancies with still growing men, and enrich many with the loss of one."

Drummond edited Ewing's sermons and published them with a brief biographical sketch—in which the above words are found— under the title *The Unsearchable Riches of Christ*.

In spite of the sad burden of his friend's death Drummond carried out his schedule of meetings in Melbourne, Adelaide and Sydney. He met the same student problems in Australia that he had in Great Britain and America, and sought to bring home the same message to "forwandered souls"—the new possibilities of faith which lie in the rational and discriminating criticism of the Old Testament (the old story of "verbal inspiration" versus "evolution"), the compatibility of science and religion, and the introduction to Christ of those who never went to church—"the great problem in these colonies is the young outsider."

He took an unanticipated side trip to the New Hebrides in the middle of his college meetings, leaving the conduct of the meetings in charge of the students. There were two reasons for going: to make and write up an objective appraisal of the political quarrel over the islands between France and England, and to investigate and report on a very crucial missionary problem which existed there. His trip proved both interesting and exciting—he saw cannibals, an active volcano in eruption, many geological "sights"; he experienced earthquake tremors, saw poisoned arrows, was touched by the condition of these primitive people, gained a good picture of both the political situation and the missionary, jotted down many notes for future use in his scientific lectures and student addresses, and wrote his reports for home consumption. His conclusion about missions there: "No finer missionary work was ever done than by these New Hebrides missionaries." He incorporated his impressions of this mission field in an address presented on his return at the opening of the college session in November: "The Problem of Foreign Missions." The influence of this paper led to many changes in the philosophy and techniques of the mission fields and quickened the thinking which culminated in the calling of the great missionary conference in Edinburgh in 1910, from which sprang the modern ecumenical movement.

On his journey home he stopped at Singapore, Saigon, Hong Kong and Shanghai, visiting the missions in each place. From China he went to Japan where he addressed university students in Tokyo. From Japan he went home through Canada.

Henry Drummond was writing constantly, but most of his "pen time" was given to a reworking and polishing of the material he had presented to live audiences. He was before all an evangelist rather than a writer, and it is in the form of his addresses, at once as an interpreter of the Bible and of human life, that his most permanent literary work was done. *Tropical Africa* was the only "book," as such, which he ever attempted. All the rest of his publications were made up of talks and addresses.

He was a careful craftsman, meticulous over the final form of his articles and books. His great aim in writing was to be lucid, while in publishing it was to be attractive. His lingering influence over seventy-five stormy and disturbing years is due primarily to his care for the printed word which carried his message far beyond his beloved Scotland and beyond his lifetime.

The justly famous address on "Love" is a good example. Given first back during the Great Mission, it was used repeatedly before student audiences. It was, at Moody's insistence, polished for the Northfield Conference of 1887 and, again at Moody's suggestion, published. Its first title was "Love: the Supreme Gift." But it is under a later title—"The Greatest Thing in the World"—that it has been known to millions and still sells today in many different editions. It was this address, reduced to print and issued first at Christmastime in 1889, which led Drummond to publish similar booklets each Christmas for five consecutive years as a new kind of "Christmas card." They are and must ever remain classics of devotional reading.

Henry Drummond went to America again in 1893 to give the Lowell Institute Lectures in Boston. In pursuit of his special studies in Biological Science, spurred on by the stream of criticism of *Natural Law* and the questions put to him by students on his Australian trip, Drummond conceived the idea of writing a book on the evolution of man from his most primitive beginnings to the point of his ascent where the individual merges his destiny in family life. Drummond describes this study as one "in embryos, in rudiments, in installations; the scene is the primeval forest; the date, the world's dawn."

He was forced to the task of putting his thinking in finished form in time for the Lowell Lectures. These lectures were prepared as a serious scientific study, primarily for scholars. On arriving in Boston and finding the wide interest in the lecture series by the general public, however, he rewrote the lectures. Even though he gave the lectures several times and they were received everywhere with enthusiastic acclaim, the book version never reached the wide circulation accorded to *Natural Law*, chiefly because these studies were not written for popular consumption—they were not simple talks addressed to working men—although he did attempt in reworking them to keep the "layman" in mind. The rich analogy and striking illuminations for the more practical application of the contents of *Natural Law* are largely lacking in *The Ascent of Man*.

On this last trip to America Drummond made his usual addresses to students and repeated his university itinerary of 1887 with several additions. He had received invitations from nearly all the leading universities, from Amherst to Chicago, and devoted most of the late spring and early fall to this work. In addition he spent some time at Chautauqua, redelivering the Lowell Lectures; at Northfield, where he gave several addresses; and on a holiday in Canada with Lord and Lady Aberdeen.

By the time he reached Northfield for his second appearance, his position on evolution and modern Biblical criticism was well known and he felt distinctly out of place in the conservative atmosphere. He went primarily because of Moody's gracious insistence. But "it was not a happy time." Upon his arrival a delegation waited on Moody and insisted he question Drummond on the "soundness of his faith" (verbal inspiration and miracles) before allowing him to speak. (Some were also critical of his smoking cigars.) Moody agreed to do it the following morning. The deputation questioned Moody right after breakfast as to his success.

"Did you see him?"

"Yes," said Mr. Moody.

"And did you speak to him about his theological views?"

"No," said Moody, "I did not. Within half an hour of his coming down this morning he gave me such proof of his being possessed of a higher Christian life than either you or I that I could not say anything to him. You can talk to him yourselves if you like."

Whereat the baffled complainers withdrew.

The present Lord Aberdeen remembers vividly the visit "Uncle Hen," as the Aberdeen children called him, paid to Canada that summer. In a letter he describes that evening of September 17: "There we were in the Citadel, overlooking the St. Lawrence flowing quietly down beneath the windows of the room where we were assembled. Only Henry Drummond could have inspired us as he did that evening. If you know Quebec and the commanding position of the Citadel, you will realize all the more the extraordinary appropriateness of the text ('There is a river, the streams whereof make glad the city of God'—Psalm 46:4) and its lessons as portrayed by one of the finest Christians that ever lived on this earth."

That 1893 trip to America bore, as usual, "fruit an hundredfold." His words, as always, touched the hearts of men and women, bringing new faith and renewed hope. However, in spite of the joy of his work, the physical strain was great, and Drummond came home looking much older, only to plunge into a winter of hard work preparing his lectures for publication.

Drummond looked on this book, published a year after presentation as lectures, as his most scientific piece of work. It was considered by the critics, both favorable and unfavorable critics, to be an important contribution to the scientific literature of his day. While *Natural Law* concentrated on the individual and his Prodigal Son experience, *Ascent* moved out into the area of the social and gave roots to the Good Samaritan story—"the path of progress and the path of altruism are one." It was described by one writer as "the New Testament of the science of evolution, as Darwin's work was the Old."

Running all through Henry Drummond's life was the side of his nature which might best be described as the "boyishness" of the man. He never lost his schoolboy instincts and their pristine bloom. His wide range of interests, his unlimited fund of magic and games and stories, his keen joy in sports, his deep knowledge and understanding of the "genus boy," won the hearts of "lads," wherever he appeared. His genuine love for boys led him to spend a lot of time with them and to give much thought to their physical and moral welfare. Boys, wherever he found them, responded to Drummond's approach, from the highest social bracket (his own nephews, the Simpson children and those of Lord and Lady Aberdeen) to the filthiest slums (the newsboys and message-boys, in the poorest and most degraded homes), from the boy living in the crowded city to the boy dwelling on the farm; Drummond appealed to them all. He learned about

them by close association in their homes, on his visits to the Penny
Gaff in Cowgate and to the closes off High Street in Edinburgh;
he studied them in his work at Riego Street Mission Hall and the
Edinburgh Free Breakfast Mission on Sunday mornings.

His nephew, J. Graham Drummond of Aberdeen, remembers a
visit to 3 Park Circus with his younger brother during the Christmas
holidays, and the wonderful time they had with their Uncle Henry.
On this visit Uncle Henry offered the little boys a prize if they could
discover how to turn on the gaslight. On another occasion they met
him at the station and he immediately pulled a handful of what
looked like angleworms out of his pocket and ate them with relish,
much to the children's horror and delight.

His endless inventions for winning youngsters' attention and
friendship culminated in furthering the work of the newly formed
Boys' Brigade, organized in 1883 in Glasgow and made national in
scope in 1885. The Boys' Brigade was started as a desperate measure
to cope with the apparently insoluble problem of "boys" and Sunday
school. A story is told of W. O. Smith (a Glasgow merchant who was
the founder and first secretary of the Boys' Brigade) and Henry
Drummond walking down the street one day. As they passed a fruit-
erer a bunch of old round strawberry boxes were tossed into the gut-
ter. Immediately the boys playing in the street swarmed over the pile,
stuck them on their heads, lined up in military formation and
marched off. Drummond is supposed to have said to Smith, "There's
an idea for you."

The military cast of the Boys' Brigade, with the round "strawberry
box" cap, a belt with shoulder strap and the usual drill routine, was a
technique for interesting and controlling large groups of boys in order
that constructive work could be done with them. Each company was
connected with a church, and a Bible study class was an integral part
of the program. The Boys' Brigade was one of the unquestioned
religious forces of Drummond's day and continues to be as vigorous
now as then in many parts of the world, especially in Scotland.

This movement spread rapidly through the United Kingdom and
the United States, chiefly because of Drummond's zeal (he even
addressed the students of Harvard University on the subject). The
new technique helped solve the problems of Sunday-school attend-

ance and discipline, and the frustration of teachers, for boys between the ages of twelve and seventeen.

The official badge of the "B. B." is an anchor with a cross in the center—reminding of the centrality of Christ in a boy's life. Its watchwords—"sure" and "steadfast"—were inspired by the massive crags of Scotland which provoked one to steadfastness. It remains both a cultural and a religious influence, and it is still going strong in Britain, although largely replaced by the Boy Scout Movement in America.

Two of Drummond's writings were published especially for the Boys' Brigade: "First," an address delivered to fourteen hundred members on his favorite theme "Seek ye first the kingdom of God and his righteousness," and the allegorical narrative of "Baxter's Second Innings" based on the game of cricket. When the latter was first published it was sent to the sports editor for review. The theme was "temptation" and how the early teen-ager might deal with it effectively. Dr. Hugh Watt, former Moderator of the Church of Scotland, declared it was the favorite of his family. It was the favorite of many boys and their families and went through several editions. For smaller children, Drummond wrote two stories during his brief interim editorship of the children's magazine *Wee Willie Winkie*—"The Monkey that Would Not Kill" and its sequel "Gum."

Henry Drummond's absorbing interest in boys paid large dividends and one could almost delete all the other work which he crowded into his comparatively short life, and still remember him as the great developer of Christian character in boys.

For one who had such a happy experience of home in his childhood, it is strange he never married and established a home of his own. He could then have studied more intimately the "genus" boy in the kind of environment which gave him such a good foundation for his own life and career. And yet, his celibacy enabled him to do for the world that which family life might have prevented, giving him the time, freedom and energy for making his long journeys, engaging in hours of writing and endless personal work—like St. Paul before him.

With the publication of *The Ascent of Man* in 1894 the golden years began drawing to a close and Drummond's public work was nearing its end.

6

1894-1897—His Greatest Witness

"ONE afternoon in his study," his newspaper friend Shelley tells us, "when we were nearly finished [with our conversation], Drummond, whose pipe had gone out during an eager debate over one point, stooped to light a spill at the fire. As he rose and straightened his tall figure again, he paused with the lighted spill and carried his hand swiftly to the small of his back. 'O, Shelley, what's that?' He had felt a sharp pain in his spine, which did not pass off for several minutes—[it was] the beginning of the end."

The disease which took him at last the doctors never were able to diagnose—a chronic disease of the bones was as close as the doctors came to knowing what it was. After this first sudden announcement of the onset, the disease came on gradually, but within a year after its first appearance, Drummond was separated from all his beloved work, and was forced at last to seek relief. He struggled through his lectures that last winter, but had to cancel his Oddfellows Hall meetings, the very hardest thing for him to give up. He wrote Dr. Simpson: "I feel it would be wrong to attempt Edinburgh in my present condition. . . . I shall add nothing as to the disappointment all this means to me."

By the early spring of 1895 he was suffering such constant pain his doctors made him quit all work. Every known treatment was tried, but his malady baffled the most skillful medical men of the day. He went to the South of France for the sunshine and the hot baths, first at Dax then at Biarritz. But he showed no improvement. He returned

58

to London and in September went to Tunbridge Wells where he remained until his death. He grew more and more helpless, and was soon completely bedridden and dependent.

Through these two years of terrible suffering which he bore so nobly, he proved his Christian faith. He had already demonstrated how fame, prosperity and wealth of brilliant gifts could be borne with unselfishness and humility. Now he was strengthened to show how to suffer uncomplainingly, endure long illness patiently, thinking more of others than of himself, and at last face death without fear. His sense of humor never left him. One Christmas he sent a picture of himself in a bath chair to his friends with the caption underneath, "The descent of man." He was able to play his favorite game of chess and to remain his own cheerful self until close to the end. He had frequent visits from his family and friends—his mother and his brother James were never absent for long, and his friend-physicians Hugh Barbour and A. R. Simpson were in almost constant attendance.

A friend who was with him seven times during his lingering illness, staying a few days on each visit, never saw him in even a slight depression but once, and said that Drummond was always ready for a discussion, a game, a story or a joke.

The present Lord Aberdeen visited him just before he died and found "Uncle Hen" his same beloved, unselfish, cheerful self.

The Alexander Whytes often drove down to see him. Miss Agnes Young, Dr. Whyte's secretary, said they often mentioned how on these visits he never talked about his own suffering, but "felt he had to prove his life in suffering—to the glory of God."

He died quietly at last, without pain, about eleven o'clock on a Thursday morning, the 11th of March, 1897. The last rites were held in Stirling at North Church in the presence of his family, friends and a crowd representing every church in town. The funeral service was conducted by his close friends and colleagues James Stalker, George Adam Smith, Professor Charteris, Alexander Whyte and Professor A. B. Bruce. The students of Free Church College, Glasgow, were there and representatives of the Boys' Brigade. Two hymns were sung: "O God our help in ages past" and Drummond's favorite hymn during his illness, sung to the tune "Martyrdom," "I'm not ashamed to own my Lord, or to defend His cause, maintain the glory of His Cross, and honor all His laws." The twenty-third Psalm was read and also David's elegy from the Old Testament—Isaiah 38:9-20, "How are the mighty fallen"; and from the New Testament—Philippians 1:21, "For to me to live is Christ, and to die is gain"; and I Corinthians 13. At the same hour in Canada Lord and Lady Aberdeen held an identical service.

The procession to the cemetery and the burial are beautifully described in the following words:

"Winter had come back to have another look o'er the land ere yielding to the sure-coming spring. The Ochils were snow-mantled down to the shoulders, and Ben Cleuch lay hidden in the mist of rain and sleet which a chill north-east wind was driving across the Links of Forth. The great rock of Stirling Castle stood grim and black against the leaden-grey sky. The fields lay sodden in the wet. . . . Through silent streets where every shop was closed, between lines of sympathetic onlookers, past picturesque old buildings and narrowing wynds, the long procession climbed the steep way which leads to the cemetery lying high up on the ridge of the Castle Rock."

They came away, leaving the earthly form of their "dear friend and master" on the slope above the dark town, under the shadow of the old Greyfriars' Church—and Henry Drummond, in Charles Lamb's phrase, so glorious for the Christian, "went home forever."

7

In Memoriam

THERE are many memorials erected in loving memory of Henry
Drummond. A beautiful drinking fountain was given to the City
of Glasgow and placed in the West End Park by Lord and Lady
Aberdeen on the fifth anniversary of his death. Affixed to the pillar
is a profile bust of Drummond circled by a laurel wreath, executed in
bronze by the distinguished King's sculptor for Scotland, James Pit-
tendrigh Macgillivray, R.S.A. Around the head is his name. Underneath is the inscription of the text used to welcome the Aberdeen
family to Quebec in 1893. "There is a river, the streams whereof make
glad the city of God." On the other side of the pillar is a bronze tab-
let with the inscription "1851 H.D. 1897." A copy of this same plaque
is in the ante-chapel of Haddo House with another inscription underneath: "In memory of Henry Drummond and the message he gave in
this place." The bas-relief is flanked on either side by the texts of the
first and last sermons he preached in that chapel. There is another
replica placed in the Governor's Residence in Quebec. There is still
another copy, mounted on white marble and placed on the second
floor of Trinity College, Glasgow, at the end of the hall opposite the
stairs. The first two replicas were given by Lord and Lady Aberdeen,
while the third one was given by Henry's oldest brother, James, in
1903. There is a stained-glass window on the stair landing in the foyer
of Trinity College, given in memory of Professors James Smith
Candlish and Henry Drummond by students and friends. The Possil-

park Church, where he did such an important work, is now named
the Henry Drummond (Memorial) Parish Church of the Church
of Scotland.

Henry Drummond's greatest memorial, however, is a living one—
his effect upon human lives by confronting them with Jesus Christ.
The testimonials are endless of Drummond's life-changing and re-
generating influence on others. From the most famous down to the
least significant come words which tell of his abiding influence on
the thinking and living of all who heard him or read his writings. One
such testimony is typical: "I owe more to him than I do any other
mortal." His influence still abides in his word; and, even though we
can never have the same wonderful privilege of standing in his bright
and exhilarating presence, accorded those fortunate ones of his era,
we can still feel the power of life through his words, which breathe
the very spirit of the Christ who was Henry Drummond's Master and
Lord. For he lived at the center of his religion.

As an added memorial the following anthology has been compiled,
"the best of Henry Drummond," so that men today might come to
grips with Drummond—the man and his message—and find in both
the impetus for a new life in Christ in the midst of this complex modern world.

Part II

HIS MESSAGE

PUBLISHER'S NOTE: In Parts II and III the introductory and explanatory material by James W. Kennedy is set in *italic*. The writing of Henry Drummond is set in roman.

1

The Essence of His Evangel

*O*NE Sunday evening, after one of Drummond's addresses in Students' Hall, Gilmorehill, Glasgow, he went for a long walk with one of his young friends. The conversation turned entirely upon religious matters. "Alluding to his selection of topics for these Glasgow addresses, he said, 'Do you mean, have I a pile of addresses which I take one by one and rip them off?—No! A man has a message.' It is impossible to forget the emphasis with which these words were uttered, and they furnish an invaluable clue to his success as an evangelist. Indeed, I am inclined to the opinion that they are the* most significant I heard from his lips. They help to account for his intense earnestness."[1]

The three keynotes of his message illustrate the reality and intensity which characterized his religious life: "Ye must be born again"—the importance of the individual life; "None of us liveth to himself"—the seriousness of the social influence; and "Seek ye first the kingdom of God"—the necessity of religion. Drummond preached Christ as Savior and master of life and insisted on the necessity of regeneration and new life received through personal encounter with Jesus Christ. His words were always the effortless utterance of a man with a consistent, appealing message, which convinced men and changed the direction of their going. His mind viewed religion—the spiritual life—not in theological but in biological terms. In presenting his message in these terms he developed a "method" which remained the distinguishing characteristic of his treatment of religious truth.

He expressed the conclusion of all his doctrine—his "message"— in the words of Christ which were most often on his lips: "Abide in me and I in you, for without me ye can do nothing."

Dr. Otto Zöckler, in defense of Drummond's message wrote the following apologia:

"And if one of the German critics . . . has found fault with the Pelagian[2] tendency of Drummond's ethic, its mitigation of the conception of sin, and its disregard of God's free pardoning grace in Christ, he does so by ignoring the profound manner in which . . . the noble Scotsman speaks of the necessity of the new birth. He forgets that the individual's utter inability to deliver himself from the yoke of sin and of death is for Drummond a fact of fundamental importance, and that, when Drummond takes the field against the superficial and shallow modes of thought of one-sided modern moralists, he at the same time declares war against Pelagianism."

In the following selections from Drummond's writings will be found the essence of his evangel, the best of what he left behind.

[1] T. Hunter Boyd, Henry Drummond: Some Recollections, (London: Headley Brothers, 1907), p. 61.

[2] The Pelagian heresy maintained, among other things, that man is the author of his own salvation and does not need the grace of God to set him right.

2

"The Contribution of Science to Christianity"

SINCE part of Drummond's method and message was inherent in his attitude toward the relation of science and religion, and all tied up with the question of authority in connection with the Bible; and since his scientific approach and terminology opened the path of his influence to university students, his inaugural address as Professor of Natural Science, later published in The Expositor, is placed first in this anthology. He gave this address—"The Contribution of Science to Christianity"—many times and it shows the trend of his thinking following Natural Law which led eventually to The Ascent of Man.

There is nothing more inspiring just now to the religious mind than the expansion of the intellectual area of Christianity. Christianity seemed for a time to have ceased to adapt itself to the widening range of secular knowledge, and the thinking world had almost left its side. But the expansion of Christianity can never be altogether contemporaneous with the growth of knowledge. For new truth must be solidified by time before it can be built into the eternal truth of the Christian system. Yet, sooner or later, the conquest comes; sooner or later, whether it be art or music, history or philosophy, Christianity utilizes the best that the world finds, and gives it a niche in the temple of God.

To the student of God's ways, who reverently marks His progressive revelation and scans the horizon for each new fulfillment, the field of science presents just now a spectacle of bewildering interest. To say that he regards it with expectation is feebly to realize the dignity and import of the time. He looks at science with awe. It is the thing that is moving, unfolding. It is the breaking of a fresh seal. It is the new chapter of the world's history. What it contains for Christianity, or against it, he knows not. What it will do or undo— for in the fulfilling it may undo—he cannot tell. The plot is just at its thickest as he opens the page; the problems are more in number and more intricate than they have ever been before, and he waits almost with excitement for the next development.

And yet this attitude of Christianity toward science is as free from false hope as it is from false fear. It has no false fear, for it knows the strange fact that this plot is always at its thickest; and its hope of a quick solution is without extravagance, for it has learned the slowness of God's unfolding and His patient tempering of revelation to the young world which has to bear the strain. . . .

The one thing to be careful about in approaching nature is, that we really come to be taught; and the same attitude is honorably due to its interpreter, science. Religion is probably only learning for the first time how to approach science. Their former intercourse, from faults on both sides, and these mainly due to juvenility, is not a thing to remember. After the first quarrel—for they began the centuries hand in hand—the question of religion to science was simply "How dare you speak at all?" Then, as science held to its right to speak just a little, the question became, "What new menace to our creed does your latest discovery portend?" By-and-by both became wiser, and the coarser conflict ceased. Then we find religion suggesting a compromise, and asking simply what particular adjustment to its last hypothesis science would demand. But we do not speak now of the right to be heard, or of menaces to our faith, or even of compromises. Our question is a much maturer one—we ask what contribution science has to bestow, what good gift the wise men are bringing now to lay at the feet of our Christ. This question marks an immense advance in the relation between science and Christianity, and we should be careful to sustain it. Nothing is more easily thrown out of working order than the balance between different spheres of thought. The least assumption of superiority on the part of one, the least hint of a challenge, even a suggestion of independence, may provoke a quarrel. In one sense religion is independent of science, but in another it is not. For science is not independent of religion, and religion dare not leave it. One notices sometimes a disposition in religious writers, not only to make light of the claims of science, to smile at its attempts to help them, to despise its patronage, but even to taunt it with its impotence to touch the higher problems of life and being at all. Now science has feelings. This impotence is a fact, but it is the limitation simply of its function in the scheme of thought; and to taunt it with its insufficiency to perform other functions is a vulgar way to make it jealous of that which does perform them. We live in an intellectual commune, and owe too much to each other to reflect on a neighbor's poverty, even when it puts on appearances.

The result of the modern systematic study of nature has been to raise up in our midst a body of truth with almost unique claims to acceptance. The grounds of this acceptance are laid bare to all the world. There is nothing esoteric about science. It has no secrets. Its facts can be seen and handled; they are facts; they are nature itself. Apart therefore from their attractiveness or utility, men feel that here at last they have something to believe in, something independent of opinion, prejudice, self-interest, or tradition. This feeling is a splendid testimony to man as well as to nature. And we do not grudge to science the vigor and devotion of its students, for, like all true devotion, it is founded on an intense faith. Now the mere presence of this body of truth, so solid, so transparent, so verifiable, immediately affects all else that lies in the field of knowledge. And it affects it in different ways. Some things it scatters to the winds at once. They have been the birthright of mankind for ages, it may be; their venerableness matters not, they must go. And the power of the newcomer is so self-evident that they require no telling, but disappear of themselves. In this way the modern world has been rid of a hundred superstitions.

Among other things which have been brought to this bar is Christianity. It knows it can approve itself to science; but it is taken by surprise, and therefore begs time. It will honestly look up its credentials, and adjust itself, if necessary, to the new relation. Now this is the position of theology at the present moment. . . . Any theology proceeds by asking science what it demands, and then borrows its instruments to carry out the improvements. This loan of the instruments constitutes the first great contribution of science to religion.

What are these instruments? We shall name two—the scientific method and the doctrine of evolution. The first is the instrument for the interpretation of nature; the second is given us as the method of nature itself. With the first of these we shall deal formally; the second will present itself in various shapes as we proceed.

In emphasizing the scientific method as a contribution from science to Christianity, it is not to be understood that science has an exclusive, or even a prior claim, either to its discovery or possession. Along with the germs of all great things, it is found in the Bible; and theologians all along have fallen into its vein at times, though they have seldom pursued it long or with entire abandonment. There are examples of work done in modern theology, German and English, by the use of this method, which for the purity, consistency, and reverence with which it is applied are not surpassed by anything that physical science has produced. At the same time, this is *par excellence* the method of science. The perfecting of the instrument, the most lucid exhibition of its powers, the education in its use, above all the intellectual revolution which has compelled its application in every field of knowledge, we owe to natural science. Theology has had its share in this great movement, how much we need not ask, or seek to prove. The day is past for quarreling over rights of discovery; and whether we owe the scientific method to Job and Paul, or to Bacon and Darwin, is just the kind of question which the possession of this instrument would warn us not to touch.

To see what the scientific method has done for Christianity, we have only to ask ourselves what it is. The things which it insists upon are mainly two—the value of facts, and the value of laws. From the first of these comes the integrity of science; from the second its beauty and force. On bare facts science from first to last is based. . . . Now if Christianity possesses anything it possesses facts. So long as the facts were presented to the world Christianity spread with marvelous rapidity. But there came a time when the facts were less exhibited to men than the evidence for the facts. Theology, that is to say, began to rest on authority. Men or manuscripts were quoted as authorities for these facts, always with a loss of impressiveness, a loss increasing rapidly as time distanced the facts themselves. Then as the facts became more and more remote the Churches became the authorities rather than individual witnesses, and this was accompanied by a still further loss of power. And the surest proof of the waning influence of the facts themselves, and the extent of the loss incurred by the transfer of their credential to authority, is found in the appeal, which quickly followed, to the secular arm. The facts, ceasing to be their own warrant, had to be enforced by the establishment of judicial relations between Church and State. . . . Now Christianity is learning from science to go back to its facts, and it is going back to facts. Critics in every tongue are engaged upon the facts; travelers in every land are unveiling facts; exegetes are at work upon the words, scholars upon the manuscripts; skeptics, believing and unbelieving, are eliminating the not-facts; and the whole field is alive with workers. And the point to mark is that these men are not manipulating, but verifying, facts.

There is one portion of this field of facts, however, which is still strangely neglected, and to which a scientific theology may turn its next attention. The evidence for Christianity is not the Evidences. The evidence for Christianity is a *Christian*. The unit of physics is the atom, of biology the cell, of philosophy the man, of theology the Christian. The natural man, his regeneration by the Holy Spirit, the spiritual man and his relations to the world and to God, these are the modern facts for a scientific theology. We may indeed talk with science on its own terms about the creation of the world, and the spirituality of nature, and the force behind nature, and the unseen universe; but our language is not less scientific, not less justified by fact, when we speak of the work of the risen Christ, and the contemporary activities of the Holy Ghost, and the facts of regeneration, and the powers which are freeing men from sin. There is a great experiment which is repeated every day, the evidence for which is as accessible as for any facts of science; its phenomena are as palpable as any in nature; its processes are as explicable, or as inexplicable; its purpose is as clear; and yet science has never been seriously asked to reckon with it, nor has theology ever granted it the place its impressive reality commands. . . .

But not less essential, in the scientific method, than the examination of facts is the arrangement of them under laws. . . .

The sense of lawlessness which pervades the spiritual world at present reacts in many subtle and injurious ways upon the personal experience of Christians. They gather the idea that things are managed differently there from anywhere else—less strictly, less consistently; that blessings or punishments are dispensed arbitrarily, and that everything is ordered rather by a Divine discretion than by a system of fixed principle. In this higher atmosphere ordinary sequences are not to be looked for—cause and effect are suspended or superseded. Accordingly, to descend to the particular, men pray for things which they are quite unable to receive, or altogether unwilling to pay the price for. They expect effects without touching the preliminary causes, and causes without calculating the tremendous nature of the effects. There is nothing more appalling than the wholesale way in which unthinking people plead to the Almighty the richest and most spiritual of His promises, and claim their immediate fulfillment, without themselves fulfilling one of the conditions either on which they are promised or can possibly be given. If the Bible is closely looked into, it will probably be found that very many of the promises have attached to them a condition—itself not unfrequently the best part of the promise. True prayer for any promise is to plead for power to fulfill the condition on which it is offered, and which, being fulfilled, is in that act given. We have need, certainly in this sense, to know more of prayer and natural law. And science could make no truer contribution to modern Christianity than to enforce upon us all, as unweariedly as in nature, the law of causation in the spiritual life. The reason why so many people get nothing from prayer is that they expect effects without causes; and this also is the reason why they give it up. It is not irreligion that makes men give up prayer, but the uselessness of their prayers.

There is one other gain to Christianity to be expected from the wider use of the scientific method which may be mentioned in passing. Besides transforming it outwardly and reforming it inwardly, it must attract an ever-increasing band of workers to theology. There is a charm in working with a true method, which, once felt, becomes for ever irresistible. The activity in theology at the present time is almost limited, and the enthusiasm almost wholly limited, to those who are working with the scientific method. Round the islands of coral skeletons in the Pacific Ocean there is a belt of living coral. Each tiny polyp on this outermost fringe, and here only, secretes a solid substance from the invisible storehouse of the sea, and lays down its life in adding it to the advancing reef. So science and so theology grow. Through these workers on the fringing reef—behind, in contact with the great solid, essential, formulated past; before, the profound sea of unknown truth—through these workers, and through these alone can knowledge grow. . . . And it is the method that attracts them. And every day theology too, as it knows this method, gets busier—not undermining the old reef, nor abandoning it to make a new one, but adding the living work of living men to this essential, formulated past.

We are warned sometimes that this method has dangers, and told not to carry it too far. It is then it becomes dangerous. The danger arises, not from the use of the scientific method, but from its use apart from the scientific spirit. For these two are not quite the same. Some men use the scientific method, but not in the scientific spirit. And as science can help Christianity with the former, Christianity may perhaps do something for science as regards the latter. Christianity is certainly wonderfully tolerant of all this upturning in theology, wonderfully generous and patient and hopeful upon the whole. And so just is the remark of "Natural Religion," that the true scientific spirit and the Christian spirit are one, that the Christian world is probably prepared to accept almost anything the most advanced theology brings, provided it be a joint product of the scientific spirit—the fearlessness and originality of the one, tempered by the modesty, caution and reverence of the other.

To preserve this confidence, and to keep this spirit pure, is a sacred duty. There is an intellectual covetousness abroad just now which is: neither the fruit nor the friend of a scientific age—a haste to be wise which, like the haste to be rich, leads men into speculation upon indifferent securities, and can only end in fallen fortunes. Theology must not be bound up with such speculation. . . .

The one safeguard is to use the intellectual method in sympathetic association with the moral spirit. The scientific method may bring to light many fresh and revolutionary ideas; the scientific spirit will see that they are not given a place as dogmas in their first exuberance, that they are held with caution, and abandoned with generosity on sufficient evidence. The scientific method may secure many new and unique possessions; the scientific spirit will wear its honors humbly, knowing that after all new truth is less the product of genius than the daughter of time. And in its splendid progress the scientific method will find some old lights dim, some cherished doctrines old-fashioned, venerable authorities superseded; the scientific spirit will be respectful to the past, checking that mockery at the old which those who lack it make unthinkingly, and remembering that the day will come for its work also to pass away.

So much for the scientific method. Let us now consider for a moment one or two of its achievements. . . . We should begin with the beginnings, and expect the first serious contribution to theology on the doctrine of creation.

And what do we find? We find that upon this subject of all others science has most to offer us. It comes to us freighted with vast treasures of newly noticed facts, but with a theory which by many thoughtful minds has been accepted as the method of creation. And, more than this, it tells us candidly it has failed—and the failures of science are among its richest contributions to Christianity—it has failed to discover any clue to the ultimate mystery of origins, any clue which can compete for a moment with the view of theology.

Consider first this impressive silence of science on the question of origins. Who creates, or evolves; whither do the atoms come, or go? These questions remain as before. Science has not found a substitute for God. And yet, in another sense, these questions are very different from before. Science has put them through its crucible. It took them from theology, and deliberately proclaimed that it would try to answer them. They are now handed back, tried, unanswered, but with a new place in theology and a new power with science. Science has attained, after this ordeal, to a new respect for theology. If there are answers to these questions, and there ought to be, theology holds them. And theology likewise, has learned a new respect for science. In its investigations of these questions science has made a discovery. It has seen plainly that atheism is unscientific. It is a remarkable thing that after trailing its black length for centuries across European thought, atheism should have had its doom pronounced by science. With its most penetrating gaze science has now looked at the back of phenomena. It says "The atheist tells us there is nothing there. We cannot believe him. We cannot tell what it is, but there is certainly something. Agnostics we may be, we can no longer be atheists."

This permission to theism to go on, this invitation to Christianity to bring forward its theory to supplement science here, and give this something a name, is a great advance. And science has not left here a mere vague void for Christianity to fill, but a carefully defined niche with suggestions of the most striking kind as to how it is to be filled. It has never been sufficiently noticed how complete is the scientific account of a creative process, and how here biology and theology have actually touched. Watch a careful worker in science for a moment, and see how nearly a man by searching has found out God. The observer is Mr. Huxley. He stands looking down the tube of a powerful microscope. Almost touching the lens, he has placed a tiny speck of matter, which he tells us is the egg of a little water-animal, the common salamander or water-newt. He is trying to describe what he sees; it is the creation or development of a life. "It is a minute spheroid," he says, "in which the best microscope will reveal nothing but a structureless sac, enclosing a glairy fluid, holding granules in suspension. But strange possibilities lie dormant in that semi-fluid globe. Let a moderate supply of warmth reach its watery cradle, and the plastic matter undergoes changes so rapid and yet so steady and *purposelike* in their succession, that one can only compare them to those operated by a *skilled modeler* upon a formless lump of clay. As with an invisible trowel the mass is divided and subdivided into smaller and smaller portions, until it is reduced to an aggregation of granules not too large to build withal the finest fabrics of the nascent organism. And then it is *as if a delicate finger* traced out the line to be occupied by the spinal column, and molded the contour of the body; pinching up the head at one end, and the tail at the other, and fashioning flank and limb into due salamandrine proportions in so artistic a way, that, after watching the process hour by hour, one is almost involuntarily possessed by the notion that *some more subtle aid to vision than an achromatic would show the hidden artist with his plan before him, striving with skillful manipulation to perfect his work.*" So near has this observer come to a creator from the purely scientific side, that he can only describe what he sees in terms of creation. From the natural side he has come within a hair-breadth of the spiritual. Science and theology are here simply touching each other. There is not room really for another link between. And it will be apparent, on a moment's reflection, that we have much more in this than the final completion of a religious doctrine. What we really have is the joining of the natural and spiritual worlds themselves. It seems such a long way, to some men, from the natural to the spiritual, that it is a relief to witness at last their actual contact even at a point. And this is also a presumption that they are in unseen contact all along the line; that as we push all other truths to the last resort they will be met at the point where they disappear, that the complementary relations of religion and science will more and more be manifest; and that the unity, though never the fusion, of the natural and the spiritual will be finally disclosed.

When we turn now to the larger question of the creation of the world itself, we find much more than silence, or a permission to go on. We find science has a definite theory on that subject. It offers, in short, to theology a doctrine of the method of creation, in its hypothesis of evolution. That this doctrine is proved, many are convinced. It will be time for theology to be unanimous about it when science is unanimous about it. Yet it would be idle to deny that in a general form it has received the widest assent from theology. But if science is satisfied, even in a general way, with its theory of the method of creation, "assent" is a cold word for theology to welcome it with. It is needless at this time of day to point out the surpassing grandeur of the new conception. How it has filled the Christian imagination and kindled to enthusiasm the soberest scientific minds, is known to all. For that splendid hypothesis we cannot be too grateful to science, and that theology can only enrich itself which gives it even temporary place. There is a sublimity about the old doctrine of creation—we are speaking of its scientific aspects—which, if one could compare sublimities, is not surpassed by the new; but there is also a baldness. Fulfillments in this direction were sure to come with time, and they have come almost before the riper mind had felt its need of them. The doctrine of evolution fills a gap at the very beginning of our religion, and no one who looks now at the transcendent spectacle of the world's past, as disclosed by science, will deny that it has filled it worthily. Yet, after all, its beauty is not the only part of its contribution to Christianity. Scientific theology required a new view, though it did not require it to come in so magnificent a form. What it wanted was a credible presentation, in view especially of astronomy, geology, and biology. These had made the former theory simply untenable. And science has supplied theology with a theory which the intellect can accept and which for the devout mind leaves everything more worthy of worship than before.

From the contemplation of the flood of light poured by science over the doctrine of Creation, we might pass on to mark the effect upon many other theological truths which rays from the same source are beginning to illuminate. Nothing could be more interesting than to trace up the doctrines one by one in order, and watch the light gradually stealing over all. This must always be a beautiful sight; for this is the light of nature, and even its dawn is lovely. We should like to mark where the last ray gilded the last hill-top, and see how many higher peaks lay still beyond in shadow. And then we should like to prophesy that another light will rise, when physical science is dim, to illuminate what remains. We do not mean an inspired word, but a further contribution from nature itself. To many men of science, judging by the small esteem in which they hold philosophy, the day of mental science apparently is past. To an enlightened theology it is the science of the future. It were strange indeed, and a contradiction of evolution, if the science of atoms and cells were a later or further development than the science of man. Theology sees the point at which physical science must cease to help it; but encouraged by that help, it will expect a science to arise to carry it through the darkness that remains. The analogies of biology may be looked to to elucidate the mysterious phenomena of regeneration. When theology has received its full contribution from natural science it will be able to present to the world a scientific account of its greatest fact. The ultimate mystery of life, whether natural or spiritual, may still remain; but the laws, if not the processes, of the second birth will take their place in that great circle of the known which science is slowly redeeming from the surrounding darkness. We shall then have an embryology, a morphology, and a physiology of the new man; and a scientific theology will add to its departments a higher biology. . . . Without theology, the sciences are incomplete, and theology can only complete itself by completing the sciences.

But we have only space at present to note one or two other examples of the contribution of physical science, and these of a somewhat general kind. One shall be the doctrine of revelation itself. That science shows the necessity for a revelation in a new way, and even hints at subtle analogies for the mode in which it is conveyed to human minds, are points well worth developing. But we can only deal now with the more familiar question of subject matter and see how that has been affected by evolution.

According to science, as we have already seen, evolution is the method of creation. Now, creation is a form of revelation; it is the oldest form of revelation, the most accessible, the most universal, and still an ever-increasing source of theological truth. It is with this revelation that science begins. If then science, familiar with this revelation, and knowing it to be an evolution, were to be told of the existence of another revelation—an inspired word—it would expect that this other revelation would also be an evolution. Such an anticipation might or might not be justified; but from the law of the uniformity of nature, there would be, to a man of science, a very strong presumption in favor of any revelation which bore this scientific hall-mark, which indicated, that is to say, that God's word had unfolded itself to men like His works.

Now, if science searches the field of theology for an additional revelation, it will find a Bible awaiting it—a Bible in two forms. The one is the Bible as it was presented to our forefathers; the other is the Bible of modern theology. The books, the chapters, the verses, and the words, are the same in each; yet in form they are two entirely different Bibles. To science the difference is immediately palpable. Judging of each of them from its own standpoint, science perceives after a brief examination that the distinction between them is one with which it has been long familiar. In point of fact, the one is constructed like the world according to the old cosmogonies, while the other is an evolution. The one represents revelation as having been produced on the creative hypothesis, the Divine-fiat hypothesis, the ready-made hypothesis; the other on the slow-growth or evolution theory. It is at once obvious which of them science would prefer—it could no more accept the first than it could accept the ready-made theory of the universe.

Nothing could be more important than to assure science that the same difficulty has for some time been felt, and with quite equal keenness, by theology. The scientific method in its hand, scientific theology has been laboriously working at a reconstruction of Biblical truth from this very viewpoint of development. And it no more pledges itself today to the interpretations of the Bible of a thousand years ago, than does science to the interpretations of nature in the time of Pythagoras. Nature is the same today as in the time of Pythagoras, and the Bible is the same today as a thousand years ago. But the Pythagorean interpretation of nature is not less objectionable to the modern mind than are many ancient interpretations of the Scriptures to the scientific theologian.

The supreme contribution of Evolution to Religion is that it has given it a clearer Bible. One great function of science is not, as many seem to suppose, to make things difficult, but to make things plain. Science is the great explainer, the great expositor, not only of nature, but of everything it touches. Its function is to arrange things, and make them reasonable. And it has arranged the Bible in a new way, and made it as different as science has made the world. It is not going too far to say that there are many things in the Bible which are hard to reconcile with our ideas of a just and good God. This is only expressing what even the most devout and simple minds constantly feel, and feel to be sorely perplexing, in reading especially the Old Testament. But these difficulties arise simply from an old-fashioned or unscientific view of what the Bible is, and are similar to the difficulties found in nature when interpreted either without the aid of science, or with the science of many centuries ago. We see now that the mind of man has been slowly developing, that the race has been gradually educated, and that revelation has been adapted from the first to the various and successive stages through which that development passed. Instead, therefore, of reading all our theology into Genesis, we see only the alphabet there. In the later books we see primers—first, second, and third: the truths stated provisionally as for children, but gaining volume and clearness as the world gets older. Centuries and centuries pass, and the mind of the disciplined race is at last deemed ripe enough to receive New Testament truth, and the revelation culminates in the person of Christ.

The moral difficulties of the Old Testament are admittedly great. But when approached from the new standpoint, when they are seen to be rudiments spoken and acted in strange ways to attract and teach children, they vanish one by one. For instance, we are told that the iniquities of the father are to be visited upon the children unto the third and fourth generations. The impression upon the early mind undoubtedly must have been that this was a solemn threat which God would carry out in anger in individual cases. We now know, however, that this is simply the doctrine of heredity. A child inherits its parents' nature not as a special punishment, but by natural law. In those days that could not be explained. Natural law was a word unknown; and the truth had to be put provisionally in a form that all could understand. And even many of the miracles may have explanations in fact or in principle, which, without destroying the idea of the miraculous, may show the naturalness of the supernatural. . . .

Theology, surely, with its great age, its eternal foundation, and its countless mysteries, has the least to lose and the most to gain from every advance of knowledge. And the development theory has done more for theology perhaps than for any other science. Evolution has given to theology some wholly new departments. It has raised it to a new rank among the sciences. It has given it a vastly more reasonable body of truth, about God and man, about sin and salvation. It has lent it a firmer base, an enlarged horizon, and a richer faith. But its general contribution, on which all these depend, is to the doctrine of revelation.

What then does this mean for revelation? It means in plain language that evolution has given Christianity a new Bible. Its peculiarity is, that in its form, it is like the world in which it is found. It is a word, but its root is now known, and we have other words from the same root. Its substance is still the unchanged language of heaven, yet it is written in a familiar tongue. The new Bible is a book whose parts, though not of unequal value, are seen to be of different kinds of value; where the casual is distinguished from the essential, the local from the universal, the subordinate from the primal end. This Bible is not a book which has been made; it has grown. Hence it is no longer a mere word-book, nor a compendium of doctrines, but a nursery of growing truths. It is not an even plane of proof text without proportion or emphasis, or light and shade; but a revelation varied as nature, with the Divine in its hidden parts, in its spirit, its tendencies, its obscurities, and its omissions. Like nature it has successive strata, and valley and hilltop, and mist and atmosphere, and rivers which are flowing still, and here and there a place which is desert, and fossils too, whose crude forms are the stepping-stones to higher things. It is a record of inspired deeds as well as of inspired words, an ascending series of inspired facts in a matrix of human history.

Now it is to be marked that this is not the product of any destructive movement, nor is this transformed book in any sense a mutilated Bible. All this has taken place, it may be, without the elimination of a book or the loss of an important word. It is simply the transformation by a method whose main warrant is that the book lends itself to it. . . .

Theology is only beginning to realize how radical is the change in mental attitude of those who have learned to think from science. Intercourse with the ways of nature breeds a mental attitude of its own. It is an attitude worthy of its master. In this presence the student is face to face with what is real. He is looking with his own eyes at facts—at what God did. He finds things in nature just as its Maker left them; and from ceaseless contact with phenomena which will not change for man, and with laws which he has never known to swerve, he fears to trust his mind to anything less. Now this Bible which has been described, is the presentation to this age of men who have learned this habit. They have studied the facts, they have looked with their own eyes at what God did; and they are giving us a book which is more than the devout man's Bible, though it is as much as ever the devout man's Bible. It is the apologist's Bible. It is long since the apologist has had a Bible. The Bible of our infancy was not an apologist's Bible. There are things in the Old Testament cast in his teeth by skeptics, to which he has simply no answer. These are the things, the miserable things, the masses have laid hold of. . . . And, surprising as it is, there are not a few honest seekers who are made timid and suspicious, not a few on the outskirts of Christianity who are kept from coming further in, by the half-truths which a new exegesis, a reconsideration of the historic setting, and a clearer view of the moral purposes of God, would change from barriers into bulwarks of the faith. Such a Bible scientific theology is giving us, and it cannot be proclaimed to the mass of the people too soon. It is no more fair to raise and brandish objections to the Bible without first studying carefully what scientific theologians have to say on the subject, than it would be fair for one who derived his views of the natural world from Pythagoras to condemn all science. It is expected in criticisms of science that the critic's knowledge should at least be up to date, that he is attacking what science really holds; and the same justice is to be awarded to the science of theology. When science makes its next attack upon theology, if indeed that shall ever be again, it will find an armament, largely furnished by itself, which has made the Bible as impregnable as nature.

One question, finally, will determine the ultimate worth of this contribution to Christianity. Does it help it practically? Does it impoverish or enrich the soul? Does it lower or exalt God? These questions, with regard to one or two of the elementary truths of religion have been partially answered already. But a closing illustration from the highest of all will show that here also science is not silent.

Science has nothing finer to offer Christianity than the exaltation of its supreme conception—God. Is it too much to say that in a practical age like the present, when the idea and practice of worship tend to be forgotten, God should wish to reveal Himself afresh in ever more striking ways? Is it too much to say, that at this distance from creation, with the eye of theology resting largely upon the incarnation and work of the man Christ Jesus, the Almighty should design with more and more impressiveness to utter Himself as the Wonderful, the Counselor, the Great and Mighty God? Whether this be so or not, it is certain that every step of science discloses the attributes of the Almighty with a growing magnificence. The author of Natural Religion tells us that "the average scientific man worships just at present a more awful, and as it were a greater Deity than the average Christian." Certain it is that the Christian view and the scientific view together frame a conception of the object of worship such as the world in its highest inspiration has never reached before. The old student of natural theology rose from his contemplation of design in nature with heightened feeling of the wisdom, goodness, and power, of the Almighty. But never before had the attributes of eternity, and immensity, and infinity, clothed themselves with language so majestic in its sublimity. It is a language for the mind alone. Yet in the presence of the slow toiling of geology, millennium after millennium, at the unfinished earth; before the unthinkable past of paleontology, both but moments and lightning-flashes to the immenser standards of astronomy: before these even the imagination reels and leaves an experience only for religion.

3

Addresses to University Students

*T*HE Oddfellows Hall, where Henry Drummond held his Edinburgh student meetings, was on Forrest Road, only a brief walk
from library or lodging or from almost any point in the University
area. The hall was cozy, similar to an amateur theater, with movable
benches arranged in neat rows in the center and permanent seats
ringing the walls on back and sides. The balcony circled all but the
platform end of the hall, having benches in tiers all the way around.
On the small platform, with steps at both ends, several chairs were
placed across the wall with a rostrum for the speaker down center.
Only two rooms opened from the main hall, a small one in the back
and another one to the side of the platform. The hall could seat almost seven hundred students, but often as many as a thousand
crowded in, pushed tightly together on the benches, sitting on the
floor and steps, and standing even out into the long hallway leading
to the front door. The hall was easy to speak in but rather small for
the many informal personal conferences held simultaneously after
the meetings.

Yellow placards were put up at the University gates on Thursday
morning announcing the Oddfellows Hall meeting on Sunday
evening with Henry Drummond making the address. The placards
were posted on the large bulletin boards lining every entranceway to
the University buildings so the students could not miss them. Also
on Thursday, Friday and Saturday, sandwichmen carried signs in

the neighborhood of the University and the Royal Infirmary, advertising the meeting.

The order of the meetings was very simple: an opening hymn, a prayer, and Scripture reading, taking about fifteen minutes in all; then the address, lasting about forty-five minutes; then a closing hymn following an invitation to remain for personal conversation. The meetings were held on Sunday evenings only, except for an occasional prayer meeting, Bible reading, or other get-together on Saturday nights in some home. The meetings were never allowed to interfere with the University work of the students nor was there any attempt to interfere with amusements or athletics.

Sometimes Drummond took a text, but he could get along very well without one. Often his address only appeared to be informal. Actually he spent endless care in preparing each address, although he used no notes. He spoke about religion in the language of young men, and in such a shining new way, that young men flocked to hear him —and these doubt-ridden, materialistic, morally burdened University students responded, with the medical men leading the way.

Recollections of these Oddfellows Hall meetings by two who were there give a vivid background and setting for those who read Drummond's addresses in cold print, far removed from the time and place they were given. Ralph Connor, the Canadian story-teller, writes of hearing Drummond speak one Sunday evening when he was a student at New College:

"The striking feature of his face was his clear, blue, steady eyes, eyes of Mesmeric power. His manner was frank, manly, and perfectly respectful. Naturalness was the keynote of Drummond's religion. You felt he could say what he was saying on that Sunday evening, thrilling with its solemn emotion, just as forcibly in the cold light of Monday morning. Drummond's religion was natural because it was his life. He was speaking of the Friend of sinners, and was commending Christ to men as a Friend worth having. His words were simple Saxon, but chosen with exquisite exactness and arranged with almost poetic grace. But they were strong, and though they flowed easily, we were conscious of the power behind them, and of feeling the more intense that it was held so in command. Yet strong as were the words, and tense the feeling, they flowed full of light and music. It gave you thought, but in a series of visions. It was the most luminous and light-giving speaking I ever listened to. And how he commended his Friend to us. With gentle, firm and quiet insistence he made us feel our need first, and then a longing for that Friend of his. With what respectful urgency he appealed to the men who had not yet discovered this Friend to seek His acquaintance; and above all and through all, how dear and well-known this Friend seemed to him. He made us feel as if he had met Him on the street that day, as if he would meet Him round the corner when he left the hall, and would take Him home with him. It was as if one comrade were speaking of another whom he trusted, loved, and championed with all the ardor of a chivalrous and loyal soul."

One of the most vivid and perhaps typical recollections of these meetings and what the message did for students, some of whom never talked with Drummond personally at all, is given by David S. Cairns in his recent Autobiography. When Cairns first entered the University in 1880 he was in great doubt and conflict over the old inherited theology and the new science. His unresolved conflict led to a serious breakdown in health after wrestling unsuccessfully with this terrifically urgent question—"What reason had I for believing in God or Christ or Immortality?" He left the University for three years to recuperate. In 1886 he returned. By then Drummond's meetings were in full swing. Cairns tells how different things were:

"During my first period at the University religious life was at low ebb. Meagerly attended prayer meetings on Saturday morning, no corporate religious life. When I came back in the winter the Odd-fellows Hall in Forrest Road was filled every Sunday night by some six hundred students and not a few students met in little groups of prayer circles. The whole spiritual atmosphere was changed. . . . Drummond understood us, for he had singular intuitive gifts, and knew that many of us students were honestly groping our way, in a very troubled period of thought, to further light. This conflict over the faith of our fathers which we could not share in that form is just where Drummond met the inner necessities of many. There is an inner region, in religion as in moral matters, in which faiths and ideals have their birth. In this inner sphere Drummond had a good deal to say to us. . . . In [his addresses] he translated the truths of that older theology into another thought form, and he did it in a most vivid and attractive form of speech. He made us feel the spiritual issue for Christ or against Him was one of life or death. I'm deeply grateful that my youth passed under so gracious an influence, and I am certainly thankful to have had him as one of my teachers in spiritual things, for he helped me greatly in a transition time at once to hold fast to what was permanent in the old tradition and at the same time go on into the new world of thought with a new freedom."

In the 1880's the students were just beginning to awaken to their own existence as a responsible part of the human race. Henry Drummond helped the coming of a new spirit, giving a sense of responsibility and dignity, taking them and their problems (moral and intellectual) seriously. Out of this awakened student consciousness came a new unity in student life and such organizations as the Student Christian Movement.

Dr. Marcus Dods, who knew Drummond so well, said that in his University student work "all his gifts told: his personality so genial and happy and sympathetic, so obviously sincere and trustworthy, so disengaged from self and so glad to be at any man's service; his intellect trained in scientific methods, quick in the intuition of truth and in the reading of character; his Christlikeness, his purity and patience with those who had fallen, his serious view of life relieved by a ceaseless playfulness and humor and gaiety." And wherever he spoke—Australia, America, Germany, Japan—it was the same. His plain, practical, intellectually respectable talks were irresistible to students, principally because of his kinship with academic life and his contagious charm. He excited not the imagination only, but reason and common sense. There was no sensation in his addresses, nor any imposition of authority; no artificiality nor false mysticism; but the style was as simple as the thinking; it was one sensible man talking to others of his own generation about things of supreme importance.

In the ten years Henry Drummond devoted to the Oddfellows Hall meetings, covering three generations of students, he gave most of his better-known addresses more than once, but always with variations

and additions suitable to the occasion. The addresses which follow
were all given to students' groups and are among the finest of his
published works. The two best collections, other than the "Christmas
Booklets," are The Ideal Life and Stones Rolled Away, available from
time to time in secondhand bookstores. These few selections will
give some insight into his style and his appeal to thinking young men.

✺

("Ill-Temper" or "The Elder Brother" was given first at the Barclay Free Church, Edinburgh (1876-1877), repeated at Possilpark
Church (1877-1881), Glasgow, used time and again with various
student groups, and published posthumously in The Ideal Life.)

Those who have studied the paintings of Sir Noel Paton must
have observed that part of their peculiar beauty lies, by a trick of Art,
in their partial ugliness. There are flowers and birds, knights and
ladies, gossamer-winged fairies and children of seraphic beauty; but
in the corner of the canvas, or just at their feet, some uncouth and
loathsome form—a toad, a lizard, a slimy snail—to lend, by contrast
with its repulsiveness, a lovelier beauty to the rest. So in ancient
sculpture the griffin and the dragon grin among the angel faces on the
cathedral front, heightening the surrounding beauty by their deformity.

Many of the literary situations of the New Testament powerfully
exhibit this species of contrast. The twelve disciples—one of them is
a devil. Jesus upon the Cross, pure and regal—on either side a thief.
And here, as conspicuously, in the fifteenth chapter of Luke, the
most exquisite painting in the Bible is touched off at the foot with
the black thundercloud of the elder brother[1]—perfect, as a mere
dramatic situation.

But this conjunction, of course, is more than artistic. Apart from
its reference to the Pharisees, the association of these two characters
—the prodigal and his brother—side by side has a deep moral significance.

When we look into Sin, not in its theological aspects, but in its

[1] Drummond uses some of this same material in discussing "Good Temper" in
The Greatest Thing in the World. J. W. K.

everyday clothes, we find that it divides itself into two kinds. We find that there are sins of the body and sins of the disposition. Or more narrowly, sins of the passions, including all forms of lust and selfishness, and sins of the temper. The prodigal is *the* instance in the New Testament of sins of passion; the elder brother, of sins of temper.

One would say, at a first glance, that it was the younger brother in this picture who was the thundercloud. It was he who had dimmed all the virtues, and covered himself and his home with shame. And men have always pointed to the runaway son in contrast with his domestic brother, as the type of all that is worst in human character. Possibly the estimate is wrong. Possibly the elder brother is the worse. We judge of sins, as we judge of most things, by their outward form. We arrange the vices of our neighbors according to a scale which society has tacitly adopted, placing the more gross and public at the foot, the slightly less gross higher up, and then by some strange process the scale becomes obliterated. Finally it vanishes into space, leaving lengths of itself unexplored, its sins unnamed, unheeded, and unshunned. But we have no balance to weigh sins. Coarser and finer are but words of our own. The chances are, if anything, that the finer are the lower. The very fact that the world sees the coarser sins so well is against the belief that they are the worst. The subtle and unseen sin, that sin in the part of the nature most near to the spiritual, ought to be more degrading than any other. Yet for many of the finer forms of sin society has yet no brand. This sin of the elder brother is a mere trifle, only a little bit of temper, and scarcely worth the recording.

Now what was this little bit of temper? For Christ saw fit to record it. The elder brother, hard-working, patient, dutiful—let him get full credit for his virtues— comes in from his long day's work in the fields. Every night for years he has plodded home like this, heavy-limbed but light-hearted, for he has done his duty and honest sweat is on his brow. But a man's sense of responsibility for his character ends too often with the day's work. And we always meet the temptation which is to expose us when we least expect it. Tonight, as he nears the old homestead, he hears the noise of mirth and music. He makes out the strain of a dancing measure—a novel sound, surely, for the dull farm. "Thy brother is come," the servant says, "and they have killed the fatted calf." His brother! Happy hour! How long they mourned for him! How glad the old man would be! How the family prayer has found him out at last and brought the erring boy to his parents' roof! But no—there is no joy on that face; it is the thundercloud. "Brother, indeed," he mutters, "the scapegrace! Killed the fatted calf, have they? More than they ever did for me. I can teach them what I think of their merry-making. And talk of the reward of virtue! Here have I been all these years unhonored and ignored, and this young roué from the swine-troughs assembles the whole country-side to do him homage. 'And he was angry, and would not go in.' "

"Oh, the baby!" one inclines to say at first; but it is more than this. It is the thundercloud, a thundercloud which has been brewing under all his virtues all his life. It is the thundercloud. The subtle fluids from a dozen sins have come together for once, and now they are scorching his soul. Jealousy, anger, pride, uncharity, cruelty, self-righteousness, sulkiness, touchiness, doggedness, all mixed up together into one—Ill Temper. This is a fair analysis. Jealousy, anger, pride, uncharity, cruelty, self-righteousness, sulkiness, touchiness, doggedness—these are the staple ingredients of Ill Temper. And yet, men laugh over it. "Only temper," they call it: a little hot-headedness, a momentary ruffling of the surface, a mere passing cloud. But here the passing cloud is composed of drops, and the drops betoken an ocean, foul and rancorous, seething somewhere within the life—an ocean made up of jealousy, anger, pride, uncharity, cruelty, self-righteousness, sulkiness, touchiness, doggedness, lashed into a raging storm.

This is why temper is significant. It is not in what it is that its significance lies, but in what it reveals. But for this it were not worth notice. It is the intermittent fever which tells of unintermittent disease; the occasional bubble escaping to the surface, betraying the rottenness underneath; a hastily prepared specimen of the hidden products of the soul, dropped involuntarily when you are off your guard. In one word, it is the lightning-form of a dozen hideous and unchristian sins.

One of the first things to startle us—leaving now mere definition—about sins of temper, is their strange *compatibility with high moral character.* The elder brother, without doubt, was a man of high principle. Years ago, when his father divided unto them his living, he had the chance to sow his wild oats if he liked. As the elder brother, there fell to him the larger portion. Now was his time to see the world, to enjoy life, and break with the monotony of home. Like a dutiful son, he chose his career. The old home should be his world, the old people his society. He would be his father's right hand, and cheer and comfort his declining years. So to the servants he became a pattern of industry; to the neighbors an example of thrift and faithfulness; a model young man to all the country, and the more so by contrast with his vagabond brother. For association with lofty character is a painful circumstance of this deformity. And it suggests strange doubts as to the real virtue of much that is reckoned virtue and gets credit for the name. In reality we have no criterion for estimating at their true worth men who figure as models of all the virtues. Everything depends on motive. The virtues may be real or only apparent, even as the vices may be real though not apparent. Some men, for instance, are kept from going astray by mere cowardice. They have not character enough to lose their character. For it often requires a strong character to go wrong. It demands a certain originality and courage, a pocketing of pride of which all are not capable, before a man can make up his mind to fall out of step with Society and scatter his reputation to the winds. So it comes to pass that many very mean men retain their outward virtue. Conversely, among the prodigal sons of the world are often found characters of singular beauty. The prodigal, no doubt, was a better man to meet and spend an hour with than his immaculate brother. A wealth of tenderness and generosity, truly sweet and noble dispositions, constantly surprise us in characters hopelessly under the ban of men. But it is an instance of misconception as to the nature of sin that with most men this counts for nothing; although in those whose defalcation is in the lower region it counts, and counts almost for everything. Many of those who sow to the flesh regard their form of sin as trifling compared with the inconsistent and unchristian graves of those who profess to sow to the spirit. Many a man, for example, who thinks nothing of getting drunk would scorn to do an ungenerous deed or speak a withering word. And, as already said, it is really a question whether he is not right. One man sins high up in his nature, the other low down; and the vinous spendthrift, on the whole, may be a better man than the acid Christian. "Verily, I say unto you," said Jesus to the priests, "the publicans and the harlots go into the kingdom of God before you."

The fact, then, that there are these two distinct sets of sins, and that few of us indulge both, but most of us indulge the one or the other, explains compatibility of virtuous conduct with much unloveliness of disposition. Now it is this very association which makes sins of temper appear so harmless. There cannot be much wrong, we fancy, where there is so much general good. How often it is urged as an apology for garrulous people, that they are the soul of kindness if we only knew them better. And how often it is maintained, as a set-off against crossness and pitiable explosions of small distempers, that those who exhibit them are, in their normal mood, above the average in demonstrative tenderness. And it is this which makes it so hard to cure. We excuse the partial failure of our characters on the ground of their general success. We can afford to be a little bad who are so good. A true logic would say we can only afford to be a little better. If the fly in the ointment is a very small fly, why have a very small fly? Temper is the vice of the virtuous. Christ's sermon on the "elder brother" is evidently a sermon pointedly to the virtuous—not to make bad people good but to make good people perfect.

Passing now from the nature and relations of sins of this peculiar class, we come briefly to look at their effects. And these are of two kinds—the influence of temper on the intellect, and on the moral and religious nature.

With reference to the first, it has sometimes been taken for granted that a bad temper is a positive acquisition to the intellect. Its fieriness is supposed to communicate combustion to surrounding faculties, and to kindle the system into intense and vigorous life. "A man, when excessively jaded," says Darwin, "will sometimes invent imaginary offences, and put himself into a passion unconsciously, for the sake of re-invigorating himself." Now, of course, passion has its legitimate place in human nature, and when really controlled, instead of controlling, becomes the most powerful stimulus to the intellectual faculties. Thus it is this to which Luther refers when he says, "I never work better than when I am inspired by anger. When I am angry, I can write, pray, and preach well; for then my whole temperament is quickened, my understanding sharpened, and all mundane vexations and temptations depart."

The point, however, at which temper interferes with the intellect is in all matters of judgment. A quick temper really incapacitates for sound judgment. Decisions are struck off at a white heat, without time to collect grounds or hear explanations. Then it takes a humbler spirit than most of us possess to reverse them when once they are made. We ourselves are prejudiced in their favor simply because we have made them, and subsequent courses must generally do homage to our first precipitancy. No doubt the elder brother secretly confessed himself a fool the moment after his back was turned on the door. But he had taken his stand; he had said, "I will not go in," and neither his father's entreaties nor his own sense of the growing absurdity of the situation—think of the man standing outside his own door—were able to shake him. Temptation betraying a man into an immature judgment, that quickly followed by an irrelevant action, and the whole having to be defended by subsequent conduct, after making such a fuss about it—such is the natural history on the side of intellect of a sin of temper.

Among the scum left behind by such an action, apart from the consequences to the individual, are results always disastrous to others. It is generally, too, the weak who are the sufferers; for temper is the prerogative of superiors, and inferiors, down to the bottom of the scale, have not only to bear the brunt of the storm, but to sink their own judgment and spend their lives in ministering to what they know to be caprice. So their whole training is systematically false, and their own mental habits become disorganized and ruined. When the young, again, are disciplined by the iron instead of on the golden rule, the consequences are still more fatal. They feel that they do not get a fair hearing. Their case is summarily dismissed untried; and that sort of nursery lynch law to which they are constantly subjected carries with it no explanation of moral principles, muzzles legitimate feelings, and really inflicts a punishment infinitely more serious than is intended, in crushing out all sense of justice.

But it is in their moral and social effects that the chief evil lies. It is astonishing how large a part of Christ's precepts is devoted solely to the inculcation of happiness. How much of His life, too, was spent simply in making people happy! There was no word more often on His lips than "blessed," and it is recognized by Him as a distinct end in life, the end for this life, to secure the happiness of others. This simple grace, too, needs little equipment. Christ had little. One need scarcely even be happy one's self. Holiness, of course, is a greater word, but we cannot produce that in others. That is reserved for God Himself, but what is put in our power is happiness, and for that each man is his brother's keeper. Now society is an arrangement for producing and sustaining human happiness, and temper is an agent for thwarting and destroying it. Look at the parable for a moment, and see how the elder brother's wretched pettishness, explosion of temper, churlishness, spoiled the happiness of a whole circle. First, it certainly spoiled his own. How ashamed of himself he must have been when the fit was over, one can well guess. Yet these things are never so quickly over as they seem. Self-disgust and humiliation may come at once, but a good deal else within has to wait till the spirit is tuned again. For instance, prayer must wait. A man cannot pray till the sourness is out of his soul. He must first forgive his brother who trespassed against him before he can go to God to have his own trespasses forgiven.

Then look at the effect on the father, or on the guests, or even on the servants—that scene outside had cast its miserable gloom on the entire company. But there was one other who felt it with a tenfold keenness—the prodigal son. We can imagine the effect on him. This was home, was it? Well, it was a pity he ever came. If this was to be the sort of thing, he had better go. Happier a thousand times among the swine than to endure the boorishness of his self-contained, self-righteous brother. Yes, we drive men from Christ's door many a time by our sorry entertainment. The Church is not spiritualized enough yet to entertain the world. We have no spiritual courtesies. We cultivate our faith and proclaim our hope, but forget that a greater than these is charity. Till men can say of us, "They suffer long and are kind, they are not easily provoked, do not behave themselves unseemly, bear all things, think no evil," we have no chance against the world. One repulsive Christian will drive away a score of prodigals. God's love for poor sinners is very wonderful, but God's patience with ill-natured saints is a deeper mystery.

The worst of the misery caused by ill-temper is that it does no good. Some misery is beneficial, but this is gratuitous woe. Nothing in the world causes such rankling, abiding, unnecessary and unblessed pain. And Christ's words, therefore, when He refers to the breach of the law of love are most severe. "If any man offend one of these little ones," He says, "it were better for him that a millstone were hanged about his neck, and that he were cast into the depth of the sea." That is to say, it is Christ's deliberate verdict that it is better not to live than not to love.

In its ultimate nature Distemper is a sin against love. And however impossible it may be to realize that now, however we may condone it as a pardonable weakness or small infirmity, there is no greater sin. A sin against love is a sin against God, for God is love. He that sinneth against love, sinneth against God.

This tracing of the sin to its root now suggests this further topic—its cure. Christianity professes to cure anything. The process may be slow, the discipline may be severe, but it can be done. But is not temper a constitutional thing? Is it not hereditary, a family failing, a matter of temperament, and can *that* be cured? Yes, if there is anything in Christianity. If there is no provision for that, then Christianity stands convicted of being unequal to human need. What course then did the father take, in the case before us, to pacify the angry passions of his ill-natured son? Mark that he made no attempt in the first instance to reason with him. To do so is a common mistake, and utterly useless both with ourselves and others. We are perfectly convinced of the puerility of it all, but that does not help us in the least to mend it. The malady has its seat in the *affections*, and therefore the father went there at once. Reason came in its place, and the son was supplied with valid arguments—stated in the last verse of the chapter—against his conduct, but he was first plied with *Love*.

"Son," said the father, "thou art ever with me, and all that I have is thine." Analyze these words, and underneath them you will find the rallying cries of all great communities. There lie Liberty, Equality, and Fraternity—the happy symbols with which men have sought to maintain governments and establish kingdoms. "Son"—there is Liberty. "Thou art ever with me"—there is Unity, Fraternity. "All that I have is thine"—there is Equality. If any appeal could rouse a man to give up himself, to abandon selfish ends, under the strong throb of a common sympathy, it is this formula of the Christian Republic. Take the last, Equality, alone—"All that I have is thine." It is absurd to talk of your rights here and your rights there. You have all rights. "All that I have is thine." There is no room for selfishness if there is nothing more that one can possess. And God has made the Equality. God has given us all, and if the memory of His great kindness, His particular kindness to us, be once moved within, the heart must melt to Him, and flow out to all mankind as brothers.

It is quite idle, by force of will, to seek to empty the angry passions out of our life. Who has not made a thousand resolutions in this direction, only and with unutterable mortification to behold them dashed to pieces with the first temptation? The soul is to be made sweet not by taking the acidulous fluids out, but by putting something in—a great love, God's great love. This is to work a chemical change upon them, to renovate and regenerate them, to dissolve them in its own rich fragrant substance. If a man let this into his life, his cure is complete; if not, it is hopeless.

The character most hard to comprehend in the New Testament is the unmerciful servant. . . . How a man can rise from his knees, where, forgiven much already, he has just been forgiven more, and go straight from the audience chamber of his God to speak hard words and do hard things, is all but incredible. This servant truly in wasting his master's money must have wasted away his own soul. But grant a man any soul at all, love must follow forgiveness.

Being forgiven much, he *must* love much, not as a duty, but as a necessary consequence; he *must* become a humbler, tenderer man, generous and brotherly. Rooted and grounded in love, his love will grow till it embraces the earth. Then only he dimly begins to understand his father's gift—"All that I have is thine." The world is his: he cannot injure his own. The ground of benevolence is proprietorship. And all who love God are the proprietors of the world. The meek inherit the earth—all that He has is theirs. All that God has—what is that? Mountain and field, tree and sky, castle and cottage, white man, black man, genius and dullard, prisoner and pauper, sick and aged—all these are mine. If noble and happy, I must enjoy them; if great and beautiful, I must delight in them; if poor and hungry, I must clothe them; if sick and in prison, I must visit them. For they are all mine, all these, and all that God has beside, and I must love all and give myself for all. . . .

Now we are learning slowly that to believe is to love; that the first commandment is to love God, and the second *like unto it*—another version of it—is to love man. Not only the happiness but the efficiency of the passive virtues, love as a power, as a practical success in the world, is coming to be recognized. The fact that Christ led no army, that He wrote no book, built no church, spent no money, but that He loved, and so conquered, this is beginning to strike men. And Paul's argument is gaining adherents, that when all prophecies are fulfilled, and all our knowledge becomes obsolete, and all tongues grow unintelligible, this thing, Love, will abide and see them all out one by one into the oblivious past. This is the hope for the world that we shall learn to love, and in learning that, unlearn all anger and wrath and evil-speaking and malice and bitterness.

And this will indeed be the world's future. This is heaven. The curtain drops on the story of the prodigal, leaving him *in*, but the elder brother out. And why is obvious. It is impossible for such a man to be in heaven. He would spoil heaven for all who were there. Except such a man be born again he cannot enter the Kingdom of God. To get to heaven we must take it in with us. . . .

All sins mar God's image, but sins of temper mar God's image and God's work and man's happiness.

❦

("To Me to Live is Christ" or "Paul's Life" was written and delivered between 1876-1881; it was probably used at both Barclay Free

Church and Possilpark Church as well as with students. It was never prepared for publication by Drummond but published posthumously in The Ideal Life.)

. . . If we were to begin by seeking an appropriate motto for Paul's life, we should not need to go further than the quotation which forms our text. This fragment from one of his own letters lets us in at once to the whole secret of his life. The true discovery of a character is the discovery of its ideals. Paul spares us any speculation in his case. "To me to live," he says, "is Christ." This is the motto of his life, the ruling passion of it, which at once explains the nature of his success and accounts for it. He lives for Christ. . . .

This being the clue to Paul's life, the instructive question next arises, What exactly did Paul mean by this principle, and how did he come to find it out? But the question, "What is this object of life?" is so closely bound up with how Paul came to have this object of life, that the answer to the last question will form at once an explanation and an illustration of the first. . . .

Paul had two lives. Many men besides Paul have had two lives, but the line is cleaner cut in Paul's case than in almost any biography we have.

Both lives were somewhat about the same length, so far as we know, but so distinct in their general features and details that Paul had not only two lives, but as if to make the distinction more strikingly, two names. Let us look for a moment at the first of these lives. . . .

Paul's first life, as we all know, was spent under the most auspicious circumstances, and for certain reasons it will be worth while running over it. Born of a family which belonged to the most select theological school of that day, the son was early looked upon as at once the promise of his parents and the hope of their religion. They sent him when a mere lad to Jerusalem, and enrolled him as a student in the most distinguished college of the time. After running a brilliant college career, and sitting for many years at the feet of the greatest learning the Jewish capital could boast, we find him bursting upon the world with his splendid talents, and taking a place at once in the troubled political movements of the day. It was impossible for such a character with his youth's enthusiasm and a Pharisee's pride to submit to the tame life of a temple Rabbi, and he sees his opportunity in the rise of the Christian sect. Here, at last, he would match his abilities in a contest which would gain him at once a field of exercise and a name. So far, doubtless, he thought his first life great.

Into his work of persecution he seems to have next entered with all an inquisitor's zest. . . .

Upon the little Church at Jerusalem he . . . wreaked his vengeance to the full. . . .

But there is no pause in the pursuit of human fame. . . . With the ambition which knows not how to rest, and in the pride of his Pharisee's heart, he strikes out [with] the idea to reverse the maxim of the crucified Leader of the hated sect, and go into all the world and suppress the gospel in every creature. He applies to the high-priest for commission and authority, and, breathing out threatenings and slaughter, the man who is going to live for Christ starts out on his Christless mission to make havoc of the Church.

This is the last act of Paul's first life. . . . We are on the bridge which separates Paul's two lives. What marks the transition is this: up to this time his life has been spent in public. It has been one prolonged whirl of excitement and applause. But no sooner have the gates of Jerusalem closed upon him than Paul begins to think. The echoes of the people's praises have died away one by one. He has gone out into the great desert. It is strangely silent and soothing, and the lull has come at last upon his soul. It is a long time, perhaps, since he has had time to think; but Saul was far too great a man to live long an unthinking life. His time for reflection has come. And as he wanders with his small escort along the banks of the Jordan or through the solitary hills of Samaria, his thoughts are busy with the past. And if Saul was far too great a man to live an unthinking life, he was also too great a man to think well of his life when he did think. Each new day as he journeyed away from the scene of his triumph, and looked back upon it all from that distance—which always gives the true perspective to man's life—his mind must have filled with many a sad reproach. And as he lay down at night in the quiet wilderness his thoughts must often have turned on the true quality of the life to which he was sacrificing his talents and his youth. With his quick perception, with his keen trained intellect, with his penetration, he must have seen that after all this life was a mistake. Minds of lesser caliber in the applauding world which he had left had told him he was great. Now, in his calmer moments, he knew he was not great. The eternal heavens stretching above him pointed to an infinity which lay behind it all; and the stars and the silence spoke to him of God. And he felt that his life was miserably small. Saul's thoughts were greater than Saul's life. How he had been living beneath himself —how he had wasted the precious years of his youth—how he had sold his life for honor and reputation, and bartered the talents God had given him for a name, he must have seen. He had been dazzled, and that was all. He had nothing really to show for his life, nothing that would stand the test of solid thought. It was all done for himself. He, Saul of Tarsus, the rising man of his time, was the center of it all. "After all," perhaps he cried in agony, "To me to live is Saul, To me to live is Saul."

Paul's first great discovery, as we have seen—and it is the discovery which precedes every true reformation of life—was the discovery of himself. When Paul said, "To me to live is *myself*," his conversion was begun. There was no retreat then for a man like him. He was too great to have such a little center to his life; or, rather, he felt life too great to be absorbed with even such a personality as his.

But the next element in the case was not so easily discovered, and it is of much more importance than the first. His first achievement was only to discover himself. His second was to discover someone better than himself. He wanted a new center to his life—where was he to find it? The unseen hand which painted his own portrait in its true colors on the dark background of his mind had painted every other life the same. The high priests at Jerusalem, the members of the Sanhedrim, his own father at Tarsus—all the men he knew were living lives like himself. They were no better—most of them worse. Must the old center of Paul's life remain there still? Is there nothing better in all the world than himself?

It may be conjecture, or it may be nearer truth, that while such questionings passed through the mind of Paul, there came into his thoughts as he journeyed some influences from a life—a life like that for which his thoughts had longed. Paul's best-known journeys are his missionary tours, and we generally associate him in our thoughts with the countries of Asia and Italy and Greece. But this time his way leads through the holy land. He has entered the land of Christ. He is crossing the very footsteps of Jesus. The villages along his route are fragrant still with what Jesus said and did. They are not the bitter things that Saul had heard before. Kind words are repeated to him, and tender acts which Jesus did are told. The peasants by the wayside and the shepherds on the hills are full of stories of a self-denying life which used to pass that way a year or two ago, but now will come no more. And the mothers at the cottage doors remember the stranger who suffered their little children to come unto Him, and got them to repeat to Saul, perhaps, the children's blessing which He left behind. Perhaps, in passing through Samaria, the traveler met a woman at a well, who tells her strange tale for the thousandth time, of a weary man who had sat there once and said He was the Christ. And Galilee and Capernaum, and Bethsaida, and the lake shore at Gennesaret, are full of memories of the one true life which surely even then had begun to cast a sacred influence over Paul. At all events, there seemed a strange preparedness in his mind for the meeting on the Damascus Road, as if the interview with Jesus then was not so much the first of his friendship as the natural outcome of something that had gone before. And no doubt the Spirit's silent working had been telling on his mind during all these quiet days, leading up his thoughts to the revelation that was to come, and preparing a pathos for the memorable question, with its otherwise unaccountable emphasis, "Why persecutest thou Me?"

What went on between Paul's heart and God we do not know. We do not know how deep repentance ran, nor where, nor how, the justifying grace came down from heaven to his soul. Whether just then he went through our formula of conversion—the process which we like to watch and describe in technical words—we do not know. But we know this—there came a difference into his life. His life was changed. It was changed at its most radical part. He had changed centers. During the process, whatever it was, this great transfer was effected. Paul deliberately removed the old center from his life, and put a new one in its place. Instead of "to me to live is Paul," it was now, "to me to live is Christ."

Of course, when the center of Paul's life was changed, he had to take his whole life to pieces and build it up again on a totally different plan. This change, therefore, is not a mere incident in a man's life. It is a revolution, a revolution of the most sweeping sort. There never was a life so filled up with anti-Christian thoughts and impulses brought so completely to a halt. There never was such a total eclipse of the most brilliant worldly prospects, nor such an abrupt transition from a career of dazzling greatness to humble and obscure ignominy.

Let those who define conversion as a certain colorless experience supposed to go on in the *feelings*, blind themselves to the real transition in this life if they will. Let them ask themselves if there ever was a more sweeping revolution in any life, for any cause, than in Paul's, when he abandoned himself, literally abandoned himself, and subordinated everything, and evermore, to this one supreme passion—"to live for Christ."

The stages by which this transcendent standpoint is to be reached are plainly now before us. They are, the discovery of self and the discovery of Christ. These two discoveries between them exhaust the whole of life. *Till* these discoveries are made, no man truly lives till *both* are made—for many discover themselves who have not yet discovered Christ. But he that hath not the Son hath not *life*. Whatever he has, *existence, continuity*, he has not *life*. The condition of living at all is to live for Christ. "He that hath the Son," and he alone, and no one else, "hath life."

Paul takes special care indeed that we should fully understand the altogether different quality of the two lives which a man may live. In his view, the first life, the ordinary life of men, was altogether a mistake. "What things were gain to me," then, he tells us, "I count loss for Christ." That brilliant career of his was loss; that mission, noble and absorbing once, was mere waste energy and misspent time. And he goes further still. His life *was* death. It was selfishness pure and simple; it was the carnal mind pure and simple; and to be carnally minded is *death*. We shall understand the theology of these letters better if we think of the writer as a man escaping *death*. And with this horrible background to his life we can see the fuller significance of his words, that for him to live was Christ.

Another thing is also made plain to us.

The ceaseless demand of the New Testament for *regeneration* is also plain to us when we study the doctrine in such a life as this. It was not Saul who wrote the letters; it was a different man altogether—Paul. It was one who was in a totally different world from the other. If it *was* Saul, he must have been *born again* before he could have done it. Nothing *less* could account for it. His interests were new, his standpoint, his resources, his friendships. *All* old things, in fact, had passed away. *All* things had become new. In a word, he was a *new* creature. The pool, polluted and stagnant, had found its way at last into the wide, pure sea; the spirit, tired of its narrow prison, disgusted with ambition which ended with itself, reaches out to the eternal freedom, and finds a worthy field of exercise in the great enterprise of Christ.

There is one class, finally, to whom this biography of Paul has a special message. The people who need Paul's change most are not those, always, who are most thought to need it. The really difficult cases—to others, but especially to themselves—are the people who cannot see really that their life could be much better. There are thousands who do not see exactly what conversion could do to them. And their great difficulty in changing their life has just been this: "What, after all, should we really have to change? Our lives at present can *scarcely* be distinguished from the real Christians around us. Had we been irreligious, or profane, or undutiful, or immoral, conversion might do something for us; but we belong to the class who feel how well we have been brought up, how much our interests are gathered round religion, and, generally, how circumspect and proper our entire outward life has been. We do not really see, indeed, what change conversion could make." Now this is a class who seldom get any sympathy, and none deserve it more. Religious people and religious books are always saying hard things of the "religiously brought up"—bitterly hard and undeserved things—until they almost come to feel as if their goodness were a crime. But there are secret rendings of the heart within these ranks—longings after God perhaps purer than anywhere else outside God's true family. And these are those who feel the difficulty of changing in surroundings so Christian-like as theirs; who feel it so keenly that their despair sometimes leads them to the dark thought of almost envying the prodigal and the open sinner, who seem to have more chance of finding the kingdom than they.

Now the change in Paul's life is exactly the case in point for them. Paul himself was one of these characters who wonder what use conversion could ever be to them. He was one of the "religiously brought up." Touching the law he was blameless. There was no stricter man with his religion in all Jerusalem than Saul; no man took his place more regularly in the temple, or kept the Sabbath with more scrupulous care. Touching the law he was blameless—just the man you would have said who never would be changed, who was far too good to be susceptible of a change. But this is the man—not far from the kingdom of God, as everyone thought him to be—who found room in his most religious heart for the most sweeping reform that ever occurred in a life.

Let those who really do not know very well what religion could do for them take a little quiet thought like Paul. Let them look once more, not at the circumstance, but at the center of their life. Let them ask one question about it: *"Is it Christ?"* There is no middle way in religion—*self* or *Christ*. The quality of the selfishness—intellectual, literary, artistic—the fact that our self's center may be of a superior order of self, does nothing to destroy this grave distinction. It is between *all* self and Christ. . . . This question, then, of centers is the vital question. "To me to live is"—what? "To me to live is myself!" Suppose that it is so. . . .

> "I lived for myself, I thought for myself,
>   For myself, and none beside,
> Just as if Jesus had never lived,
>   As if he had never died."

This leads naturally to the other point—the discovery of Christ. And here once more we draw abundant encouragement from our biography of Paul. And it brings us not only to a hopeful thought, but to a very solemn thought. *We have all in some way made the discovery of Christ*—we know more about Christ than Paul did when he became a Christian. When he made Him the center of his life, he knew less of Him perhaps than most of us. It is a startling truth, at all events, that we are as near the center of life—the center of the universe—as Paul. We have heard of Him from our infancy; the features of His life are as familiar as our own; we have no hatred to Him as Paul had once. And if the few days' quietness in the Holy Land, which Paul had on the threshold of his change, were in any way a preparation for the crisis of his life, how much more has our past life been a preparation for a change in ours! We call Paul's change a sudden conversion—we do not know how sudden it was. But if our life was changed today, it would be no sudden conversion. Our whole past has been leading up to these two discoveries of life. Our preparation, so far as knowledge of the new center goes, is complete. The change, so far as that is concerned, might happen now. We have the responsibility of being so near eternal life as that.

The question comes to be then, finally, simply a question of transfer. To me to live is myself, or to me to live is Christ. To live for Christ is not simply the sublime doctrine which it includes of *Christ our life*. It is not so much Christ our life, but rather our *life for Christ*.

Shall it be, then, our life for Christ? "To me to live is Christ." Contrast it with all the other objects of life; take all the centers out of all the great lives, and compare them one by one. Can you match the life-creed of Paul—"to me to live is Christ?"

"To me to live is"—*what? What* are we living for? . . . What was the first thought that came into our hearts just then? What word trembled first on our lip just now—"to me to live is"—was it business, was it money, was it ourself, was it Christ?

. . . The time will come when we shall ask ourselves why we ever crushed this infinite substance of our life within these narrow bounds, and centered that which lasts for ever on what must pass away. In the perspective of eternity all lives will seem poor, and small, and lost, and self-condemned beside a life for Christ. There will be plenty then to gather round the Cross. But who will do it now? Who will do it now? There are plenty [of] men to die for Him, there are plenty to spend eternity with Christ; but where is the man who will live for Christ? Death and Eternity in their place. Christ wants lives. No fear about death being gain if we have lived for Christ. So let it be. "To me to live is Christ." There is but one alternative—the putting on of Christ; Paul's alternative, the discovery of Christ. We have all in some sense, indeed, already made the discovery of Christ. We may be as near it now as Paul when he left Jerusalem. There was no notice given that he was to change masters. The new Master simply crossed his path one day, and the great change was come. How often has He crossed our path? We know what to do the next time: we know how our life can be made worthy and great—how only; we know how death can become gain—how only. Many, indeed, tell us death will be gain. Many long for life to be done that they may rest, as they say, in the quiet grave. Let no cheap sentimentalism deceive us. Death can only be gain when to have lived was Christ.

❦

(*"Dealing with Doubt"—given to a student conference at North-field in the summer of 1887 and repeated with many other student groups, and published first in a volume of the addresses delivered at Northfield that summer—The College of Colleges.*)

There is a subject which I think we . . . cannot afford to keep out of sight—I mean the subject of "Doubt." We are forced to face it . . . and I say that the men who are perplexed—the men who come to you with serious and honest difficulties—are the best men. They are men of intellectual honesty, and cannot allow themselves to be put to rest by words, or phrases, or traditions, or theologies, but who must get to the bottom of things for themselves. And if I am not mistaken, Christ was very fond of these men. The outsiders always interested Him, and touched Him. The orthodox people—the Pharisees—He was much less interested in. He went with publicans and sinners—with people who were in revolt against respectability, intellectual and religious, of the day. And following Him, we are entitled to give sympathetic consideration to those whom He loved and took trouble with.

First, let me speak for a moment or two about the origin of doubt.

In the first place, we are born questioners. Look at the wonderment of a little child in its eyes before it can speak. The child's great word when it begins to speak is "Why?" Every child is full of every kind of question, about every kind of thing that moves, and shines, and changes, in the little world in which it lives. That is the incipient doubt in the nature of man. Respect doubt for its origin. It is an inevitable thing. It is not a thing to be crushed. It is a part of man as God made him. . . . Doubt is the prelude of knowledge.

Secondly: The world is a Sphinx. It is a vast riddle—an unfathomable mystery; and on every side there is temptation to questioning. In every leaf, in every cell of every leaf, there are a hundrd problems. There are ten good years of a man's life in investigating what is in a leaf, and there are five good years more in investigating the things that are in the things that are in the leaf. God has planned the world to incite men to intellectual activity.

Thirdly: The instrument with which we attempt to investigate truth is impaired. Some say it fell, and the glass is broken. Some say prejudice, heredity, or sin, have spoiled its sight, and have blinded our eyes and deadened our ears. In any case the instruments with which we work upon truth, even the strongest men, are feeble and inadequate to their tremendous task.

And in the fourth place, all religious truths are doubtable. There is no absolute proof for any one of them. Even that fundamental truth—the existence of God—no man can prove by reason. The ordinary proof for the existence of God involves either an assumption, argument in a circle, or a contradiction. The impression of God is kept up by experience; not by logic. And hence, when the experimental religion of a man, of a community, or of a nation, wanes, religion wanes—their idea of God grows indistinct, and that man, community or nation becomes infidel. Bear in mind, then, that all religious truths are doubtable—even those which we hold most strongly.

What does this brief account of the origin of doubt teach us? It teaches us great intellectual humility. It teaches us sympathy and toleration with all men who venture upon the ocean of truth to find out a path through it for themselves. . . .

What has been the Church's treatment of doubt in the past? It

has been very simple. "There is a heretic. Burn him!" That is all.
"There is a man who has gone off the road. Bring him back and torture him!" We have got past that physically; have we got past it
morally? . . . I have spoken already of His [Christ's] strange partiality
for the outsiders—for the scattered heretics up and down the
country; of the care with which He loved to deal with them, and
of the respect in which He held their intellectual difficulties.
Christ never failed to distinguish between doubt and unbelief. Doubt
is *can't believe*; unbelief is *won't believe*. Doubt is honesty; unbelief
is obstinacy. Doubt is looking for light; unbelief is content with darkness. Loving darkness rather than light—that is what Christ attacked,
and attacked unsparingly. But for the intellectual questioning of
Thomas, and Philip, and Nicodemus, and the many others who came
to Him to have their great problems solved, He was respectful and
generous and tolerant.

And how did He meet their doubts? . . . Christ said, "Teach him."
He destroyed by fulfilling. When Thomas came to Him and denied
His very resurrection, and stood before Him waiting for the scathing
words and lashing for his unbelief, they never came. Christ gave him
facts—facts. No man can go around facts. Christ said, "Behold my
hands and my feet." The great god of science at the present time is a
fact. It works with facts. Its cry is, "Give me facts." Found anything
you like upon facts and we will believe it. The spirit of Christ was the
scientific spirit. He founded His religion upon facts; and He asked all
men to found their religion upon facts. Now, gentlemen, get up the
facts of Christianity, and take men to the facts. Theologies—and I
am not speaking disrespectfully of theology; theology is as scientific
a thing as any other science of facts—but theologies are human versions of Divine truths, and hence the varieties of the versions, and the
inconsistencies of them. I would allow a man to select whichever
version of this truth he liked *afterward*; but I would ask him to begin
with no version, but go back to the facts and base his Christian life
upon that. That is the great lesson of the New Testament way of
looking at doubt—of Christ's treatment of doubt. It is not "Brand
him!"—but lovingly, wisely, and tenderly to teach him. Faith is never
opposed to reason in the New Testament; it is opposed to sight. You

will find that a principle worth thinking over. *Faith is never opposed to reason in the New Testament, but to sight.*

Well, now, with these principles in mind as to the origin of doubt, and as to Christ's treatment of it, how are we ourselves to deal with our fellow-students who are in intellectual difficulty? In the first place, I think we must make all the concessions to them that we conscientiously can. When a doubter first encounters you he pours out a deluge of abuse of churches, and ministers, and creeds, and Christians. Nine-tenths of what he says is probably true. Make concessions. Agree with him. It does him good to unburden himself of these things. He has been cherishing them for years—laying them up against Christians, against the Church, and against Christianity; and now he is startled to find the first Christian with whom he has talked over the thing almost entirely agrees with him. We are, of course, not responsible for everything that is said in the name of Christianity; but a man does not give up medicine because there are quack doctors, and no man has a right to give up Christianity because there are spurious or inconsistent Christians. Then, as I already said, creeds are human versions of Divine truths; and we do not ask a man to accept all the creeds, any more than we ask him to accept all the Christians. We ask him to accept Christ, and the facts about Christ, and the words of Christ. But you will find the battle is half won when you have endorsed the man's objections, and possibly added a great many more to the charges which he has against ourselves. These men are in revolt against the kind of religion which we exhibit to the world—against the cant that is taught in the name of Christianity. And if the men that have never seen the real thing—if you could show them that, they would receive it as eagerly as you do. They are merely in revolt against the imperfections and inconsistencies of those who represent Christ to the world.

Secondly: Beg them to set aside, by an act of will, all unsolved problems: such as the problem of the origin of evil, the problem of the Trinity, the problem of the relation of human will and predestination, and so on—problems which have been investigated for thousands of years without results—ask them to set those problems aside as insoluble in the meantime, just as a man who is studying mathematics may be asked to set aside the problem of squaring the circle. Let him go on with what can be done, and what has been done, and leave out of sight the impossible. You will find that will relieve the skeptic's mind of a great deal of unnecessary cargo that has been in his way.

Thirdly: Talking about difficulties, as a rule, only aggravates them. Entire satisfaction to the intellect is unattainable about any of the greater problems, and if you try to get to the bottom of them by argument, there is no bottom there; and therefore you make the matter worse. But I would say what is known, and what can be honestly and philosophically and scientifically said about one or two of the difficulties that the doubter raises, just to show him that you can do it—to show him that you are not a fool—that you are not merely groping in the dark yourself, but you have found whatever basis is possible. But I would not go around all the doctrines. I would simply do that with one or two; because the moment you cut off one, a hundred other heads will grow in its place. It would be a pity if all these problems could be solved. The joy of the intellectual life would be largely gone. I would not rob a man of his problems, nor would I have another man rob me of my problems. They are the delight of life, and the whole intellectual world would be stale and unprofitable if we knew everything.

Fourthly—and this is the great point: Turn away from the reason, and go into the man's moral life. I don't mean, go into his moral life and see if the man is living in conscious sin, which is the great blinder of the eyes—I am speaking of honest doubt; but open a new door into the practical side of man's nature. Entreat him not to postpone life and his life's uselessness until he has settled all the problems of the universe. Tell him those problems will never all be settled; that his life will be done before he has begun to settle them; and ask him what he is doing with his life meantime. Charge him with wasting his life and his usefulness; and invite him to deal with the moral and practical difficulties of the world, and leave the intellectual difficulties as he goes along. To spend time upon these is proving the less important before the more important; and, as the French say, "The good is the enemy of the best." It is a good thing to think; it is a better thing to work—it is a better thing to do good. And you have him there, you see. He can't get beyond that. You have to tell him, in fact, that there are two organs of knowledge: the one reason, the other obedience. And now tell him, as he has tried the first and found the little in it, just for a moment or two to join you in trying the second. And when he asks whom he is to obey, you tell him there is but One, and lead him to the great historical figure who calls all men to Him: the one perfect life—the one Savior of mankind—the one Light of the world. Ask him to begin to obey Christ; and, doing His will, he shall know of the doctrine whether it be of God.

That, I think, is about the only thing you can do with a man: to get him into practical contact with the needs of the world, and to let him lose his intellectual difficulties meantime. Don't ask him to give them up altogether. Tell him to solve them afterward one by one if he can, but meantime to give his life to Christ and his time to the kingdom of God. And, you see, you fetch him completely around when you do that. You have taken him away from the false side of nature, and to the practical and moral side of his nature; and for the first time in his life, perhaps, he puts things in their true place. He puts his nature in the relations in which it ought to be, and he then only begins to live. And by obedience—by obedience—he will soon become a learner and pupil for himself, and Christ will teach him things, and he will find whatever problems are solvable gradually solved as he goes along the path of practical duty.

Now, let me, in closing, give a couple of instances of how to deal with specific points. The commonest thing that we hear nowadays by young men is, "What about evolution? How am I to reconcile my religion, or any religion, with the doctrine of evolution?" That upsets more men than perhaps anything else at the present hour. How would you deal with it? I would say to a man that Christianity is the further evolution. I don't know any better definition than that. It is the further evolution—the higher evolution. . . . I take [a man] at his own terms. He says evolution is that which pushes the man on from the simple to the complex, from the lower to the higher. Very well; that is what Christianity does. It pushes the man farther on. It takes him where nature has left him, and carries him on to heights which on the plain of nature he could never reach. That is evolution. "Lead me to the Rock that is higher than I." That is evolution. It is the development of the whole man in the highest directions—the drawing out of his spiritual being. Show an evolutionist that, and you have taken the wind out of his sails. "I came not to destroy. . . ." Put a larger meaning into it.

The other instance—the next commonest question perhaps—is the question of miracles. It is impossible, of course, to discuss that now—miracles; but that question is thrown at my head every second day: "What do you say to a man when he says to you, 'Why do you believe in miracles?' " I say, "Because I have seen them." He says, "When?" I say, "Yesterday." He says, "Where?" "Down such-and-such a street I saw a man who was a drunkard redeemed by the power of an unseen Christ and saved from sin. That is a miracle." The best apologetic for Christianity is a Christian. That is a fact which the man cannot get over. There are fifty other arguments for miracles, but none so good as that you have seen them. Perhaps you are one yourself. But take you a man and show him a miracle with his own eyes. Then he will believe.

❦

(*"The Perfected Life"* or *"The Greatest Need of the World"* was published first in 1887, after having been given at Northfield. Mrs. A. R. Simpson labeled it "Very precious." Some parts of it are in common with *"The Changed Life"* and *"Modes of Sanctification."* It is found in A College of Colleges and separately in booklet form.)

God is all for quality; man is for quantity. But the immediate need of the world at this moment is not more of us, but, if I may use the expression, a better brand of us. To secure ten men of an improved type would be better than if we had ten thousand more of the average Christians distributed all over the world. There is such a thing in the evangelistic sense as winning the whole world and losing our own soul. And the first consideration is our own life—our spiritual relations to God—our own likeness to Christ. And I am anxious, briefly, to look at the right and wrong way of becoming like Christ— of becoming better men . . .

One of the futile methods of sanctifying ourselves is trying; effort —struggle—agonizing. I suppose you have all tried that, and I appeal to your own life when I ask if it has not failed. Crossing the Atlantic, the *Etruria*, in which I was sailing, suddenly stopped in mid-ocean— something had broken down. There were a thousand people on board that ship. Do you think we could have made it go if we had all gathered together and pushed against the sides or against the masts? When a man hopes to sanctify himself by trying, he is like a man trying to make the boat go that carries him by pushing it—he is like a man drowning in the water and trying to save himself by pulling the hair of his own head. It is impossible. Christ held up the mode of sanctification almost to ridicule when He said: "Which of you by taking thought can add a cubit to his stature?" Put down that method forever as futile.

Another man says: "That is not my way. I have given up that. Trying has its place, but that is not where it comes in. My method is to concentrate on some single sin, and to work away upon that until I have got rid of it." Now, in the first place, life is too short for that process to succeed. Their name is legion. In the second place, that leaves the rest of the nature for a long time untouched. In the third place, it does not touch the seed or root of the disease. If you dam up a stream at one place, it will simply overflow higher up. And for a fourth reason: Religion does not consist in negatives—in stopping this sin and stopping that sin.

Another man says: "Very well; I am not trying to stop sins in succession; but I am trying to copy the character of Christ, bit by bit, point by point, into my life." The difficulty about that method is, that it is too mechanical. It makes an over-balanced life; and there is always the mark of the tool about such a life—about such a nature. It is like a wax-flower as compared with a natural flower.

There is another method. I suppose you have tried it. I have. It is to get a book of blank paper and make columns for the days of the week, and then put down a list of the virtues with spaces against each for marks, and then follow it up with a great many rules, and determine to live by rule. That is how Franklin did; and I suppose that many men in this day could tell how they had hung up in their bedroom, or laid away in their secret drawers, the rules they had drawn up for themselves. Again I appeal to life. You bear me witness that that method has failed. And it failed for very matter-of-fact reasons—likely because you forgot the rules. As a matter of fact, that is a false method of sanctification; and, like all the others, must come to nothing.

All these methods that I have named are perfectly human, perfectly futile. I do not say we must abandon them; but they are futile to accomplish the real end that we seek.

Now, what is the true method? There is one method which is as simple and effectual as the others are complicated and useless. It is laid down in a single verse in the Bible; and it is so practical that any man can apply it to his own life, and as certain in its action as a law of nature. It is a case of cause and effect. The verse I refer to is in II Corinthians; and I take it from the immensely improved text in this instance of the Revised Version—the 18th verse of the 3rd chapter of II Corinthians: "We all, with unveiled face, reflecting in a mirror the glory of the Lord, are changed into the same image from glory to glory even as by the Lord, the Spirit."

Observe: "We are changed." The mistake we have been making is that we have been trying to change ourselves. That is not possible. We are changed into the same image. Now, if we are to get the benefit of the relief that these words ought to give to the man who has been spending half his nights and half his life in a frenzied struggle for holiness without having fulfilled the necessary conditions, let us carefully mark the condition demanded. For that condition being fulfilled, we are infallibly changed into the same image. The condition is that we reflect in a mirror the glory of Christ. That condition I shall refer to in a moment; but one word requires an explanation in passing. "Reflecting in a mirror the glory of the Lord." What is the glory of the Lord? The word "glory" suggests effulgence —radiance. It recalls the halo that the old masters delighted to paint around the heads of their saints and *Ecce Homos*. But this is all material. What does that halo, that radiance, symbolize? It symbolizes the most radiant and beautiful thing in man, as in the man Christ Jesus; and that is, character. *Character*. The glory of Christ is in character. I make a challenge. Does any man know anything more glorious in man or in God than character? God's name was His character—Himself. Do not be misled by the vagueness of that word "glory" in modern usage. We lose the force of it because we do not employ the word in current speech. When it is in your mind, substitute "character" for "glory." "We are all, with unveiled face, reflecting in a mirror the character of Christ, are changed into the same image from character to character"—from the character a little better to the character a little better still, the character getting nobler and nobler by slight and imperceptible degrees. Now, read that verse once more with all these meanings brought out: "We all, with unveiled face, reflecting in a mirror the character of the Lord, are changed into the 'same image from character to character."

How to get character: Stand in Christ's presence and mirror His character, and you will be changed in spite of yourself, into the same image from character to character. Every man is a reflector. That is the principle upon which this is based. In your face you reflect your nationality. I ask a man a question, and I find out in ten seconds whether his is a Northerner, or Southerner, or a Canadian, or an Englishman. He has reflected in his very voice his country. I ask him another question, and another, and another, and I see reflections flit over the mirror from all points of the compass. I find out in five minutes that he has a good mother. I see reflected in a mirror that he has been reading Herbert Spencer, and Huxley, and Darwin; and as I go on watching him as he stands and talks to me, his whole life is reflected back from it. I see the kind of set he has been living in—the kind of companions he has had. He cannot help reflecting. He cannot help himself showing the environment in which he has lived—the influences that have played around him. As Tennyson says: "I am a part of all that I have met." Now, we become like those whom we habitually reflect. I could prove from science that that applies even to the physical framework of animals—that they are influenced and organically changed by the environment in which they live. We all know how every man is influenced by the people and the things that surround him. I remember two fellow-students who lived for eight years together, and by the end of that time they had become so like one another in their methods of thinking, in their opinions, in their ways of looking at things, that they were practically one. When you asked a question it was immaterial to which you addressed it, and when you made a remark you knew exactly the impression it would make on both of them. They had been changed into the same image. There was a savor of Jonathan about David, and a savor of David about Jonathan. You sometimes see husband and wife, after a half century of fellowship, changed entirely into the same image. They have gone on reflecting one another so often—without trying, and perhaps even trying to prevent it—that they have become largely made up of the same qualities and characteristics. That is the grand doctrine of influence—that we become like those whom we habitually associate with.

What, then, is the practical lesson? It is obvious. *Make Christ your most constant companion.* Be more under His influence than any other influence. Five minutes spent in the companionship of Christ every morning—aye, two minutes, if it is face to face and heart to heart—will change the whole day, will make every thought and feeling different, will enable you to do things for His sake that you would not have done for your own sake, or for anyone's sake. And the supreme and the sole secret of a sanctified nature and a Christlike character and life, is to be ever with Christ and reflecting Him—catching His nature, His mind and spirit, insensibly and unconsciously, by mere proximity and contagion.

You say, "How can a man make Christ, the absent Christ, his most constant companion?" Why; friendship is a spiritual thing. Think over it for a moment, and you will find that your friend influences you just about as much in his absence as when he is with you. Christ might have influenced us more, perhaps, if He had been here, and yet I do not know. It would have been an ineffable experience to have lived at that time. . . . And yet, if Christ were to come into the world again, few of us probably would ever have a chance of seeing Him. I have never seen my own Queen in our little country of Britain. There are millions of her subjects who have never seen her. And there would be thousands of the subjects of the Lord Jesus who could never get within speaking distance of Him if He came to the world now. We remember He said: "It is expedient for you (not Me) that I go away"; because by going away He could really be nearer to us than He would have been if He had stayed here. It would have been geographically and physically impossible for most of us to have been influenced by His person had He remained. And so, our communion with Him is a spiritual companionship; but not different from most companionships, which when you press them down to the roots, you will find to be essentially spiritual.

All friendship, all love, human and Divine, is spiritual. So that it is no difficulty in reflecting the character of Christ that we have never been in visible contact with Him. He does not appeal to the eye; He appeals to the soul: and is reflected not from the body, but from the soul. The thing you love in a friend is not the thing you see. . . .

Let me say a word or two about the effects which necessarily must follow from this contact, or fellowship, with Christ—I need not quote the texts upon the subject—the texts about abiding in Christ—"He that abideth in Him sinneth not." You cannot sin when you are standing in front of Christ. You simply cannot do it. "Whosoever committeth sin hath not seen Him, neither known Him." Sin is abashed and disappears in the presence of Christ. Again: "If ye abide in Me, and My words abide in you, ye shall ask what ye will, and it shall be done unto you." Think of that! That is another inevitable consequence. And there is yet another. "He that abideth in Me, the same bringeth forth much fruit." Sinlessness—answered prayer—much fruit. But in addition to these things, see how many of the highest Christian virtues and experiences necessarily flow from the assumption of that attitude toward Christ. For instance, the moment you assume that relation to Christ you begin to know what the child-spirit is. You stand before Christ, and He becomes your Teacher, and you instinctively become docile. Then you learn also to become charitable and tolerant; because you are learning of Him, and He is "meek and lowly in heart," and you catch that spirit. That is a bit of His character being reflected into yours. Instead of being critical and self-asserting, you become humble and have the mind of a little child. I think, further, the only way of learning what faith is is to know Christ and be in His company. You hear sermons about the nine different kinds of faith—distinctions drawn between the right kind of faith and the wrong—and sermons telling you how to get faith. So far as I can see, there is only one way in which faith is got, and it is the same in the religious world as in the world of men and women. I learn to trust you, my brother, just as I get to know you, and neither more nor less; and you get to trust me just as you get to know me. I do not trust you as a stranger. But as I come into contact with you, and watch you, and live with you, I find out that you are trustworthy, and I come to trust myself to you, and to lean upon you. But I do not do that to a stranger.

The way to trust Christ is to know Christ. You cannot help trusting Him then. You are changed. By knowing Him faith is begotten in you, as cause and effect. To trust Him as thousands do, is not faith, but credulity. I believe a great deal of prayer for faith is thrown away. What we should pray for is that we may be able to fulfill the condition, and when we have fulfilled the condition, the faith necessarily follows. The way, therefore, to increase our faith is to increase our intimacy with Christ. We trust Him more and more the better we know Him.

And then another immediate effect of this way of sanctifying the character is the tranquillity that it brings over the Christian life. How disturbed and distressed and anxious Christian people are about their growth in grace! Now, the moment you give that over into Christ's care—the moment you see that you are being changed—that anxiety passes away. You see that it must follow by an inevitable process and by a natural law if you fulfill the simple condition; so that peace is the reward of that life and fellowship with Christ. Peace is not a thing that comes down solid, as it were, and is fitted somehow into a man's nature. We have very gross conceptions of peace, joy, and other Christian experiences; but they are all simply effects and causes. We fulfill the condition; we cannot help the experiences following. I have spoken about peace, but how about joy? In the 15th of John you will see when Christ gave His disciples the Parable of the Vine, He said: "I will tell you why I have told you that parable. It is that your joy might be full." Did you ever notice that? He did not merely throw it into space as a fine illustration. It was not merely a statement of the doctrine of the indwelling Christ. It was that, but it was more. "These words have I spoken unto you," He said, "That My joy might remain in you, and that your joy might be full." That is the way to get joy. It is to abide in Christ. Out of this simple relationship we have faith, we have peace, we have joy. Many other things follow. A man's usefulness depends to a large extent upon his fellowship with Christ. That is obvious. Only Christ can influence the world; but all that the world sees of Christ is what it sees of you and me. Christ said: "The world seeth Me no more, but ye see Me." You see Him, and standing in front of Him, reflect Him, and the world sees the reflection. It cannot see Him. So that a Christian's usefulness depends solely upon that relationship.

Now, I have pointed out a few of the things that follow from the standing before Christ—from the abiding in Christ. You will find, if you run over the texts about abiding in Christ, many other things will suggest themselves in the same relation. Almost everything in Christian experience and character follows, and follows necessarily, from standing before Christ and reflecting His character. But the supreme consummation is that we are changed into *the same image*, "even as by the Lord the Spirit." That is to say, that in some way, unknown to us, but possibly not more mysterious than the doctrine of personal influence, we are changed into the image of Christ.

This method cannot fail. I am not setting before you an opinion or a theory, but this is a certainly successful means of sanctification (perfecting one's life). "We all, with unveiled face, reflecting in a mirror the glory of Christ (the character of Christ) assuredly—without any miscarriage—are changed into the same image." It is an immense thing to be anchored in some great principle like that. Emerson says: "The hero is the man who is immovably centered. . . ." Do not be carried away by the hundred and one theories of sanctification that are floating about in the religious literature of the country at the present time; but go to the bottom of the thing for yourself, and see the *rationale* of it for yourself, and you will come to see that it is a matter of cause and effect, and that if you will fulfill the condition laid down by Christ, the effect must follow by a natural law.

What a prospect! To be changed into the same image. Think of that! That is what we are here for. That is what we are elected for. Not to be saved, in the common acceptance, but "whom He did foreknow He also did predestinate to be conformed to the image of His Son." Not merely to be saved, but *to be conformed to the image of His Son*. Conserve that principle. And as we must spend time in cultivating our earthly friendships if we are to have their blessings, so we must spend time in cultivating the fellowship and companionship of Christ. And there is nothing so much worth taking into our lives as a profounder sense of what is to be had by living in communion with Christ, and by getting nearer to Him. It will matter much if we take away with us some of the thoughts about theology, and some of the new light that has been shed upon the text of Scripture; it will matter infinitely more if our fellowship with the Lord Jesus become a little closer, and our theory of holy living a little more rational. And then as we go forth, men will take knowledge of us, that we have been with Jesus, and as we reflect Him upon them, they will begin to be changed into the same image.

It seems to me the preaching is of infinitely smaller account than the life which mirrors Christ. That is bound to tell; without speech or language—like the voices of the stars. It throws out its impressions upon every side. The one simple thing we have to do is to be there— in the right relation; to go through life hand in hand with Him; to have Him in the room with us, and keeping us company wherever we go; to depend upon Him and lean upon Him, and so have His life reflected in the fullness of its beauty and perfection into ours. . . .

The work of creation is not done. Geology is still toiling today at the unfinished earth; and the Spirit of God which brooded upon the waters thousands of years ago, is busy now creating men, within these commonplace lives of ours, in the image of God.

❦

(*"Stones Rolled Away"*—*an address delivered to the students of Harvard University, in April, 1893, and repeated before many other student gatherings, was finally published in a book of the same title posthumously.*)

Gentlemen, I am very much astonished at this spectacle. I told you last night it was against our principles in Scotland to have religious meetings on a week night. It seems to me that if you come to a meeting of this kind you mean business, and you may just as well own it. If a man comes to a shorthand class, it means that he wants to learn shorthand; and, if a man turns up at what I suppose I must call a religious meeting, it means that he is less or more interested in the subject.

Now I should say that I think a man has to give himself the benefit of that desire, and he should not be ashamed of it. The facts of religion are real; and, as mere students of life, you and I are bound to take cognizance of them. Of course, many very fair-minded men are kept away from going into this subject as they would like by a number of exceedingly surface reasons. I cannot help calling them surface reasons. For instance, you meet a man who tells you that he doesn't like Christians, that they always put his back up.

Now, Christians often put my back up. There are many of them I find, with whom it takes all my time to get along. But that is not peculiar with Christians. It is only peculiar to peculiar Christians, and there are just as many of the other sort. A man might just as well say, I don't like sinners. A man might just as well keep out of the world because he doesn't like some people in the world, as to keep out of Christian circles because there are objectionable creatures in it. We cannot be too fastidious. We cannot join any sect without having the weaker brethren in it. We cannot get on in this world entirely by ourselves. We must join this thing and that if we are going to be of any service at all, so that I think the difficulty of having to join ourselves with objectionable men applies pretty much all around.

Other men are kept away from Christianity by what I might call its phrases. A great many people, not so much in your country as in ours, talk in a dialect. The older people especially, our grandmothers, have a set of phrases in which all their religion is imbedded, and they can't talk to us about religion without using those phrases; and when we talk to them, if we do not use those phrases, we are put out of the synagogue. Now what we can do in this case is to translate their dialect into our own language, and then translate into their dialect when we speak back. It is a different dialect. We would put it upon a different basis; but after all we mean pretty much the same thing, and if we can once get into this habit of translating our more modern way of putting things into this antique language that those worthy people use to us we will find ourselves more at one with them than we think.

I meet another set of men who tell me that they don't like churches, that they find sermons stale, flat and unprofitable. Now, if any man here hates a dull sermon, I am with him. I have intense sympathy with any man who hates dullness. I think the world is far too dull, and that is one of the greatest reasons why the brightest men should throw themselves into Christianity to give it a broader phase to other people. One must confess that some church work, at all events, is not of a very cheerful or lively order. But of course that is not an argument why one should abstain from religious service. There are many reasons why we should even sacrifice ourselves and submit to a little dullness now and again if it is going to gain for us a greater good. After all, we live by institutions, and by fixed institutions. There are very few men who are able to get along without steady institutions of one kind and another. Some men are so tremendously free that they hate to be tied down to hours, to places and to seasons; but there are very few men big enough to stand that for a long time. If we look about for it, we will find some place that we can go and get some good. When a man goes to church really hungry and goes because he is hungry, he will pick up something, no matter where it is. Christ himself went to church, and even if we know something more than the minister knows, the fellowship, the sense of the solidarity of the Christian church throughout the whole world, the prayer and the inspiration of the hymn and the reading will at least do us some good. . . .

The religious life needs keeping up just as the other parts of our life need keeping up. There is nothing more impossible than for a man to live a religious life on an hour's work or an hour's thought a week. A man could not learn French, German or Latin by giving an hour per week to it; and how can we expect a man to get in this great world of the spirit, this great moral world, this great ideal region, and learn anything about it by merely dabbing in it now and again? We must make it a regular business, and, if the religious part is a vital part of the whole nature, we may as well attend to it.

You may remember a passage in Mr. Darwin's life. He says: "In one respect my mind has changed during the last twenty or thirty years. Up to the age of thirty, or beyond it, the poetry of many kinds, such as the works of Milton, Gray, Byron, Coleridge and Shelley, gave me great pleasure; and even as a school boy I took intense delight in Shakespeare, and especially in the historical plays. I have always said that pictures gave me considerable, and music very great, delight. But now for many years I cannot endure to read a line of poetry. I have tried lately to read Shakespeare, but found it so intolerably dull that it nauseated me. I have also lost my taste for pictures and music. My mind seems to have become a kind of machine for grinding general laws out of large collections of facts. But why this should have caused the atrophy of that part of the brain, I cannot conceive. If I had my life to live over again" (this is the point) "I would have made the rule to read some poetry and listen to some music at least once every week." There is the greatest authority on degeneration confessing to his own personal degeneration, and in the same paragraph telling us how we may avoid it. He says by leaving these things out of his life for so many years, although he had a real liking for them, his nature at these points began to atrophy, and when he went back to them he found that they disgusted him; and then he says that, if he had his life to live again, he would have made it a rule to read some poetry and listen to some music at least once a week, and that would have kept the thing up. There is nothing magical about religion. If a man is to keep it up, he must use the means, just as he would use the means to keep up the violin, or his interest in art of any kind.

I find another set of men who have never got beyond this difficulty, that they find the Bible a somewhat arid and slow book. Now, in the first place, I want to say that I have, again, great sympathy with that objector because, as a matter of fact, there are whole tracts of the Bible which are distinctly dull, which are written in an archaic language, and about departments of history in the past which haven't any great living interest for us now. One must remember that the Bible is not a book, but a library consisting of a large number of books. By an accident, we have these books bound up in one as if they were one book; and to say that all the books of the Bible are dull is simply to pass a literary judgment which is incorrect. It is not true, as a matter of fact, that all these books of the Bible are dull. Of course a sailing directory is very flat on the shore; but when a man is at sea and wants to steer his way through difficult and dangerous wastes, where the currents are strong and the passages narrow, he wants the best chart he can get, and he wants to use it as carefully as he can; and when a man wakens up to the difficulty of life and the reality of its temptations, he wants some such chart as he gets in that book to help him through.

As a mere literary work, there are books there that are unsurpassed in the English tongue, and for their teaching, for their beauty and for their truth they have never been surpassed. Christ's words, of course, are beyond comparison; but even Paul had a far greater brain than almost any writer of history. . . .

If a man doesn't like the Bible, it is because he has never struck the best parts of it, or because he has never felt any great need in his own life for its teaching. As a matter of fact, however, reading the Bible is a new thing. There were Christians for hundreds and hundreds of years before there was any people's Bible; so that it is not even essential, if you can't overcome this matter of taste, that you should read the Bible. There are hundreds of Christians at this moment who cannot read the Bible. There are Christians in heathen lands in whose language there is as yet no Bible;[2] so that you see there is no absolute connection between these two things. Besides that, the Bible has now become diffused through literature to such an extent that you can often get the heart of the Bible in a very bright and living and practical form through other forms of literature. . . .

A man may get his nourishment straight out of the Bible . . . but he may also get his nourishment mixed up with other ingredients, and it will do him just as much good.

There is another class of men, however, whom none of these minor difficulties touch—men who have come up to college, and who have got upset on almost all the main doctrines of Christianity. Now, I

[2] Today the Bible has been translated into more than a thousand tongues. J. W. K.

want to confess to you that, so far as I know my old friends, they have all passed through that stage. Every man who is worth a button passes through that stage. He loses all the forms of truth which he got in the Sunday School; and, if he is true to himself, gains them all back again in a richer and larger and more permanent form. But, between the loss and the gain, there is sometimes a very painful and dismal interlude, during which the man thinks that he is never going to believe again, when everything lies in ruin, and he doesn't see where any reconstruction is to come in. These are dark days and dark years in a man's life, and they are inevitable to every man who thinks. They are inevitable, because we are all born doubters. We came into the world asking questions. The world itself is a sphinx and tempts us to keep on asking questions. There are no great truths in the world which are not to some extent doubtable; and the instrument with which we look at truth is largely impaired, and has to be corrected by long years of experience for its early aberration. So that when we look at truth we only see part of it, and we see that part of it distorted. The result is a certain amount of twilight where we expected full day. One consolation to give that man is to tell him that we have all been through that. We take it like the measles. It lasts a certain number of months or years, and then we come out with our constitutions better than ever. There is a real rationale for that. Everything in the world passes through these stages, provided it be growing. You remember how the philosophers describe it. They describe the three great stages as position, opposition and composition. Position: Somebody lays down a truth, you look at it and say, "Yes, that is truth." I heard a clergyman say that when I was a boy, and I believed it. Then, one day, you read a book or hear someone else talk, and he put a query on it; and then there came the revolt against it, and for a long time your mind was seething with opposition to this original thing which was positive. And then you went on and put all these contradictory things together and composed them into a unity again. You reached the third stage—that of composition.

It is the same with everything. You begin to learn the piano, and after you have played about a year you think you know all about it; and you tackle the most difficult pieces, dash away at them, and think you can do it as well as anybody. Then you go into Boston and hear some great pianist, and come home a sad man. You see you know nothing about it. For the next six months you do not touch a single piece. You play scales day after day and practice finger exercises. Then, after six months, you say: "What is the use of playing scales? Music does not exist for scales"; and you turn to your old pieces and play them over again in an entirely different way. You have got it all back again. There are men here going through the scale period with regard to religious questions. What is the use of all this opposition? Is it not time to go back again, you ask, and put all this experience into something, and get at some truth at the other side? You see the same truth in a novel. Volume I, they will. Volume II, they won't. Volume III, they do.

We see the same thing in art. A man paints a picture. He thinks he has painted a grand one. After a few months, someone comes along and says: "Look here! Look at that boat! You don't call that a boat? And look at that leaf! That is not a leaf." And you discover that you have never looked at a boat and never seen a leaf. You are disheartened and do nothing the next six months but draw boats and leaves; and, after you have drawn boats and leaves until you are sick, you say: "What is the use of drawing boats and leaves?" and try again and produce your first landscape. But it is altogether a different thing from the picture you painted before. Now, when a man is working over the details of the Christian religion and struggling to get one thing adjusted and another, he will very soon find out that that does not amount to much. It is a useful thing, and he has to go through it, but he has to come out the other side also and put these things together.

The best advice, I think, that can be given to a man who is in this difficulty is, in the first place, to read the best authorities on the subject; not to put himself off with cheap tracts and popular sermons, but to go to the scientific authorities. There are as great scientific authorities in Germany, in England and in America on all the subject matter of theology as there are on the subject matter of chemistry or geology. Go to the authorities. You may not agree with them when you have read them. But if a man reads all the books on the opposition side he will very naturally get a distorted view of it. So, for every book he reads on the one side, he should, in justice, read a book on the other side.

Next, let a man remember that the great thing is not to think about religion, but to do it. We do not live in a "think" world. It is a real world. You do not believe that botany lies in the pages of Sachs. Botany lies out there in the flowers and in the trees, and it is living. And religion does not live in the pages of the doctrinal books, but in human life—in conflict with our own temptations, and in the conduct and character of our fellow-beings. When we abandon this "think-world" of ours and get out into the real world, we will find that, after all, these doubts are not of such immense importance, and that we can do a great deal of good in the world.

For my part, I have as many doubts on all the great subjects connected with theology as probably any one here; but they do not interfere in the very slightest with my trying, in what humble way I can, to follow out the religion of Christ. They do not even touch that region; and I don't want to lose these doubts. I don't want any man to rob me of my problem. I have no liking and little respect for the cocksure Christian—a man who can demonstrate some of the most tremendous verities of the faith, as he can the Fifth Book of Euclid. I want a religion and theology with some of the infinite about it, and some of the shadow as well as some of the light; and if, by reading up one of the great doctrines for five or six years, I get some little light upon it, it is only to find there are a hundred upon which I could spend another hundred lives. And if I should try to meet some specific point upon which you are at sea tonight, it would not do you much good. Tomorrow a new difficulty would start in your mind, and you would be simply where you were. I would be stopping up only one of your wells. You would open another out of the first book you read. Try to separate theological doctrine from practical religion. Believe me that you can follow Christ in this University without having solved any of these problems. Why, there was a skeptic among the first twelve disciples, and one of the best of them, and one of the most loyal of them. That man sat down at the first Lord's table, and Christ never said any hard words against him. He tried to teach him. That is the only attitude, it seems to me, we can take to Christ still. We can enter His school as scholars, and sit at His feet and learn what we can; and by doing His will in the practical things of life, we shall know of this and that doctrine, whether it be of God. The only use of truth is that it can do somebody some good. The only use of truth is in its sanctifying power; and that is the peculiarity of the truth of Christianity, that it has this sanctifying power and makes men better.

Now you say: "What am to do? If I am to block up this avenue and am not to expect very much along the line of mere belief, in what direction am I to shape my Christian life?" Well, I cannot in the least answer that. Every man must shape his Christian life for himself, according as his own talents may lead him; but the great thing to do is simply to become a follower of Christ. That is to become a Christian. There is nothing difficult or mysterious about it. A Darwinian is a man who follows Darwin, studies his books, accepts his views and says, "I am a Darwinian." You look into Christ's life, into His influence; you look at the needs of the world; you see how the one meets the other; you look into your own life and see how Christ's life meets your life; and you say, "I shall follow this teacher and leader until I get a better." From the time you do that, you are a Christian. You may be a very poor one. A man who enlists is a very poor soldier for the first few years, but he is a soldier from the moment he enlists; and the moment a man takes Christ to be the center of his life that man becomes a Christian. Of course that makes a great change in his life. His friends will know it tomorrow. On the steam engine you have seen the apparatus at the side called the eccentric. It has a different center from all the other wheels. Now, the Christian man is to some extent an eccentric. His life revolves around a different center from many people round about him. Of course, it is the other people who are eccentric because the true center of life is the most perfect life, the most perfect man, the most perfect ideal; and the man who is circulating around that is living the most perfect. At the same time, that man's life will to some extent be different from the lives round about him, and to some extent he will be a marked man.

But what difference will it make to a man himself? For one thing, it will keep you straight. I fancy most of the men here are living straight lives as it is; but it is impossible that every man here is. Well, I will tell you how to keep your life straight from this time—how your hunger after righteousness can be met. If you become a Christian, you will lead a straight life. That is not all. If you become a Christian, you will help other men to lead straight lives. Seek first the kingdom of God and His righteousness. The only chance that this world has of becoming a righteous world is by the contagion of the Christian men in it. I do not know any country with the splendid pretensions and achievements of America where there is so much unrighteousness in politics and to some extent in commerce, and where shady things are not only winked at, but admired. That is acknowledged and deplored by every right thinking man in the country. I get it, not from observation, but from yourselves. There is not a day passes that I do not find men deploring political corruption and the want of commercial integrity, in some districts of this country, at all events. Now nothing can change that state of affairs unless such men as yourselves throw your influence on to the side of righteousness and determine that you will live to make this country a little straighter than you found it.

There is a career in Christianity as well as an individual life. How do you test the greatness of a career? You test it by its influence. Well, can you point me to any influence in the world in the past which has had anything like the influence of the name to which I have asked you to give your life's adherence? That life started without a chance of succeeding in anything, according to the received theories of a successful life. Christ was born in a manger. If you and I had been born in a manger, the shame of it would have accompanied us through our whole lives; and yet there is not one of us born today who is not baptized in the name of Christ and who has not a Christian name. Christ went to no university, and had no education; and there is not a university in Europe or in America which is not founded in the name of Christ. Aye, and the very money which has gone to build the universities of the world has come from the followers of Christ. The education of the world, gentlemen, has been done by the followers of Jesus Christ. Christ had no political influence, and sought none;

yet there is not a President placed in the White House, there is not a sovereign in Europe placed upon a throne, but acknowledges, in the doing of it and in public, that the power to do it has come from Christ, and that the object in doing it is to secure the coming of Christ's kingdom. Take it in any direction, and you will find that this influence, judged from mere worldly standards of success, has been supreme.

Napoleon said, "I do not understand that man. He must have been more than human. I used to be able," he said on St. Helena, "to get people to die for me. I got hundreds of thousands of them, but I had to be there. Now that I am here on this island, I can't get a man. But He," said he, "gets hundreds of thousands of the best men in the world to lay down their whole lives for Him every day." Judged as mere influence from the standpoint of an ambitious man like Napoleon, you see that that Life was supreme.

You remember the dinner that Charles Lamb gave to some literary men, and how they were discussing after dinner what their attitude would be if certain great figures of the past were to come into their dining room. After they had all spoken, Lamb said:

"Well, it looks to me like this, that if Shakespeare entered the room I should rise up to greet him; but if Christ entered the room, I should kneel down and keep silent."

And so I ask you if you have feelings of that kind about any figure in history compared to the feelings that spring into your mind when you try to contemplate that Life. Some of you have never read Christ's life. You have picked up a parable here and a miracle there, and a scrap of history between; but you have never read that biography as you have read the biography of Washington, Webster, or the life of Columbus. Read it. Go home and read one of the four little books which tell you about His life. Take Matthew, for instance; and if you don't run aground in the 5th chapter and find yourself compelled to spend a week over it, you haven't much moral nature left. I have known men who have tried that experiment, who have begun to read the gospel of Matthew, and by the time they had finished reading the 5th chapter, they had thrown in their lot with the Person who forms the subject of that book. There is no other way of getting to know about Christ unless you read His life, at least as a beginning. If you want to become a Christian you must read up, and that is the thing to read. If you like, after that you can read the other lives of Christ. How do men get to know one another? They simply take to one another. Two men meet here tonight. They go downstairs and exchange greetings. Tomorrow night they meet in each other's rooms. By the end of a month they have got to know each other a little, and after another year of college life they have become sworn friends.

A man becomes a little attracted to Christ. That grows and grows, into a brighter friendship, and that grows into a great passion, and the man gives his life to Christ's interest. He counts it the highest ambition he can have to become a man such as Christ was. You see there is nothing profound about a religion of that kind. It is a religion that lies in the line of the ideals a young man forms, and that all the reading that he meets with from day to day fashions. In fact, it is a man's ideal turning up, and the man who turns his back upon that is simply turning his back upon his one chance of happiness in life and of making anything of life. Every life that is not lived in that line is out of the true current of history, to say nothing else. It is out of the stream—the main stream that is running through the ages, and that is going to sweep everything before it. A man who does not live that life may not be a bad man. The Bible does not say that everybody who is not a Christian is a notorious sinner; but it says that the man who lives outside that is wasting his life. He may not be doing wrong, but his life is lost. "He that loveth his life," Christ said, "shall lose it; and he that hateth his life in this world shall keep it unto life eternal." I am not ashamed to quote that to you; and I ask you to regard it with the same validity, and more, that you will give to any other quotation.

You will not accuse me of cant because I have used sacred words in this talk. There are technical terms in religion just as in science and philosophy. Just as in science I should speak of protoplasm, of oxygen or carbonic acid gas, so in talking of religion I must talk about faith and Jesus Christ. Just as I should quote authorities in speaking of chemistry or political economy, so I must use authorities in speaking about Christ. You will not take the words that I have said tonight as a mere expression of phraseology of a cant description, because it is not that; and I would ask those of you who are very much frightened to use such words to consider whether it is not a rational thing and a necessary thing, if you speak at all on this subject, to use these words. We must not be too fastidious, or thin-skinned, or particular on a point like that. While we are not in any degree to advertize our Christianity by our language, there are occasions, and this is one, when these things are necessary. . . .

Now I have no acquaintance with you whatever; but I have been asking up and down this district what sort of men the Harvard men are, and I want to let you know that you have a fairly good character. . . . Now live up to it. Let this university in the years to come be famous over America not only for its education, but for its sense of honor and manliness, and purity and Christianity. Seek first the kingdom of God. You know the whole truth. Live it. Want of interest in religion does not acquit you of taking your share in it. Why should I be here to talk to you? A Scotsman hates talking. . . . Well, I say want of religion does not absolve you from taking your share of it. The fact that you do not care about Christ does not alter the fact that Christ cares about you, that He wants you men, and that His kingdom cannot go on unless He gets such men as you. Are we to leave the greatest scheme that has ever been propounded to be carried out by duffers? It is easier, somebody says, to criticize the greatest scheme superbly than to do the smallest thing possible. The man who is looking on from the outside sees things in the game that the players do not see. He sees this bit of bad play and that. Well, stop criticizing the game. Take off your coat, and come and help us. Our side is strong, and it is getting stronger; but we want the best men. Christianity ought to have the superlative men here in every department—in classics, in poetry, in literature, in humor, in everything that goes to the making of a man. The best gifts should be given to Christ. We are apt to despise Christianity and keep away from it because there are many weak-minded people in it. That is one reason why we ought to take off our coats and throw ourselves into it, heart and soul. . . .

4

The "Christmas Booklets"

AS THE fame of Natural Law spread, the public clamored for more published writing from the pen of its author. In response Henry Drummond conceived the idea of printing a series of his addresses as "Christmas Cards." They appeared in the following order: "The Greatest Thing in the World"—1889; "Pax Vobiscum"—1890; "The Program of Christianity"—1891; "The City without a Church"—1892; and "The Changed Life"—1893.

All five of these "Christmas Booklets" were translated into many languages and reprinted again and again in innumerable editions. Through them Henry Drummond reached a wider public than he ever dreamed of, and the total issue and "spread" of them made his name a household word around the world. The message of these little books is still as fresh and pertinent as ever. One can prove it by reading any of them with the date line removed.

"Pax Vobiscum" was the second address published. It had been given many times before student audiences, appearing first as the second address of his Oddfellows Hall series in 1885. It tells how to find rest, joy and peace under the yoke of Christ.

❦

. . . Nothing that happens in the world happens by chance. God is a God of order. Everything is arranged upon definite principles, and never at random. The world, even the religious world, is governed by law. Character is governed by law. Happiness is governed by law.

131

The Christian experiences are governed by law. Men, forgetting this expect Rest, Joy, Peace, Faith to drop into their souls from the air like snow or rain. But in point of fact they do not do so; and if they did they would no less have their origin in previous activities and be controlled by natural laws. Rain and snow do drop from the air, but not without a long previous history. They are the mature effects of former causes. Equally so are Rest, and Peace, and Joy. They, too, have each a previous history. Storms and winds and calms are not accidents, but are brought about by antecedent circumstances. Rest and Peace are but calms in man's inward nature, and arise through causes as definite and as inevitable.

Realize it thoroughly: it is a methodical not an accidental world. If a housewife turns out a good cake, it is the result of a sound receipt, carefully applied. She cannot mix the assigned ingredients and fire them for the appropriate time without producing the result. It is not she who has made the cake; it is nature. She brings related things together; sets causes at work; these causes bring about the result. She is not a creator, but an intermediary. She does not expect random causes to produce specific effects—random ingredients would only produce random cakes. So it is in the making of Christian experiences. Certain lines are followed; certain effects are the result. These effects cannot but be the result. But the result can never take place without the previous cause. To expect results without antecedents is to expect cakes without ingredients. That impossibility is precisely the almost universal expectation.

Now what I mainly wish to do is to help you firmly to grasp this simple principle of Cause and Effect in the spiritual world. And instead of applying the principle generally to each of the Christian experiences in turn, I shall examine its application to one in some little detail. The one I shall select is Rest. And I think any one who follows the application in this single instance will be able to apply it for himself to all the others.

Take such a sentence as this: African explorers are subject to fevers which cause restlessness and delirium. Note the expression, "cause restlessness." *Restlessness has a cause.* Clearly, then, anyone who wished to get rid of restlessness would proceed at once to deal with the cause. If that were not removed, a doctor might prescribe a hundred things, and all might be taken in turn, without producing the least effect. Things are so arranged in the original planning of the world that certain effects must follow certain causes, and certain causes must be abolished before certain effects can be removed. Certain parts of Africa are inseparably linked with the physical experience called fever; this fever is in turn infallibly linked with a mental experience called restlessness and delirium. To abolish the mental experience the radical method would be to abolish the physical experience, and the way of abolishing the physical experience would be to abolish Africa, or to cease to go there. Now this holds good for all other forms of Restlessness. Every other form and kind of Restlessness in the world has a definite cause, and the particular kind of Restlessness can only be removed by removing the allotted cause.

All this is also true of Rest. Restlessness has a cause: must not Rest have a cause? Necessarily. If it were a chance world we would not expect this; but, being a methodical world, it cannot be otherwise. Rest, physical rest, moral rest, spiritual rest, every kind of rest has a cause, as certainly as restlessness. Now causes are discriminating. There is one kind of cause for every particular effect, and no other; and if one particular effect is desired, the corresponding cause must be set in motion. It is no use proposing finely devised schemes, or going through general pious exercises in the hope that somehow Rest will come. The Christian life is not casual but causal. All nature is a standing protest against the absurdity of expecting to secure spiritual effects, or any effects, without the employment of appropriate causes. The Great Teacher dealt what ought to have been the final blow to this infinite irrelevancy by a single question, "Do men gather grapes of thorns or figs of thistles?"

Why, then, did the Great Teacher not educate His followers fully? Why did He not tell us, for example, how such a thing as Rest might be obtained? The answer is, that He did. But plainly, explicitly, in so many words? Yes, plainly, explicitly, in so many words. He assigned Rest to its cause, in words with which each of us has been familiar from his earliest childhood. . . .

"Come unto me," He says, "and I will give you Rest."

Rest, apparently, was a favor to be bestowed; men had but to come to Him; He would give it to every applicant. But the next sentence takes that all back. The qualification, indeed, is added instantaneously. For what the first sentence seemed to give was next thing to an impossibility. For how, in a literal sense, can Rest be *given?* One could no more give away Rest than he could give away Laughter. We speak of "causing" laughter, which we can do; but we cannot give it away. When we speak of giving pain, we know perfectly well we cannot give pain away. And when we aim at giving pleasure, all that we do is to arrange a set of circumstances in such a way as that these shall cause pleasure. Of course there is a sense, and a very wonderful sense, in which a Great Personality breathes upon all who come within its influence an abiding peace and trust. Men can be to other men as the shadow of a great rock in a thirsty land. Much more Christ; much more Christ as Perfect Man; much more still as Savior of the world. But it is not this of which I speak. When Christ said He would give men Rest, He meant simply that He would put them in the way of it. By no act of conveyance would, or could, He make over His own Rest to them. He could give them His receipt for it. That was all. But He would not make it for them; for one thing, it was not in His plan to make it for them; for another thing, it was a thousand times better that they should make it for themselves.

That this is the meaning becomes obvious from the wording of the second sentence: "Learn of Me and ye shall find Rest." Rest, that is to say, is not a thing that can be given, but a thing to be *acquired.* It comes not by an act, but by a process. It is not to be found in a happy hour, as one finds a treasure; but slowly, as one finds knowledge. It could indeed be no more found in a moment than could knowledge. A soil has to be prepared for it. Like a fine fruit, it will grow in one climate and not in another; at one altitude and not at another. Like all growths it will have an orderly development and mature by slow degrees.

The nature of this slow process Christ clearly defines when He says we are to achieve Rest by *learning.* "Learn of Me," He says, "and ye shall find rest to your souls." Now consider the extraordinary originality of this utterance. How novel the connection between these two words, "Learn" and "Rest"? How few of us have ever associated them—ever thought that Rest was a thing to be learned; ever laid ourselves out for it as we would to learn a language; ever practiced it as we would practice the violin? Does it not show how entirely new Christ's teaching still is to the world, that so old and threadbare an aphorism should still be so little applied? The last thing most of us would have thought of would have been to associate *Rest* with *Work*.

What must one work at? What is that which if duly learned will find the soul of man in Rest? Christ answers without the least hesitation. He specifies two things—Meekness and Lowliness. "Learn of Me," He says, "for I am meek and lowly in heart." Now these two things are not chosen at random. To these accomplishments, in a special way, Rest is attached. Learn these, in short, and you have already found Rest. These as they stand are direct causes of Rest; will produce it at once; cannot but produce it at once. And if you think for a single moment, you will see how this is necessarily so, for causes are never arbitrary, and the connection between antecedent and consequent here and everywhere lies deep in the nature of things.

What is the connection, then? I answer by a further question. What are the chief causes of *Unrest*? If you know yourself, you will answer Pride, Selfishness, Ambition. As you look back upon the past years of your life, is it not true that its unhappiness has chiefly come from the succession of personal mortifications and almost trivial disappointments which the intercourse of life has brought you? Great trials come at lengthened intervals, and we rise to breast them; but it is the petty friction of our every-day life with one another, the jar of business or of work, the discord of the domestic circle, the collapse of our ambition, the crossing of our will or the taking down of our conceit, which make inward peace impossible. Wounded vanity, then, disappointed hopes, unsatisfied selfishness—these are the old, vulgar, universal sources of man's unrest.

Now it is obvious why Christ pointed out as the two chief objects for attainment the exact opposites of these. To Meekness and Lowliness these things simply do not exist. They cure unrest by making it impossible. These remedies do not trifle with surface symptoms; they strike at once at removing causes. The ceaseless chagrin of a self-centered life can be removed at once by learning Meekness and Lowliness of heart. He who learns them is forever proof against it. He lives henceforth a charmed life. Christianity is a fine inoculation, a transfusion of healthy blood into an anemic or poisoned soul. No fever can attack a perfectly sound body; no fever or unrest can disturb a soul which has breathed the air or learned the ways of Christ. Men sigh for the wings of a dove that they may fly away and be at Rest. But flying away will not help us. "The kingdom of God is *within* you." We aspire to the top to look for Rest; it lies at the bottom. Water rests only when it gets to the lowest place. So do men. Hence, be lowly. The man who has no opinion of himself at all can never be hurt if others do not acknowledge him. Hence, be meek. He who is without expectation cannot fret if nothing comes to him. It is self-evident that these things are so. The lowly man and the meek man are really above all other men, above all other things. They dominate the world because they do not care for it. The miser does not possess gold, gold possesses him. But the meek possess it. "The meek," said Christ, "inherit the earth." They do not buy it; they do not conquer it; but they inherit it.

There are people who go about the world looking out for slights, and they are necessarily miserable, for they find them at every turn— especially the imaginary ones. One has the same pity for such men as for the very poor. They are the morally illiterate. They have had no real education, for they have never learned how to live. Few men know how to live. We grow up at random, carrying into mature life the merely animal methods and motives which we had as little children. And it does not occur to us that all this must be changed; that much of it must be reversed; that life is the finest of the Fine Arts; that it has to be learned with lifelong patience, and that the years of our pilgrimage are all too short to master it triumphantly.

Yet this is what Christianity is for—to teach men the Art of Life. And its whole curriculum lies in one word—"Learn of me." Unlike most education, this is almost purely personal; it is not to be had from books or lectures or creeds or doctrines. It is a study from the life. Christ never said much in mere words about the Christian graces. He lived them, He was them. Yet we do not merely copy Him. We learn His art by living with Him, like the old apprentices with their masters.

Now do we understand it all? Christ's invitation to the weary and heavy-laden is a call to begin life over again upon a new principle—

upon His own principle. "Watch My way of doing things," He says. "Follow Me. Take life as I take it. Be meek and lowly and you will find Rest."

I do not say, remember, that the Christian life to every man, or to any man, can be a bed of roses. No educational process can be this. And perhaps if some men knew how much was involved in the simple "learn" of Christ, they would not enter His school with so irresponsible a heart. For there is not only much to learn, but much to unlearn. Many men never go to this school at all till their disposition is already half-ruined and character has taken on its fatal set. To learn arithmetic is difficult at fifty—much more to learn Christianity. To learn simply what it is to be meek and lowly, in the case of one who has had no lessons in that in childhood, may cost him half of what he values most on earth. Do we realize, for instance, that the way of teaching humility is generally by *humiliation?* There is probably no other school for it. When a man enters himself as a pupil in such a school it means a very great thing. There is much Rest there, but there is also much Work.

I should be wrong, even though my theme is the brighter side, to ignore the cross and minimize the cost. Only it gives to the cross a more definite meaning, and a rarer value, to connect it thus directly and *causally* with the growth of the inner life. Our platitudes on the "benefits of affliction" are usually about as vague as our theories of Christian Experience. "Somehow," we believe affliction does us good. But it is not a question of "Somehow." The result is definite, calculable, necessary. It is under the strictest law of cause and effect. The first effect of losing one's fortune, for instance, is humiliation; and the effect of humiliation, as we have just seen, is to make one humble; and the effect of being humble is to produce Rest. It is a roundabout way, apparently, of producing Rest; but Nature generally works by circular processes; and it is not certain that there is any other way of becoming humble, or of finding Rest. If a man could make himself humble to order, it might simplify matters, but we do not find that this happens. Hence we must all go through the mill. Hence death, death to the lower self, is the nearest gate and the quickest road to life.

Yet this is only half the truth. Christ's life outwardly was one of the most troubled lives that was ever lived: Tempest and tumult, tumult and tempest, the waves breaking over it all the time till the worn body was laid in the grave. But the inner life was a sea of glass. The great calm was always there. At any moment you might have gone to Him and found Rest. And even when the bloodhounds were dogging him in the streets of Jerusalem, He turned to His disciples and offered them, as a last legacy, "My peace." Nothing ever for a moment broke the serenity of Christ's life on earth. Misfortune could not reach Him; He had no fortune. Food, raiment, money—fountain-heads of half the world's weariness—He simply did not care for; they played no part in His life; He "took no thought" for them. It was impossible to affect Him by lowering His reputation; He had already made Himself of no reputation. He was dumb before insult. When He was reviled He reviled not again. In fact, there was nothing that the world could do to Him that could ruffle the surface of His spirit.

Such living, as mere living, is altogether unique. It is only when we see what it was in Him that we can know what the word Rest means. It lies not in emotions, nor in the absence of emotions. It is not a hallowed feeling that comes over us in church. It is not something that the preacher has in his voice. It is not in nature, or in poetry, or in music—though in all these there is soothing. It is the mind at leisure from itself. It is the perfect poise of the soul; the absolute adjustment of the inward man to the stress of all outward things; the preparedness against every emergency; the stability of assured con-victions; the eternal calm of an invulnerable faith; the repose of a heart set deep in God. It is the mood of the man who says, with Browning, "God's in His Heaven, all's well with the world."

Two painters each painted a picture to illustrate his conception of rest. The first chose for his scene a still, lone lake among the far-off mountains. The second threw on his canvas a thundering waterfall, with a fragile birch-tree bending over the foam; at the fork of a branch, almost wet with the cataract's spray, a robin sat on its nest. The first was only *Stagnation*; the last was *Rest*. For in Rest there are always two elements—tranquillity and energy; silence and turbu-lence; creation and destruction; fearlessness and fearfulness. This it was in Christ.

It is quite plain from all this that whatever else He claimed to be or to do, He at least knew how to live. All this is the perfection of living, of living in the mere sense of passing through the world in the best way. Hence His anxiety to communicate His idea of life to others. He came, He said, to give men life, true life, a more abundant life than they were living; "the life," as the fine phrase in the Revised Version has it, "that is life indeed." This is what He himself possessed, and it was this which He offers to all mankind. And hence His direct appeal for all to come to Him who had not made much of life, who were weary and heavy-laden. These He would teach His secret. They, also, should know "the life that is life indeed."

There is still one doubt to clear up. After the statement, "Learn of Me," Christ throws in the disconcerting qualification, "*Take My yoke upon you and learn of Me.*" Why, if all this be true, does He call it a yoke? Why, while professing to give Rest, does He with the next breath whisper "*burden*"? Is the Christian life, after all, what its enemies take it for—an additional weight to the already great woe of life, some extra punctiliousness about duty, some painful devotion to observances, some heavy restriction and trammeling of all that is joyous and free in the world? Is life not hard and sorrowful enough without being fettered with yet another yoke?

It is astounding how so glaring a misunderstanding of this plain sentence should ever have passed into currency. Did you ever stop to ask what a yoke is really for? Is it to be a burden to the animal which wears it? It is just the opposite. It is to make its burden light. Attached to the oxen in any other way than by a yoke, the plough would be intolerable. Worked by means of a yoke, it is light. A yoke is not an instrument of torture; it is an instrument of mercy. It is not a malicious contrivance for making work hard; it is a gentle device to make hard labor light. It is not meant to give pain, but to save pain. And yet men speak of the yoke of Christ as if it were a slavery, and look upon those who wear it as objects of compassion. For generations we have had homilies on "The Yoke of Christ," some delighting in portraying its narrow exactions; some seeking in these exactions the marks of its divinity; others apologizing for it, and toning it down; still others assuring us that, although it be very bad, it is not to be compared with the positive blessings of Christianity. How many, especially among the young, has this one mistaken phrase driven forever away from the kingdom of God? Instead of making Christ attractive, it makes Him out a taskmaster, narrowing life by petty restrictions, calling for self-denial where none is necessary, making misery a virtue under the plea that it is the yoke of Christ, and happiness criminal because it now and then evades it. According to this conception, Christians are at best the victims of a depressing fate; their life is a penance; and their hope for the next world purchased by a slow martyrdom in this.

The mistake has arisen from taking the word "yoke" here in the same sense as in the expressions "under the yoke," or "wear the yoke in his youth." But in Christ's illustration it is . . . the simple "harness" or "ox-collar" of the Eastern peasant. It is the literal wooden yoke which He, with His own hands in the carpenter shop, had probably often made. He knew the difference between a smooth yoke and a rough one, a bad fit and a good fit; the difference also it made to the patient animal which had to wear it. The rough yoke galled, and the burden was heavy; the smooth yoke caused no pain, and the load was lightly drawn. The badly fitted harness was a misery; the well-fitted collar was "easy."

And what was the "burden"? It was not some special burden laid upon the Christian, some unique infliction that they alone must bear. It was what all men bear. It was simply life, human life itself, the general burden of life which all must carry with them from the cradle to the grave. Christ saw that men took life painfully. To some it was a weariness, to others a failure, to many a tragedy, to all a struggle and a pain. How to carry this burden of life had been the whole world's problem. It is still the whole world's problem. And here is Christ's solution: "Carry it as I do. Take life as I take it. Look at it from My point of view. Interpret it upon My principles. Take My yoke and learn of Me, and you will find it easy. For my Yoke is easy, works easily, sits right upon the shoulders, and therefore My burden is light."

There is no suggestion here that religion will absolve any man from bearing burdens. That would be to absolve him from living, since it is life itself that is the burden. What Christianity does propose is to make it tolerable. Christ's yoke is simply His secret for the alleviation of human life, His prescription for the best and happiest method of living. Men harness themselves to the work and stress of the world in clumsy and unnatural ways. The harness they put on is antiquated. A rough, ill-fitted collar at the best, they make its strain and friction past enduring, by placing it where the neck is most sensitive; and by mere continuous irritation this sensitiveness increases until the whole nature is quick and sore.

This is the origin, among other things, of a disease called "touchiness"—a disease which, in spite of its innocent name, is one of the gravest sources of restlessness in the world. Touchiness, when it becomes chronic, is a morbid condition of the inward disposition. It is self-love inflamed to the acute point; conceit, with a hair-trigger. The cure is to shift the yoke to some other place; to let men and things touch us through some new and perhaps as yet unused part of our nature; to become meek and lowly in heart while the old nature is becoming numb from want of use. It is the beautiful work of Christianity everywhere to adjust the burden of life to those who bear it, and them to it. It has a perfectly miraculous gift of healing. Without doing any violence to human nature it sets it right with life, harmonizing it with all surrounding things, and restoring those who are jaded with the fatigue and dust of the world to a new grace of living. In the mere matter of altering the perspective of life and changing the proportions of things, its function in lightening the care of man is altogether its own. The weight of a load depends upon the attraction of the earth. But suppose the attraction of the earth were removed? A ton on some other planet, where the attraction of gravity is less, does not weigh half a ton. Now Christianity removes the attraction of the earth; and this is one way in which it diminishes men's burden. It makes them citizens of another world. What was a ton yesterday is not half a ton today. So without changing one's circumstances, merely by offering a wider horizon and a different standard, it alters the whole aspect of the world.

Christianity as Christ taught is the truest philosophy of life ever spoken. But let us be quite sure when we speak of Christianity that we mean Christ's Christianity. Other versions are either caricatures, or exaggerations, or misunderstandings, or shortsighted and surface readings. For the most part their attainment is hopeless and the results wretched. But I care not who the person is, or through what vale of tears he has passed, or is about to pass, there is a new life for him along this path.

Were Rest my subject, there are other things I should wish to say about it, and other kinds of Rest of which I should like to speak. But that is not my subject. My theme is that the Christian experiences are not the work of magic, but come under the law of Cause and Effect. And I have chosen Rest only as a single illustration of the working of that principle. If there were time I might next run over all the Christian experiences in turn, and show how the same wide law applies to each. But I think it may serve the better purpose if I leave this further exercise to yourselves. I know no Bible study that you will find more full of fruit, or which will take you nearer to the ways of God, or make the Christian life itself more solid or more sure. . . .

No man can make things grow. He can get them to grow by arranging all the circumstances and fulfilling all the conditions. But the growing is done by God. Causes and effects are eternal arrangements, set in the constitution of the world; fixed beyond man's ordering. What man can do is to place himself in the midst of a chain of sequences. Thus he can get things to grow: thus he himself can grow. But the grower is the Spirit of God.

What more need I add but this—test the method by experiment. Do not imagine that you have got these things because you know how to get them. As well try to feed upon a cookery book. But I think I can promise that if you try in this simple and natural way, you will not fail. Spend the time you have spent in sighing for fruits in fulfilling the conditions of their growth. The fruits will come, must come. We have hitherto paid immense attention to effects, to the mere experiences themselves; we have described them, extolled them, advised them, prayed for them—done everything but find out what caused them. Henceforth let us deal with causes. "To be," says Lotze, "is to be in relations."[1] About every other method of living the Chris-

---

[1] Today a new phrase has emerged from this statement—"relationship theology." J. W. K.

tian life there is an uncertainty. About every other method of acquiring the Christian experiences there is a "perhaps." But in so far as this method is the way of nature, it can not fail. Its guarantee is the laws of the universe, and these are "the Hands of the Living God."

The third of the "Christmas Booklets" was The Program of Christianity. This address was given from rather sketchy notes to the Possilpark congregation in 1882. When Drummond delivered it at the Oddfellows Hall every student present received a tastefully printed card on which the details of Christ's commission were set down in categorical form. The familiar words from the sixty-first chapter of Isaiah were both Scripture lesson and long text for this address which set forth "the importance of Christianity as a social factor, the fountainhead of all genuine altruism."

W. R. Nicoll, editor of The British Weekly, heard Drummond give this address at Grosvenor House and commented in a letter to a friend that he was pleased and that the address was excellent, "and his manner was even better than his matter—both manly and modest —just the right thing. Text: 'The Lord hath anointed me.' First part showed how Christianity takes in everything. Then he gave a kind of sermon on the text—very good. Fine audience. I have seldom seen so many characteristic heads, and the address could do nothing but good."

Drummond's social vision had expanded since the publication of Natural Law, as we see in the following essay; he concludes his commentary on the venerable fragment from Isaiah by this thought: "Men, then, are the only means God's Spirit has of accomplishing His purpose." But he makes it clear that "Sanctification will come to masses only as it comes to individual men; and to work with Christ's Program and ignore Christ is to [try to] utilize the sun's light without its energy."

❦

"What does God do all day?" once asked a little boy. One could wish that more grown-up people would ask so very real a question. Unfortunately, most of us are not even boys in religious intelligence, but only very unthinking children. It no more occurs to us that God

is engaged in any particular work in the world than it occurs to a
little child that its father does anything except be its father. Its father
may be a Cabinet member absorbed in the nation's work, or an
inventor deep in schemes for the world's good; but to this master-
egoist he is father, and nothing more. Childhood, whether in the
physical or moral world, is the great self-centered period of life; and
a personal God who satisfies personal ends is all that for a long time
many a Christian understands.

But as clearly as there comes to the growing child a knowledge of
his father's part in the world, and a sense of what real life means,
there must come to every Christian whose growth is true some richer
sense of the meaning of Christianity and a larger view of Christ's
purpose for mankind. To miss this is to miss the whole splendor and
glory of Christ's religion. Next to losing the sense of a personal Christ,
the worst evil that can befall a Christian is to have no sense of anything else. To grow up in complacent belief that God has no business
in this great groaning world of human beings except to attend to a
few saved souls is the negation of all religion. The first great epoch
in a Christian's life, after the awe and wonder of its dawn, is when
there breaks into his mind some sense that Christ has a purpose for
mankind, a purpose beyond him and his needs, beyond the churches
and their creeds, beyond Heaven and its saints—a purpose which
embraces every man and woman born, every kindred and nation
formed, which regards not their spiritual good alone, but their
welfare in every part, their progress, their health, their work, their
wages, their happiness in this present world.

What, then, does Christ do all day? By what further conception
shall we augment the selfish view of why Christ lived and died?

I shall mislead no one, I hope, if I say—for I wish to put the social
side of Christianity in its strongest light—that Christ did not come
into the world to give men religion. He never mentioned the word
religion. Religion was in the world before Christ came, and it lives
today in a million souls who have never heard His name. What God
does all day is not to sit waiting in churches for people to come and
worship Him. It is true that God is in churches and in all kinds of
churches, and is found by many in churches more immediately than

anywhere else. It is also true, that, while Christ did not give men religion, He gave a new direction to the religious aspiration bursting forth then and now and always from the whole world's heart. But it was His purpose to enlist these aspirations on behalf of some definite practical good. The religious people of those days did nothing with their religion except attend to its observances. Even the priest, after he had been to the temple, thought his work was done; when he met the wounded man he passed by on the other side. Christ reversed all this—tried to reverse it, for He is only now beginning to succeed. The tendency of the religious of all time has been to care more for religion than for humanity; Christ cared more for humanity than for religion—rather, His care for humanity was the chief expression of His religion. He was not indifferent to observances, but the practices of the people bulked in His thoughts before the practices of the Church. It has been pointed out as a blemish on the immortal allegory of Bunyan that the Pilgrim never did anything— anything but save his soul. The remark is scarcely fair, for the allegory is designedly the story of a soul in a single relation; and, besides, he did do a little. But the warning may well be weighed. The Pilgrim's one thought, his work by day, his dream by night, was escape. He took little part in the world through which he passed. He was a Pilgrim traveling through it; his business was to get through safe. Whatever this is, it is not Christianity. Christ's conception of Christianity was heavens removed from that of a man setting out from the City of Destruction to save his soul. It was rather that of a man dwelling amidst the Destructions of the City and planning escapes for the souls of others—escapes not to the other world, but to purity and peace and righteousness in this. In reality Christ never said "Save your soul." It is a mistranslation which says that. What He said was, "Save your life." And this not because the first is nothing, but only because it is so very great a thing that only the second can accomplish it. But the new word altruism—the translation of "love thy neighbor as thyself"—is slowly finding its way into current Christian speech. The People's Progress, not less than the Pilgrim's Progress, is daily becoming a graver concern to the Church. A popular theology with unselfishness as part at least of its root, a theology which appeals no longer to fear, but to the generous heart in man, has already dawned, and more clearly than ever men are beginning to see what Christ really came into this world to do.

What Christ came here for was to make a better world. The world in which we live is an unfinished world. It is not wise, it is not happy, it is not pure, it is not good—it is not even sanitary. Humanity is little more than raw material. Almost everything has yet to be done in it. Before the days of Geology people thought the earth was finished. It is by no means finished. The work of Creation is going on. Before the spectroscope, men thought the universe was finished. We know now it is just beginning. And this teeming universe of men in which we live has almost its finer color and beauty yet to take. Christ came to complete it. The fires of its passions were not yet cool; their heat had to be transformed into finer energies. The ideals for its future were all to shape, the forces to realize them were not yet born. The poison of its sins had met no antidote, the gloom of its doubt no light, the weight of its sorrow no rest. These the Savior of the World, the Light of men, would do and be. This, roughly, was His scheme.

Now this was a prodigious task—to recreate the world. How was it to be done? God's way of making worlds is to make them make themselves. When He made the earth He made a rough ball of matter and supplied it with a multitude of tools to mold it into form—the raindrop to carve it, the glacier to smooth it, the river to nourish it, the flower to adorn it. God works always with agents, and this is our way when we want any great thing done, and this was Christ's way when He undertook the finishing of Humanity. He had a vast, intractable mass of matter to deal with, and He required a multitude of tools. Christ's tools were men. Hence His first business in the world was to make a collection of men. In other words, He founded a Society.

It is a somewhat startling thought—it will not be misunderstood—that Christ probably did not save many people while He was here. Many an evangelist, in that direction, has done much more. He never intended to finish the world single-handed, but announced from the first that others would not only take part, but do "greater things" than He. For, amazing as was the attention He was able to give to individuals, this was not the whole aim He had in view. His immediate

work was to enlist men in His enterprise, to rally them into a great
company or Society for the carrying out of His plans.

The name by which this Society was known was *The Kingdom of
God.* Christ did not coin this name; it was an old expression, and
good men had always hoped and prayed that some such Society
would be born in their midst. But it was never either defined or set
going in earnest until Christ made its realization the passion of His
life.

How keenly He felt regarding His task, how enthusiastically He set
about it, every page of His life bears witness. All reformers have one
or two great words which they use incessantly, and by mere reitera-
tion imbed indelibly in the thought and history of their time. Christ's
great word was the Kingdom of God. Of all the words of His that
have come down to us this is by far the commonest. One hundred
times it occurs in the Gospels. When He preached He had almost
always this for a text. His sermons were explanations of the aims of
His Society, of the different things it was like, of whom its membership consisted, what they were to do or to be, or not do or not be.
And, even when He does not actually use the word, it is easy to see
that all He said and did had reference to this. Philosophers talk
about thinking in categories—the mind living, as it were, in a particular room with its own special furniture, pictures, and viewpoints,
these giving a consistent direction and color to all that is thought or
expressed. It was in the category of the Kingdom that Christ's
thought moved. Though one time He said He came to save the lost,
or at another time to give men life, or to do His Father's will, these
were all included among the objects of His Society.

No one can ever know what Christianity is till He has grasped
this leading thought in the mind of Christ. Peter and Paul have many
wonderful and necessary things to tell us about what Christ was and
did; but we are looking now at what Christ's own thought was. Do
not think this is a mere modern theory. These are His own life-
plans taken from His own life. Do not allow any isolated text, even
though it seems to sum up for you the Christian life, to keep you
from trying to understand Christ's Program as a whole. The perspective of Christ's teaching is not everything, but without it everything

will be distorted and untrue. There is much good in a verse, but often much evil. To see some small soul pirouetting throughout life on a single text, and judging all the world because it cannot find a partner, is not a Christian sight. Christianity does not grudge such souls their comfort. What it grudges is that they make Christ's Kingdom uninhabitable to thoughtful minds. Be sure that whenever the religion of Christ appears small, or forbidding, or narrow, or inhuman, you are dealing not with the whole—which is a matchless moral symmetry—nor even with an arch or column—but with some cold stone removed from its place and suggesting nothing of the glorious structure from which it came.

Tens of thousands of persons who are familiar with religious truths have not noticed yet that Christ ever founded a Society at all. The reason is partly that people have read texts instead of reading their Bible, partly that they have studied Theology instead of studying Christianity, and partly because of the noiselessness and invisibility of the Kingdom of God itself. Nothing truer was ever said of this Kingdom than that "It cometh without observation." Its first discovery, therefore, comes to the Christian with all the force of a revelation. The sense of belonging to such a Society transforms life. It is the difference between being a solitary knight tilting single-handed, and often defeated, at whatever enemy one chances to meet on one's little acre of life, and the feel of belonging to a mighty army marching throughout all time to a certain victory. This note of universality given to even the humblest work we do, this sense of comradeship, this link with history, this thought of a definite campaign, this promise of success, is the possession of every obscurest unit in the Kingdom of God.

Hundreds of years before Christ's Society was formed, its Program had been issued to the world. I cannot think of any scene in history more dramatic than when Jesus entered the church in Nazareth and read it to the people. Not that when He appropriated to Himself that venerable fragment from Isaiah He was uttering a manifesto or announcing His formal Program. Christ never did things formally. We think of the words, as He probably thought of them, not in their old-world historical significance, nor as a full expression of His future aims, but as a summary of great moral facts now and always to be realized in the world since He appeared.

Remember as you read the words to what grim reality they refer. Recall what Christ's problem really was, what His Society was founded for. This Program deals with a real world. Think of it as you read—not of the surface-world, but of the world as it is, as it sins and weeps, and curses and suffers, and sends up its long cry to God. Limit it if you like to the world around your door, but think of it—of the city and the hospital and the dungeon and the graveyard, of the sweat-shop and the pawnshop and the drink-shop; think of the cold, the cruelty, the fever, the famine, the ugliness, the loneliness, the pain. And then try to keep down the lump in your throat as you take up His Program and read: "To bind up the broken-hearted; to proclaim liberty to the captives; to comfort all that mourn; to give them beauty for ashes, the oil of joy for mourning, the garment of praise for the spirit of heaviness."[2]

What an exchange—Beauty for Ashes, Joy for Mourning, Liberty for Chains! No marvel "the eyes of all them that were in the synagogue were fastened on Him" as He read; or that they "wondered at the gracious words which proceeded out of His lips." Only one man in that congregation, only one man in the world today could hear these accents with dismay—the man, the culprit, who has said hard words of Christ.

We are all familiar with the protest, "Of course"—as if there were no other alternative to a person of culture—"Of course I am not a Christian, but I always speak respectfully of Christianity." Respectfully of Christianity! No remark fills one's soul with such sadness. One can understand a man as he reads these words being stricken speechless; one can see the soul within him rise to a white heat as each fresh benediction falls upon his ear and drives him, a half-mad enthusiast, to bear them to the world. But in what school has he learned of Christ who offers the Savior of the world his respect?

Men repudiate Christ's religion because they think it a small and limited thing, a scheme with no large human interests to commend it to this great social age. I ask you to note that there is not one burn-

2 Isaiah 61:1-3 and St. Luke 4:16-21.

ing interest of the human race which is not represented here. What are the great words of Christianity according to this Program? Take as specimens these: Liberty, Comfort, Beauty, Joy. These are among the greatest words of life. Give them their due extension, the significance which Christ undoubtedly saw in them and which Christianity undoubtedly yields, and there is almost no great want or interest of mankind which they do not cover.

These are not only the greatest words of life but they are the best. This Program, to those who have misread Christianity, is a series of surprises. Observe the most prominent note in it. It is gladness. Its first word is "good-tidings," its last is "joy." The saddest words of life are also there—but there as the diseases which Christianity comes to cure. No life that is occupied with such an enterprise could be other than radiant. The contribution of Christianity to the joy of living, perhaps even more than to the joy of *thinking*, is unspeakable. The joyful life is the life of the larger mission, the disinterested life, the life of the overflow from self, the "more abundant life" which comes from following Christ. And the joy of thinking is the larger thinking, the thinking of the man who holds in his hand some Program for Humanity. . . .

But that is not all. Man's greatest needs are often very homely. And it is almost as much in its fearless recognition of the commonplace woes of life, and its deliberate offerings to minor needs, that the claims of Christianity to be a religion for Humanity stand. Look, for instance, at the closing sentence of this Program. Who would have expected to find among the special of Christ's Solicitude the *Spirit of Heaviness*? Supreme needs, many and varied, had been already dealt with on this Program; many applicants had been met; the list is about to close. Suddenly the writer remembers the nameless malady of the poor—that mysterious disease which the rich share but cannot alleviate, which is too subtle for doctors, too incurable for Parliaments, too unpicturesque for philanthropy, too common even for sympathy. Can Christ melt that?

If Christianity could even deal with the world's Depression, could cure mere dull spirits, it would be the Physician of Humanity. But it can. It has the secret, a hundred secrets, for the lifting of the world's gloom. It cannot immediately remove the physiological causes of dullness—though obedience to its principles can do an infinity to prevent them, and its inspirations can do even more to lift the mind above them. But where the causes are moral or mental or social the remedy is in every Christian's hand. Think of anyone at this moment whom the Spirit of Heaviness haunts. You think of a certain old woman. But you know for a fact that you can cure her. You did so, perfectly, only a week ago. A mere visit, and a little present, or the visit without any present, set her up for seven long days and seven long nights. The machinery of the Kingdom is very simple and very silent, and the most silent parts do most, and we all believe so little in the medicines of Christ that we do not know what ripples of healing are set in motion when we simply smile on one another. Christianity wants nothing so much in the world as sunny people, and the old are hungrier for love than for bread, and the Oil of Joy is very cheap, and if you can help the poor on with a Garment of Praise it will be better for them than blankets.

Or perhaps you know someone who is dull—not an old woman this time, but a very rich and important man. But you also know perfectly what makes him dull. It is either his riches or his importance. Christianity can cure either of these—though you may not be the person to apply the cure—at a single hearing. Or here is a third case, one of your own servants. It is the case of monotony. Prescribe more variety, leisure, variation—anything to relieve the wearing strain. A fourth case—your most honored guest: Condition—leisure, health, accomplishments, means; Disease—Spiritual Obesity; Treatment—talent to be put out to usury. And so on down the whole list of life's dejection and ennui.

Perhaps you tell me this is not Christianity at all; that everybody could do that. The curious thing is that everybody does not. Goodwill to men came into the world with Christ, and wherever that is found, in Christian or heathen land, there Christ is, and there His Spirit works. And if you say that the chief end of Christianity is not the world's happiness, I agree; it was never meant to be; but the strange fact is that, without making it its chief end, it wholly and infallibly, and quite universally, leads to it. Hence the note of Joy, though not the highest on Christ's Program, is a loud and ringing note, and none who serve in His Society can be long without its music. Time was when a Christian used to apologize for being happy. But the day has always been when he ought to apologize for being miserable.

Christianity, you will observe, really works. And it succeeds not only because it is divine, but because it is so very human—because it is common-sense. Why should the Garment of Praise destroy the Spirit of Heaviness? Because an old woman cannot sing and cry at the same moment. The Society of Christ is a sane Society. Its methods are rational. The principle in the old woman's case is simply that one emotion destroys another. Christianity works, as a railway man would say, with points. It switches souls from valley lines to mountain lines, not stemming the currents of life but diverting them. In the rich man's case the principle of cure is different, but it is again principle, not necromancy. His spirit of heaviness is caused, like any other heaviness, by the earth's attraction. Take away the earth and you take away the attraction. But if Christianity can do anything it can take away the earth. By the wider extension of horizon which it gives, by the new standard of values, by the setting of life's small pomps and interests and admirations in the light of the Eternal, it dissipates the world with a breath. All tends to abolish worldliness tends to abolish unrest, and hence, in the rush of modern life, one far-reaching good of all even commonplace Christian preaching, all Christian literature, all which holds the world doggedly to the idea of a God and a future life, and reminds mankind of Infinity and Eternity.

Side by side, with these influences, yet taking the world at a wholly different angle, works another great Christian force. How many opponents of religion are aware that one of the specific objects of Christ's Society is Beauty? The charge of vulgarity against Christianity is an old one. If it means that Christianity deals with the ruder elements in human nature, it is true, and that is its glory. But if it means that it has no respect for the finer qualities, the charge is baseless. For Christianity not only encourages whatsoever things are lovely, but wars against that whole theory of life which would exclude them. It prescribes estheticism; it proscribes asceticism. And for those who preach to Christians that in these enlightened days they must raise the masses by giving them noble sculptures and beautiful paintings and music and public parks, the answer is that these things are all already being given, and given daily, and with an increasing sense of their importance, by the Society of Christ. Take away from the world the beautiful things which have not come from Christ and you will make it poorer scarcely at all. Take away from modern cities the paintings, the monuments, the music for the people, the museums and the parks which are not the gifts of Christian men and Christian municipalities, and in ninety cases out of a hundred you will leave them unbereft of so much as a well-shaped lamp-post.

It is impossible to doubt that the Decorator of the World shall not continue to serve to His later children, and in ever finer forms, the inspirations of beautiful things. More fearlessly than he has ever done, the Christian of modern life will use the noble spiritual lever-ages of art. That this world, the people's world, is a bleak and ugly world, we do not forget; it is ever with us. But we esteem too little the mission of Beautiful Things in haunting the mind with higher thoughts and begetting the mood which leads to God. Physical beauty makes moral beauty. Loveliness does more than destroy ugli-ness; it destroys matter. A mere touch of it in a room, in a street, even on a door-knocker, is a spiritual force. Ask the workingman's wife, and she will tell you there is a moral effect even in a clean table-cloth. If a barrel-organ in a slum can but drown a curse, let no Christian silence it. The mere light and color of the wall-advertise-ments are a gift of God to the poor man's somber world. . . .

But do not misunderstand me. . . . Our Program must go deeper. Beauty may arrest the drunkard, but it cannot cure him.

It is here that Christianity asserts itself with a supreme individu-ality. It is here that it parts company with Civilization, with politics, with all secular schemes of Social Reform. In its diagnosis of human nature it finds that which most other systems ignore; which, if they see, they cannot cure; which, left undestroyed, makes every reform futile, and every inspiration vain. That thing is Sin. Christianity, of all other philanthropies, recognizes that man's devouring need is Liberty—liberty to stop sinning; to leave the prison of his passions, and shake off the fetters of his past. To surround Captives with statues and pictures, to offer Them-that-are-Bound a higher wage or a cleaner street or a few more cubit feet of air per head, is solemn trifling. It is a cleaner soul they want; a purer air, or any air at all, for their higher selves.

And where the cleaner soul is to come from apart from Christ I cannot tell. . . . The power to set the heart right, to renew the springs of action, comes from Christ. The sense of the infinite worth of the single soul, and the recoverableness of man at his worst, are the gifts of Christ. The freedom from guilt, the forgiveness of sins, come from Christ's Cross; the hope of immortality springs from Christ's grave. We believe in the gospel of better laws and an improved environment; we hold the religion of Christ to be a social religion; we magnify and call Christian the work of reformers, statesmen, philanthropists, educators, inventors, sanitary officers, and all who directly or remotely aid, abet, or further the higher progress of mankind; but in Him alone, in the fullness of that word, do we see the Savior of the world.

There are earnest and gifted lives today at work among the poor whose lips at least will not name the name of Christ. I speak of them with respect; their shoe-latchets many of us are not worthy to unloose. But because the creed of the neighboring mission-hall is a travesty of religion they refuse to acknowledge the power of the living Christ to stop man's sin, of the dying Christ to forgive it. . . . Because there are ignorant doctors do I yet rail at medicine or start an hospital of my own? Because the poor raw evangelist, or the narrow ecclesiastic, offer their little all to the poor, shall I repudiate all they do not know of Christ because of the little they do know? Of gospels for the poor which have not some theory, state it how you will, of personal conversion one cannot have much hope. Personal conversion means for life a personal religion; a personal trust in God, a personal debt to Christ, a personal dedication to His cause. These, brought about how you will, are supreme things to aim at, supreme losses if they are missed. Sanctification will come to the masses only as it comes to individual men; and to work with Christ's Program and ignore Christ is [to try] to utilize the sun's light without its energy.

But this is not the only point at which the uniqueness of this Society appears. There is yet another depth in humanity which no other system even attempts to sound. We live in a world not only of sin but of sorrow. . . .

At that moment the gospels of the world are on trial. In the presence of Death how will they act? Act! They are blotted out of existence. Philosophy, Politics, Reforms are no more. The Picture Galleries close. The Sculptures hide. The committees disperse. There is crape on the door; the world withdraws. Observe, it withdraws. It has no mission.

So awful in its loneliness was this hour that the Romans paid a professional class to step in with its mummeries and try to fill it. But that is Christ's own hour. Next to Righteousness the greatest word of Christianity is Comfort. Christianity has almost a monopoly of Comfort. . . . Christ's Program is full of comfort, studded with comfort: "to bind up the broken-hearted, to comfort all that mourn, to give unto them that mourn in Zion." Even the "good tidings to the meek" are, in the Hebrew, a message to the "afflicted" or "the poor." The word Gospel itself comes down through the Greek from this very passage, so that whatever else Christ's Gospel means it is first an Evangel for suffering men.

One note in this Program jars with all the rest. When Christ read from Isaiah that day He never finished the passage. A terrible word Vengeance, yawned like a precipice across His path; and in the middle of a sentence "He closed the Book, and gave it again to the minister, and sat down." A Day of Vengeance from our God—these were the words before which Christ paused. When the prophet proclaimed it some great historical fulfillment was in his mind. Had the people to whom Christ read been able to understand its ethical equivalents He would probably have read on. For, so understood, instead of filling the mind with fear, the thought of this dread Day inspires it with a solemn gratitude. The work of the Avenger is a necessity. It is part of God's philanthropy.

For I have but touched the surface in speaking of the sorrow of the world as if it came from people dying. It comes from people living. Before even the Broken-Hearted can be healed a hundred greater causes of suffering than death must be destroyed. Before the captive can be free a vaster prison than his own sins must be demolished. There are hells on earth into which no breath of Heaven can ever come; these must be swept away. There are social soils in which only unrighteousness can flourish; these must be broken up.

And that is the work of the Day of Vengeance. When is that day? It is now. Who is the Avenger? Law. What Law? Criminal Law, Sanitary Law, Social Law, Natural Law. Wherever the poor are trodden upon or tread upon one another; wherever the air is poison and the water foul; wherever want stares, and vice reigns, and rags rot—there the Avenger takes his stand. Whatever makes it more difficult for the drunkard to reform, for the children to be pure, for the widow to earn a wage, for any of the wheels of progress to revolve—with these he deals. Delay him not. He is the messenger of Christ. Despair of him not, distrust him not. His Day dawns slowly, but his work is sure. Though evil stalks the world, it is on the way to execution; though wrong reigns, it must end in self-combustion. The very nature of things is God's Avenger; the very story of civilization is the history of Christ's Throne.

Prevention is Christian as well as cure; and Christianity travels sometimes by the most circuitous paths. It is given to some to work for immediate results, and from year to year they are privileged to reckon up a balance of success. But these are not always the greatest in the Kingdom of God. The men who get no stimulus from any visible reward, whose lives pass while the objects for which they toil are still too far away to comfort them; the men who hold aloof from dazzling schemes and earn the misunderstanding of the crowd because they foresee remoter issues, who even oppose a seeming good because a deeper evil lurks beyond—these are the statesmen of the Kingdom of God.

Such in dimmest outline is the Program of Christ's Society. Did you know that all this was going on in the world? Did you know that Christianity was such a living and purpose-like thing? Look back to the day when that Program was given and you will see that it was not merely written on paper. Watch the drama of the moral order rise up, scene after scene in history. Study the social evolution of humanity, the spread of righteousness, the amelioration of life, the freeing of slaves, the elevation of woman, the purification of religion, and ask what these can be if not the coming of the Kingdom of God on earth. For it is precisely through the movements of nations and the lives of men that this Kingdom comes. Christ might have done all this work Himself, with His own hands. But He did not. The crowning wonder of His scheme is that He entrusted it to men. It is the supreme glory of humanity that the machinery for its redemption should have been placed within itself. I think the saddest thing in Christ's life was that after founding a Society with aims so glorious He had to go away and leave it.

But in reality He did not leave it. The old theory that God made the world, made it as an inventor would make a machine, and then stood looking on to see it work, has passed away. God is no longer a remote spectator of the natural world, but immanent in it, pervading matter by His present Spirit, and ordering it by His Will. So Christ is immanent in men. His work is to move the hearts and inspire the lives of men, and through such hearts to move and reach the world. Men, only men, can carry out this work. This humanness, this inwardness, of the Kingdom is one reason why some scarcely see that it exists at all. We measure great movements by the loudness of their advertisement, or the place their externals fill in the public eye. This Kingdom has no externals. The usual methods of propagating a great cause were entirely discarded by Christ. The sword He declined; money He had none; literature He never used; the Church disowned Him; the State crucified Him. Planting His ideals in the hearts of a few poor men, He started them out unheralded to revolutionize the world. They did it by making friends—and by making enemies; they went out, did good, sowed seed, died, and lived again in the lives of those they helped. Those in turn, a fraction of them, did the same. They met, they prayed, they talked of Christ, they loved, they went among other men, and by act and word passed on their secret. The machinery of the Kingdom of God is purely social. It acts, not by commandments, but by contagion; not by fiat, but by friendship.

"The Kingdom of God is like unto leaven, which a woman took and hid in three measures of meal till the whole was leavened."

After all, like all great discoveries once they are made, this seems absolutely the most feasible method that could have been devised. Men must live among men. Men must influence men. . . . The only fluid in the world is man. War might have won for Christ a passing victory; wealth might have purchased a superficial triumph; political power might have gained a temporary success. But in these there is no note of universality, of solidarity, of immortality. To live through the centuries and pervade the uttermost ends of the earth, to stand while kingdoms tottered and civilizations changed . . . there was no soil for the Kingdom of God like the hearts of common men. Some who have written about this Kingdom have emphasized its moral grandeur, others its universality, others its adaptation to man's needs. One great writer speaks of its prodigious originality, another notices its success. I confess what always strikes me most is the miracle of its simplicity.

Men, then, are the only means God's Spirit has of accomplishing His purpose. What men? You. Is it worth doing, or is it not? Is it worth while joining Christ's Society, or is it not? What do you do all day? What is your personal stake in the coming of the Kingdom of Christ on earth? This is a real world, not a think world. Treat it as a real world—act. Think by all means, but think also of what is actual, of what like the stern world is, of how much even you could do to make it better. The thing to be anxious about is not to be right with man, but with mankind. And, so far as I know, there is nothing so on all fours with mankind as Christianity.

There are versions of Christianity, it is true, which no self-respecting mind can do other than disown—versions so hard, so narrow, so unreal, so super-theological, that practical men can find in them neither outlet for their lives nor resting-place for their thoughts. With these we have nothing to do. With these Christ had nothing to do—except to oppose them with every word and act of His life. It too seldom occurs to those who repudiate Christianity because of its narrowness or its unpracticalness, its sanctimoniousness or its dullness, that these were the very things which Christ strove against and unweariedly condemned. It was the one risk of His religion being given to the common people—an inevitable risk which He took without reserve—that its infinite luster should be tarnished in the fingering of the crowd or have its great truths narrowed into mean and unworthy molds as they passed from lip to lip. But though the crowd is the object of Christianity, it is not its custodian. Deal with the Founder of this great commonwealth Himself. Any man of honest purpose who will take the trouble to inquire at first hand what Christianity really is will find it a thing he cannot get away from. Without either argument or pressure, by the mere practicalness of its aims and the pathos of its compassions, it forces its august claim upon every serious life.

He who joins this Society finds himself in a large place. The Kingdom of God is a Society of the best men, working for the best ends, according to the best methods. Its membership is a multitude whom no man can number; its methods are as various as human nature; its field is the world. It is a commonwealth, yet it honors a King; it is a Social Brotherhood, but it acknowledges the Fatherhood of God. Though not a Philosophy the world turns to it for light; though not political it is the incubator of all great laws. It is more human than the State, for it deals with deeper needs; more Catholic than the Church, for it includes whom the Church rejects. It is a Propaganda, yet it works not by agitation but by ideals. It is a Religion, yet it holds the worship of God to be mainly the service of man. Though not a Scientific Society its watchword is Evolution; though not an Ethic it possesses the Sermon on the Mount. This mysterious Society owns no wealth but distributes fortunes. It has no minutes for history keeps them; no member's roll for no one could make it. Its entry-money is nothing; its subscription, all you have. The Society never meets and it never adjourns. Its law is one word—loyalty; its Gospel one message—love. Verily "Whosoever will lose his life for My sake shall find it."

The program for the other life is not out yet. For this world, for these faculties, for this one short life, I know nothing that is offered to man to compare with membership in the Kingdom of God. Among the mysteries which compass the world beyond, none is

160 HENRY DRUMMOND: AN ANTHOLOGY

greater than how there can be in store for man a work more wonderful, a life more God-like than this. If you know anything better, live for it; if not, in the name of God and of Humanity, carry out Christ's plan.

"The Greatest Thing in the World" was given in many places after it achieved instant success at Northfield in 1887. Drummond repeated it during the Oddfellows Hall meetings and in his second series at Grosvenor House. This first "Christmas Booklet" was beautifully printed and attractively bound. It caught the public fancy and the sale was enormous. It is still possible from time to time, to pick up a copy in the original edition at secondhand bookstores.

Shortly after Drummond's return from Africa, in June, 1884, he was a guest in the country home of Mr. Edward Denny. He had been invited along with Moody and others engaged in the work of the London Mission. The story of how this first "Christmas Booklet" originated on this beautiful Sunday evening is told by Moody.

"As we sat around the fire, they asked me to read and expound some portion of Scripture. Being tired after the services of the day, I told them they'd been hearing me for eight months and that I was quite exhausted, and to ask Henry Drummond, who would give us a Bible reading. After some urging and characteristic reluctance he drew a small New Testament from his pocket, opened it at the thirteenth chapter of First Corinthians, and without a note, in the most informal way, began to speak on the subject of love. It seemed to me that I had never heard anything so beautiful." Moody tells of his determination then not to rest until he had brought Henry Drummond to Northfield to deliver that address on "Love," which he did three years later. Mr. Moody also wrote that "some men take an occasional journey into the thirteenth of First Corinthians, but Henry Drummond was a man who lived there constantly, appropriating its blessings and exemplifying its teachings." He also said it would be a good thing to have this chapter of Corinthians read once a month in every church until it was known by heart. For Moody, Drummond was "the sweetest tempered Christian I ever knew," and he loved him like a son to the very end of his life.

First published in 1887, immediately after the Northfield conference, under the title "Love—the Supreme Gift," it was printed in de luxe form in December 1889 to launch the "Christmas Booklet" series. It is by far the most popular of Drummond's writings and is still being published and affecting people's lives. One clergyman gives a copy to each newlywed couple because of its excellent description of what love really is.

This masterpiece of lyric utterance had the unusual distinction of being "hawked" at the street corners of Boston by enterprizing newsboys during and after Drummond's second visit to America in 1893.

After reading this essay a rough miner in the Rocky Mountains gave the following verdict "Say, if that's religion, you can't get me onto it too quick." The remarkable booklet made such men as these see the "use" in religion, and made them desire to know something more about it by the experience of its beauty and power. Drummond showed them, as another miner expressed it, "a religion with some good to it besides preachin' and singin' yourself, and sendin' everybody else to blazes."

One of Scotland's greatest painters, G. F. Watts, acknowledged the influence of "The Greatest Thing" on his life and on his choice of themes for his paintings.

Every one has asked the great question of antiquity as of the modern world: What is the supreme good? You have life before you. Once only can you live it. What is the noblest object of desire, the supreme gift to covet?

We have been accustomed to be told that the greatest thing in the religious world is Faith. That great word has been the key-note for centuries of the popular religion; and we have easily learned to look upon it as the greatest thing in the world. Well, we are wrong. If we have been told that, we may miss the mark. . . . [In the thirteenth chapter of First Corinthians] we read "the greatest . . . is love." It is not an oversight. Paul was speaking of faith just a moment before. He says, "If I have all faith, so that I can remove mountains, and have not love, I am nothing." So far from forgetting he deliberately contrasts them, "Now abideth Faith, Hope, Love," and without a moment's hesitation the decision falls, "The greatest of these is Love."

And it is not prejudice. A man is apt to recommend to others his own strong point. Love was not Paul's strong point. The observing student can detect a beautiful tenderness growing and ripening all through his character as Paul gets old; but the hand that wrote, "The greatest of these is love," when we meet it first, is stained with blood.

Nor is this letter to the Corinthians peculiar in singling out love as the *summum bonum*. The masterpieces of Christianity are agreed about it. Peter says, "Above all things have fervent love among yourselves." And you remember the profound remark which Paul makes elsewhere, "Love is the fulfilling of the law." Did you ever think what he meant by that? In those days men were working their passage to Heaven by keeping the Ten Commandments, and the hundred and ten other commandments which they had manufactured out of them. Christ said, I will show you a more simple way. If you do one thing, you will do these hundred and ten things, without ever thinking about them. If you love, you will unconsciously fulfill the whole law. And you can readily see for yourselves how that must be so. Take any of the commandments. "Thou shalt have no other gods before Me." If a man love God, you will not require to tell him that. Love is the fulfilling of that law. "Take not His name in vain." Would he ever dream of taking His name in vain if he loved Him? "Remember the Sabbath day to keep it holy." Would he not be too glad to have one day in seven to dedicate more exclusively to the object of his affection? Love would fulfill all these laws regarding God. And so, if he loved Man, you would never think of telling him to honor his father and mother. He could not do anything else. It would be preposterous to tell him not to kill. You could only insult him if you suggested that he should not steal—how could he steal from those he loved? It would be superfluous to beg him not to bear false witness against his neighbor. If he loved him it would be the last thing he would do. And you would never dream of urging him not to covet what his neighbors had. He would rather they possessed it than himself. In this way "Love is the fulfilling of the law." It is the rule for fulfilling all rules, the new commandment for keeping all the old commandments, Christ's one secret of the Christian life.

Now Paul had learned that; and in this noble eulogy he has given us the most wonderful and original account extant of the *summum bonum.* . . .

Paul, in three verses, very short, gives us an amazing analysis of what this supreme thing is. . . . It is a compound thing, he tells us. It is like light. As you have seen a man of science take a beam of light and pass it through a crystal prism, as you have seen it come out on the other side of the prism broken up into its component colors— red, and blue, and yellow, and violet, and orange, and all the colors of the rainbow—so Paul passes this thing, Love, through the magnificent prism of his inspired intellect, and it comes out on the other side broken up into its elements. And in these few words we have what one might call the Spectrum of Love, the analysis of Love. Will you observe what its elements are? Will you notice that they have common names; that they are virtues which we hear about every day, that they are things which can be practiced by every man in every place in life; and how, by a multitude of small things and ordinary virtues, the supreme thing . . . is made up?

The Spectrum of Love has nine ingredients: Patience—"Love suffereth long"; Kindness—"and is kind"; Generosity—"Love envieth not"; Humility—"Love vaunteth not itself, is not puffed up"; Courtesy—"Doth not behave itself unseemly"; Unselfishness— "Seeketh not her own"; Good Temper—"Is not easily provoked"; Guilelessness—"Thinketh no evil"; Sincerity—"Rejoiceth not in iniquity, but rejoiceth in the truth." . . . These make up the supreme gift, the stature of the perfect man. . . .

There is no time to do more than make a passing note upon each of these ingredients. Love is *Patience.* This is the normal attitude of Love; . . . Love waiting to begin; . . . ready to do its work when the summons comes, but meantime wearing the ornament of a . . . quiet spirit. . . . For Love understands, and therefore waits.

Kindness. . . . Have you ever noticed how much of Christ's life was spent in doing kind things—in *merely* doing kind things? Run over it with that in view, and you will find that He spent a great proportion of His time simply in making people happy, in doing good turns to people. There is only one thing greater than happiness in the world, and that is holiness; and it is not in our keeping; but what God *has* put in our power is the happiness of those about us, and that is largely to be secured by our being kind to them. "The greatest thing," says someone, "a man can do for his Heavenly Father is to be kind to some of His other children." I wonder why it is that we are not all kinder than we are? How much the world needs it. How easily it is done. How instantaneously it acts. How infallibly it is remembered. How super-abundantly it pays itself back. . . . Where Love is, God is. He that dwelleth in Love dwelleth in God. God is Love. Therefore *love*. Without distinction, without calculation, without procrastination, love. Lavish it upon the poor, where it is very easy; especially upon the rich, who often need it most; most of all upon our equals, where it is very difficult, and for whom perhaps we each do least of all. There is a difference between *trying to please* and *giving pleasure*. Give pleasure. Lose no chance of giving pleasure. For that is the ceaseless and anonymous triumph of a truly loving spirit. "I shall pass through this world but once. Any good thing therefore that I can do, or any kindness that I can show to any human being, let me do it now. Let me not defer it or neglect it, for I shall not pass this way again."

Generosity. "Love envieth not." This is love in competition with others. Whenever you attempt a good work you will find other men doing the same kind of work, and probably doing it better. Envy them not. Envy is a feeling of ill-will to those who are in the same line as ourselves, a spirit of covetousness and detraction. How little Christian work even is protection against un-Christian feeling. That most despicable of all the unworthy moods which cloud a Christian's soul assuredly waits for us on the threshold of every work, unless we are fortified with this grace of magnanimity. Only one thing truly need the Christian envy, the large, rich, generous soul which "envieth not."

And then, after having learned all that, you have to learn this further thing, *Humility*—to put a seal upon your lips and forget what you have done. After you have been kind, after Love has stolen forth into the world and done its beautiful work, go back into the shade again and say nothing about it. Love hides even from itself. Love waives even self-satisfaction. "Love vaunteth not itself, is not puffed up."

The fifth ingredient is a somewhat strange one to find: *Courtesy*. This is Love in society, Love in relation to etiquette. "Love doth not behave itself unseemly." Politeness has been defined as love in trifles. Courtesy is said to be love in little things. And the one secret of politeness is to love. Love *cannot* behave itself unseemly. You can put the most untutored persons into the highest society, and if they have a reservoir of Love in their heart, they will not behave themselves unseemly. They simply cannot do it. Carlyle said of Robert Burns that there was no truer gentleman in Europe than the ploughman-poet. It was because he loved everything—the mouse, and the daisy, and all the things, great and small, that God hath made. So with this simple passport he could mingle with any society, and enter courts and palaces from his little cottage on the banks of the Ayr. You know the meaning of the word "gentleman." It means a gentle man—a man who does things gently with love. And that is the whole art and mystery of it. The gentle man cannot in the nature of things do an ungentle, an ungentlemanly thing. The ungentle soul, the inconsiderate, unsympathetic nature cannot do anything else. "Love doth not behave itself unseemly."

Unselfishness. "Love seeketh not her own." Seeketh not even that which is her own. . . . Paul does not summon us to give up our rights. Love strikes much deeper. It would have us not seek them at all, ignore them, eliminate the personal element altogether from our calculations. It is not hard to give up our rights. They are often external. The difficult thing is to give up ourselves. The more difficult thing still is not to seek things for ourselves at all . . . Why? Because there is no greatness in *things*. Things cannot be great. The only greatness is unselfish love. Even self-denial in itself is nothing. . . . It is more difficult . . . not to seek our own at all, than, having sought it, to give it up. . . . Nothing is a hardship to Love, and nothing is hard. I believe that Christ's yoke is easy. Christ's "yoke" is just His way of taking life. And I believe it is an easier way than any other. I believe it is a happier way than any other. The most obvious lesson in Christ's teaching is that there is no happiness in having and getting anything, but only in giving. I repeat, *there is no happiness in having or in getting, but only in giving*. And half the world is on the wrong scent in the pursuit of happiness. They think it consists in having and getting, and in being served by others. It consists in giving, and in serving others. He that would be great among you, said Christ, let him serve. He that would be happy, let him remember that there is but one way—it is more blessed, it is more happy, to give than to receive.

The next ingredient is a very remarkable one: *Good Temper.* "Love is not easily provoked." Nothing could be more striking than to find this here. We are inclined to look upon bad temper as a very harmless weakness. We speak of it as a mere infirmity of nature, a family failing, a matter of temperament, not a thing to take into very serious account in estimating a man's character. And yet here, right in the heart of this analysis of love, it finds a place; and the Bible again and again returns to condemn it as one of the most destructive elements in human nature. . . .[3]

Guilelessness and *Sincerity* may be dismissed almost with a word. Guilelessness is the grace for suspicious people. And the possession of it is the great secret of personal influence. You will find, if you think for a moment, that the people who influence you are people who believe in you. In an atmosphere of suspicion men shrivel up, but in that atmosphere they expand, and find encouragement and educative fellowship. It is a wonderful thing that here and there in this hard, uncharitable world there should still be left a few rare souls who think no evil. This is the great unworldliness. Love "thinketh no evil," imputes no motive, sees the bright side, puts the best construction on every action. What a delightful state of mind to live in! What a stimulus and benediction even to meet with it for a day! To be trusted is to be saved. And if we try to influence or elevate others, we shall soon see that success is in proportion to their belief of our belief in them. For the respect of another is the first restoration of the self-respect a man has lost; our ideal of what he is becomes to him the hope and pattern of what he may become.

"Love rejoiceth not in iniquity, but rejoiceth in the truth." I have called this *Sincerity,* from the words rendered in the Authorized Version by "rejoiceth in the truth." And, certainly, were this the real translation, nothing could be more just. For he who loves will

[3] See pp. 86-95 for a full treatment of "ill-temper." J. W. K.

love Truth not less than men. He will rejoice in the Truth—rejoice not in what he has been taught to believe; not in this Church's doctrine or in that; not in this ism or in that ism; but "in the Truth." He will accept only what is real; he will strive to get at facts, he will search for Truth with a humble and unbiased mind, and cherish whatever he finds at any sacrifice. But the more literal translation of the Revised Version calls for just such a sacrifice for truth's sake here. For what Paul really meant is, as we there read, "Rejoiceth not in unrighteousness, but rejoiceth with the truth," a quality which probably no one English word—and certainly not Sincerity—adequately defines. It includes, perhaps more strictly, the self-restraint which refuses to make capital out of others' faults; the charity which delights not in exposing the weakness of others, but "covereth all things"; the sincerity of purpose which endeavors to see things as they are, and rejoices to find them better than suspicion feared or calumny denounced. . . .

Now the business of our lives is to have these things fitted into our characters. That is the supreme work to which we need to address ourselves in this world, to learn Love. Is life not full of opportunities for learning Love? Every man and woman every day has a thousand of them. The world is not a play ground; it is a schoolroom. Life is not a holiday, but an education. And the one eternal lesson for us all is how better we can love. What makes a man a good cricketer? Practice. What makes a man a good artist, a good sculptor, a good musician? Practice. What makes a man a good linguist, a good stenographer? Practice. What makes a man a good man? Practice. Nothing else. There is nothing capricious about religion. We do not get the soul in different ways, under different laws, from those in which we get the body and the mind. If a man does not exercise his arm he develops no biceps muscle; and if a man does not exercise his soul, he acquires no muscle in his soul, no strength of character, no vigor of moral fiber, nor beauty of spiritual growth. Love is not a thing of enthusiastic emotion. It is a rich, strong, manly, vigorous expression of the whole round Christian character—the Christlike nature in its fullest development. And the constituents of this great character are only to be built up by ceaseless practice.

What was Christ doing in the carpenter's shop? Practicing. Though perfect, we read that He *learned* obedience, and grew in wisdom and in favor with God. Do not quarrel therefore with your lot in life. Do not complain of its never-ceasing cares, its petty environment, the vexations you have to stand, the small and sordid souls you have to live and work with. Above all, do not resent temptation; do not be perplexed because it seems to thicken round you more and more, and ceases neither for effort nor for agony nor prayer. That is your practice. That is the practice which God appoints you; and it is having its work in making you patient, and humble, and generous, and unselfish, and kind, and courteous. Do not grudge the hand that is molding the still too shapeless image within you. It is growing more beautiful, though you see it not, and every touch of temptation may add to its perfection. Therefore keep in the midst of life. Do not isolate yourself. Be among men, and among things, and among troubles, and difficulties, and obstacles. . . . Character grows in the stream of the world's life. That chiefly is where men are to learn love. . . .

Love itself can never be defined. Light is a something more than the sum of its ingredients—a glowing, dazzling, tremulous ether. And love is something more than all its elements—a palpitating, quivering, sensitive, living thing. By synthesis of all the colors, men can make whiteness, they cannot make light. By synthesis of all the virtues, men can make virtue, they cannot make love. How then are we to have this transcendent living whole conveyed into our souls? We brace our wills to secure it. We try to copy those who have it. We lay down rules about it. We watch. We pray. But these things alone will not bring Love into our nature. Love is an *effect*. And only as we fulfill the right condition can we have the effect produced. Shall I tell you what the *cause* is?

If you turn to the Revised Version of the First Epistle of John you will find these words: "We love because He first loved us." "We love," not "We love *Him*." That is the way the old version has it, and it is quite wrong. "We *love*—because He first loved us." Look at that word "because." It is the *cause* of which I have spoken. "*Because* He first loved us," the effect follows that we love, we love Him, we love all men. We cannot help it. Because He loved us, we love, we love everybody. Our heart is slowly changed. Contemplate the love of Christ, and you will love. Stand before that mirror, reflect Christ's character, and you will be changed into the same image from tenderness to tenderness. There is no other way. You cannot love to order. You can only look at the lovely object, and fall in love with it, and grow into likeness to it. And so look at this Perfect Character, this perfect Life. Look at the great Sacrifice as He laid down Himself, all through life, and upon the Cross of Calvary; and you must love Him. And loving Him, you must become like Him. Love begets love. It is a process of induction. Put a piece of iron in the presence of an electrified body, and that piece of iron for a time becomes electrified. It is changed into a temporary magnet in the mere presence of a permanent magnet, and as long as you leave the two side by side, they are both magnets alike. Remain side by side with Him who loved us, and gave Himself for us, and you too will become a permanent magnet, a permanently attractive force; and like Him you will draw all men unto you, like Him you will be drawn unto all men. That is the inevitable effect of Love. Any man who fulfills that cause must have that effect produced in him. Try to give up the idea that religion comes to us by chance, or by mystery, or by caprice. It comes to us by natural law, or by supernatural law, for all law is Divine. Edward Irving went to see a dying boy once, and when he entered the room he just put his hand on the sufferer's head, and said, "My boy, God loves you," and went away. And the boy started from his bed, and called out to the people in the house, "God loves me! God loves me!" It changed that boy. The sense that God loved him overpowered him, melted him down, and began the creating of a new heart in him. And that is how the love of God melts down the unlovely heart in man, and begets in him the new creature, who is patient and humble and gentle and unselfish. And there is no other way to get it. There is no mystery about it. We love others, we love everybody, we love our enemies, because He first loved us.

Now I have a closing sentence or two to add about Paul's reason for singling out love as the supreme possession. It is a very remarkable reason. In a single word it is this: *it lasts.* "Love," urges Paul, "never

faileth." Then he begins again one of his marvelous lists of the great
things of the day, and exposes them one by one. He runs over the
things that men thought were going to last, and shows that they are
all fleeting, temporary, passing away. . . .

[Then he declares] Love is eternal. Did you ever notice how
continually John [also] associates love and faith with eternal life? I
was not told when I was a boy that "God so loved the world that He
gave His only begotten Son, that whosoever believeth in Him should
have everlasting life." What I was told, I remember, was, that God
so loved the world that, if I trusted in Him, I was to have a thing
called peace, or I was to have rest, or I was to have joy, or I was to
have safety. But I had to find out for myself that whosoever trusteth
in Him—that is, whosoever loveth Him, for trust is only the avenue
to Love—hath everlasting *life*. The Gospel offers a man life. Never
offer men a thimbleful of Gospel. Do not offer them merely joy, or
merely peace, or merely rest, or merely safety; tell them how Christ
came to give men a more abundant life than they have, a life abundant in love, and therefore abundant in salvation for themselves, and
large in enterprise for the alleviation and redemption of the world.
Then only can the Gospel take hold of the whole of a man, body,
soul, and spirit, and give to each part of his nature its exercise and
reward. Many of the current Gospels are addressed only to a part of
man's nature. They offer peace, not life; faith, not Love; justification,
not regeneration. And men slip back again from such religion because
it has never really held them. Their nature was not all in it. It offered
no deeper and gladder life-current than the life that was lived before.
Surely it stands to reason that only a fuller love can compete with the
love of this world.

To love abundantly is to live abundantly, and to love for ever is
to live for ever. Hence, eternal life is inextricably bound up with love.
We want to live for ever for the same reason that we want to live
tomorrow. Why do you want to live tomorrow? It is because there
is some one who loves you, and whom you want to see tomorrow,
and be with, and love back. There is no other reason why we should
live on than that we love and are beloved. It is when a man has no
one to love him that he commits suicide. So long as he has friends,

those who love him and whom he loves, he will live; because to live is to love. Be it but the love of a dog, it will keep him in life; but let that go and he has no contact with life, no reason to live. He dies by his own hand. Eternal life also is to know God, and God is love. This is Christ's own definition. Ponder it. "This is life eternal, that they might know Thee the only true God, and Jesus Christ whom Thou hast sent." Love must be eternal. It is what God is. On the last analysis, then, love is life. Love never faileth, and life never faileth, so long as there is love. That is the philosophy of what Paul is showing us; the reason why in the nature of things Love should be the supreme thing—because it is going to last; because in the nature of things it is an Eternal Life. It is a thing that we are living now. No worse fate can befall a man in this world than to live and grow old alone, unloving, and unloved. To be lost is to live in an unregenerate condition, loveless and unloved; and to be saved is to love; and he that dwelleth in love dwelleth already in God. For God is love.

Now I have all but finished. How many of you will join me in reading this chapter once a week for the next three months? A man did that once and it changed his whole life. Will you do it? It is for the greatest thing in the world. You might begin by reading it every day, especially the verses which describe the perfect character. "Love suffereth long, and is kind; love envieth not; love vaunteth not itself." Get these ingredients into your life. Then everything that you do is eternal. It is worth doing. It is worth giving time to. No man can become a saint in his sleep; and to fulfill the condition required demands a certain amount of prayer and meditation and time, just as improvement in any direction, bodily or mental, requires preparation and care. Address yourselves to that one thing; at any cost have this transcendent character exchanged for yours. You will find as you look back upon your life that the moments that stand out, the moments when you have really lived, are the moments when you have done things in a spirit of love. As memory scans the past, above and beyond all the transitory pleasures of life, there leap forward those supreme hours when you have been enabled to do unnoticed kindnesses to those round about you, things too trifling to speak about, but which you feel have entered into your eternal life. I have seen almost all the beautiful things God has made; I have enjoyed almost every pleasure that He has planned for man; and yet as I look back I see standing out above all the life that has gone four or five short experiences when the love of God reflected itself in some poor imitation, some small act of love of mine, and these seem to be the things which alone of all one's life abide. Everything else in all our lives is transitory. Every other good is visionary. But the acts of love which no man knows about, or can ever know about—they never fail. . . .

5

"The New Evangelism"

*A*LMOST twenty years after presenting his address on "Spiritual Diagnosis," Drummond prepared another paper out of the richness of his experience, in which he attempted to make clear what he called "The New Evangelism." This was read before the Free Church Theological Society, Glasgow. He extended this paper for the same society in January, 1892, speaking on "The Method of the New Theology." Both of these addresses enlarged on what he considered the best methods for the Church to use in its approach to people. Together with "Spiritual Diagnosis" they summarize Drummond's amazingly successful methods of dealing with the doubts and failings of humanity.

The "new" evangelism of Drummond's day was similar to the new resurgence of evangelism today as a major concern of the Christian Churches. Just as Drummond knew that evangelism without theology makes a man's religion rootless, so today the revival of evangelism is closely connected with a clear statement and understanding of the Christian doctrine of nature, man, and God. Both Drummond's aim and ours is to know God's revelation of Himself in Jesus Christ, and to make that revelation known.

And yet the same "Gospel" must be ever restated in contemporary terms both as theology and evangel. The language of yesterday cannot always convey the challenge of the Christian message with sufficient impact to win a response from "modern" man. As Paul Tillich puts it, "we must receive the ever contemporary Christ in our own contemporary way employing whatever artistic forms, liturgical patterns, theological concepts and social diagnosis that can best enable us, here and now, to re-encounter the God of history and to reapprehend and actually receive His eternal time—oriented Word."

In this sense, theology and evangelism are always "new," and both use the creative and constructive assistance of every age—philosophical, scientific, artistic, political, and social—so long as these forces bring man and God together and fulfill Paul's words "if any man be in Christ he is a new creature."

Drummond gives us clues to the making of "a new creature," in his address, "The New Evangelism."[1]

❧

. . . The old theology was largely a product of reason. It was an elaborate, logical construction. The complaint against it is that, as a logical construction, it was arrived at by a faculty of the mind, and not by a faculty of the soul. On close scrutiny it turns out to be really nothing more or less than rationalism.

. . . It does not take a religious man to be a theologian; it simply takes a man with fair reasoning powers.[2] This man happens to apply these powers to doctrinal subjects, but in no other sense than he might apply them to astronomy or physics. . . . It is equally unnecessary to point out that if reason is the exclusive or primary faculty in theology, theology itself breaks down under rigid tests at almost every point. Its first principle, for example, that God is, contains a distinct contradiction, as has been repeatedly pointed out. Many philosophers, therefore, in being presented with theology as the expression of the Christian religion, have had no alternative but to become atheists. The reasoning faculty then cannot be the organ of the new evangelism, for its conclusions are philosophically assailable. But I am not dealing here with philosophy, and it is not to be understood that I am using terms—reason, for instance—in any particular

[1] By the word "evangelism" Drummond meant, "The methods of presenting Christian truth to men's minds in any form." By the "new evangelism" he meant, "The particular substance or form of evangel which is adapted to the present state of men's minds." The "New Evangelism" is "the Gospel for the age."

[2] Canon B. H. Streeter, a great scholar, was not "converted" until age 72. J. W. K.

philosophical sense. I am looking at the question exclusively from its practical side. And the question I ask myself is, "When I apprehend spiritual truth, what faculty do I employ?" When I say it is not the reason, I do not purposely make the distinction between the understanding and the reason . . . making the understanding the logical faculty and the reason the intuitive faculty. I use the word in its ordinary working sense, meaning by it, if you like, the logical understanding of the writer's mind.

What faculty do I employ, then, in apprehending spiritual truth? What is the primary faculty of the new evangelism if it is not the reason? Leaving philosophical distinctions aside again, I think it is the IMAGINATION. Overlook the awkwardness of this mere word, and ask yourself if this is not the organ of your mind which gives you a vision of the truth. The subject-matter of the new evangelism must be largely the words of Christ, the circle of ideas of Christ in their harmony, and especially in their perspective. Sit down for a moment and hear Him speak. Take almost any of His words. To what faculty do they appeal? Almost without exception to the imagination. . . . I do not merely refer to His parables, to His allusions to nature, to the miracles, to His endless symbolism—the comparisons between Himself and bread, water, vine, wine, shepherd, doctor, light, life, and a score of others. But all His most important sayings are put up in such form as to make it perfectly clear that they were deliberately designed for the imagination.

You cannot indeed really put up religious truth in any other form. You can put up facts, information, but God's truth will not go into a word. You must put it in an image. God Himself could not put truth in a word, therefore He made the Word flesh. There are few things less comprehended than this relation of truth to language. . . .

The purpose of revelation is to exhibit the mind of God. . . . The vehicle is words. . . . What words? Words which are windows and not prisons. Words of the intellect cannot hold God—the finite cannot hold the infinite. But an image can. So God has made it possible for us by giving us an external world to make *image-words*. The external world is not a place to work in, or to feed in, but to see in. It is a world of images, the external everywhere revealing the eternal. The key to the external world is to look not at the things which are seen, but in looking at the things which are seen to see through them to the things that are unseen. Look at the ocean. It is mere water—a thing which is seen; but look again, look through that which is seen, and you see the limitlessness of Eternity. Look at a river, another of God's images of the unseen. It is also water, but God has given it another form to image a different truth. There is Time, swift and silent. There is Life, irrevocable, passing. But the most singular truth of this is the Incarnation. There was no word in the world's vocabulary for Himself. In nature we had images of Time and Eternity. The seasons spoke of change, the mountains of stability. The home-life imaged Love. Law and Justice were in the Civil system. The snow was Purity, the rain, Fertility. By using these metaphors we could realize feebly Time and Eternity, Stability and Change. But there was no image of Himself. So God made one. He gave a word in Flesh—a word in Image-form. He gave the man Christ Jesus the *express image* of His person. This was the one image that was wanting in the image-vocabulary of truth, and the Incarnation supplied it.

God had really supplied this image before, but man had spoilt it, disfigured it to such an extent that it was unrecognizable. God made man in His own image; that was, a word made flesh. From its ruins man might have reconstructed an image of God, but the audacity of the attempt repelled him, and for centuries men had forgotten that the image of God was in themselves.

How, then, do you characterize that irreverent elaboration of theology which attempts to show you in words what God has had to do in the slow unfolding of Himself in history, and by that final resort, when words were useless, of incarnating the Word, giving us the manifestation of a living God in a living Word. These doctrines stand apart. They are above words. It is a mockery for the Reason to define and formulate here, as if by heaping up words she could drive the truth into a corner and dispense it in phrases as required. It is just as clear, as a simple question of rhetoric, that Christ's words were positively protected against the mere touch of reason. They were put up in such form in many cases as to challenge reason to make beginning, middle, or end of them. Try to reason out a parable. Try to read into it theology, as our forefathers often did; or dispensational truth,[3] as certain erratic theologians do today, and it becomes either utterly contemptible or utterly unintelligible.

You see a parable, you discern it; it enters your mind as an image, you image it, you imagine it. I am the Bread of Life. With what faculty do we apprehend that? We look at it long and earnestly, and at first are utterly baffled by it. But as we look it grows more and more transparent, and we see through it. We do not understand it; if we were asked what we saw, we should be surprised at the difficulty we had in defining it. Some image rose out of the word Bread, became slowly living, sank into our soul, and vanished. The peculiarity of this expression is that it is not a simile. "I am like bread." Christ does not say that. I am bread—the thing itself. And that faculty, standing face to face with truth, draws aside the veil, or pierces it, seizes the living substance, absorbs it; and the soul is nourished.

Besides the parable, the metaphor, and the metaphor which is no metaphor, Christ has two other favorite modes of expression. These are the axiom and the paradox. The axiom is the basis of certainty; the reason is inoperative without it, but it is not apprehended by reason. It is seen, not proved. Again, therefore, we are dealing with the Imagination. The paradox is the darkest of all figures. "He that loveth his life shall lose it, and he that hateth his life shall find it." What can reason make of that? It is an utter blank; it absolutely repels reason. But for that very cause it is the richest mine for the imagination. It is not the darkest figure, but the lightest, because the rays come from exactly opposite sides, and meet as truth in the middle. The shell of words, once burst, reveals a whole world, in which the illuminated mind runs riot, and revels in the boundlessness of truth.

Had the reason been able to sink its shaft, it might have brought up a nugget. . . . As it is, it is without end, limitless, infinite truth, incapable in that form of becoming uninteresting, unreal, included in a human phrase. It is this sense of depth about Christ's words which is the sure test of their truth. They shade off, every one, into the unknown, and the roots of the known are always in the unknown. . . .

As a faculty, then, the reason is not large enough to be the organ

[3] Like "indulgences" in the Medieval Church. J. W. K.

of Christianity. It has a very high and prominent place to play in Christianity, but *prima facie* it lacks the first and the second qualities of a religious faculty. The first of these qualities is that just mentioned, largeness and penetration. The second is universality. All men cannot reason, but all men can *see*. In the rudest savage and in the youngest child, the imagination is strong. And Christ addressed His religion to the most unlettered, to the youngest child. He boldly asserted that His religion was for the youngest child. He directly appealed again and again to the child-spirit. "Except ye become as a little child, ye shall in no wise enter into the kingdom of heaven." To object to this that Christ was speaking to the Oriental mind is of course beside the mark. Christ was not an Oriental speaking to the Oriental. He was the Son of man speaking to man in the universal language of truth. I have already apologized for using this word Imagination, but I think I have made clear the idea. I am not concerned longer, therefore, about retaining it. I am not sure that it is the right word. You might perhaps prefer to call it faith or intuition, or the spirit of discernment, or a subjective idealism, but the name is of no moment. The idea I have tried to make clear is that this is the faculty which works with the eyes, as contrasted with reason, which works with the hands. . . .

After the old Evangelism, this is a new world to live in. There is air here. Take the Gospel as a gift to the Imagination, and you are entered into a large place. It is like a conversion. . . . I once saw an hotel-keeper on a starlit night in autumn erect an electric light to show his guests Niagara. It never occurred to the creature that God's dim, mystic starlight was ten millions times more brilliant to man's soul than ten million carbons. When will it occur to us that God's truth is Light—self-luminous; to be seen because self-luminous? When shall we understand that it has no speech nor language, that men are to come to the naked truth with their naked eyes, bringing no candle? . . . We have a Gospel in the new Evangelism which for a hundred years the world has been waiting for. We have a Gospel which those who even faintly see it thank God that they live, and live to preach it. But I am not quite done yet. What will be, what are, the main hindrances to the acceptance of the new Evangelism? They are mainly two: (1) Unspirituality and (2) Laziness. . . .

The carnal mind is enmity against God—hates any spiritual exercise or effort. . . . There is nothing a man will not do to evade spirituality. Do we not all know moods in which we would rather walk twenty miles than take family worship? And there are moods in which men find it of all efforts least easy to come into contact with living truth. This is always difficult: to know His doctrine, a man must do the will of God. The supreme factor in arriving at spiritual knowledge is not theology, it is consecration. But for years and years —and it is one of the saddest truths in this world—a preacher may go on manipulating his theological forms without the slightest exercise of religion, unknown to himself, and unnoticed by his people.

The second obstacle is laziness. To make doctrinal sermons requires no effort. A man has simply to take down his Hodge, and there it is. Every Sabbath, though not formally expressed, he has the same heads. And the people understand it, or at least they understood it twenty years ago, when he preached, and preached well and with real heart, in the bloom of his early ministry. But for years now he has been a mere mechanic, a repeater of phrases, a reproducer of Hodge. And the people—they too are spared all effort. They are delighted with their minister. He in these days preaches the Gospel.

A caution may be necessary. In His exhaustless wisdom, in speaking on these subjects the Lord Jesus said: "No man having tasted the old wine straightway desireth new." We can speak of these things broadly to one another here, but we cannot with too much delicacy insinuate the new Evangelism upon the Church. The old is better, men say; and if any man really feels that it is better, I do not know that we should urge it upon him at all. There are many saints in our Churches, and if the old wine is really their life-blood, we can but wish them God-speed with all humility. Younger men will come to us, too, when our wine is old and the sun has set upon our new theology; but to the many who are waiting for the dawn, and these are many, our evangel may perhaps bring some light and fulfill gladness and liberty.

Least of all have we anything to do with willfully destroying the old. Christ was never destructive in His methods. It was very exquisite tact, a true understanding of men and a delicate respect for them that made Him say, "I came not to destroy but to fulfill."

6

"Natural Law"

*N*ATURAL LAW appeared at a time when the world was ready for it. The old orthodox faith, especially the story of Creation, was driven into a corner by science, and there seemed no escape from the dilemma of choosing Moses' or Darwin's version of Creation. Henry Drummond came along at the psychological moment of unbearable crisis and spoke to the condition. He made it clear that it was no longer necessary to hang in mid-air between a Christianity and a science which would not come together nor to be smashed between two "worlds in collision." He pointed out that science and religion were not two discordant languages, but that all which could be learned by studying nature only added to the riches of the glory of God.

This "naturalness of the spiritual world" proclaimed by Henry Drummond helped transform Christianity from the closed system of hermetically sealed faith, open only from above, to the wide-open vehicle for God's truth accepted from wherever it might come.

Drummond was a pioneer. Others have followed along the paths he opened up. Scientists and historians and men of religion have enlarged on his themes and added proof to some of Drummond's insights and intuitions. Social Law in the Spiritual World by Rufus M. Jones, Human Destiny by Pierre Lecomte du Noüy, A Study of History by Arnold J. Toynbee, and other writings have confirmed a great many of Drummond's intuitive insights, guesses and surmises in the realm of the natural-spiritual, the scientific-religious.

Drummond never gave up the basic conviction enunciated in Natural Law in the Spiritual World, namely, that the fabric of God's universe was woven as a whole, without seam, throughout. He held to his belief that the lower beginnings of life in the natural world developed into higher and higher forms until the highest forms of mind and spirit completed the evolutionary plan of God's creation.

All of his critics agreed that the book was beautifully written—"earnest, eloquent and fascinating," a book of "remarkable vigor and freshness," presenting some "new and striking analogies between the natural and spiritual world." The reviews stressed in his favor the "valuable parables," "the remarkable illustrations of religious truth" found in the field of modern science, the "practical religion" well fitted to reach the conscience, the power of the new scientific metaphors to drive home the old familiar lessons and warnings. Few, even today, would fail to grant the true and searching nature of its contents as a book of practical religion.

Obviously all of Natural Law cannot, and need not, be reprinted within the limits of this volume, but enough of it can be given to show the "suggestiveness" of the laws Drummond deals with in this book. The samples indicate the values still present for stirring the mind, and bringing deeper and more pertinent thoughts into action along the lines of such laws. The suggestiveness is apparent and the themes so stimulating and different they challenge the mind on almost every page.

Drummond did his best to satisfy the hunger of those disturbed by the new Biblical criticism and the theory of evolution, who were hungry for an authoritative voice proclaiming the reconciliation of science and religion. Today, as then, critical scholars and scientists will find serious flaws in the argument and conclusions of Drummond's thesis. But also today, as then, to plain Christians who want the foundations of their Gospel strengthened, this book still speaks.

The first edition of a thousand copies appeared April 5, 1883. It was immediately successful and became the most talked of religious book of his generation.

☙

Chapter VIII. Environment

Students of Biography will observe that in all well-written Lives attention is concentrated for the first few chapters upon two points. We are first introduced to the family to which the subject of memoir belonged. The grandparents, or even the more remote ancestors, are briefly sketched and their chief characteristics brought prominently into view. Then the parents themselves are photographed in detail. Their appearance and physique, their character, their disposition, their mental qualities, are set before us in a critical analysis. And finally we are asked to observe how much the father and the mother respectively have transmitted of their peculiar nature to their offspring. How faithfully the ancestral lines have met in the latest product, how mysteriously the joint characteristics of body and mind have blended, and how unexpected yet how entirely natural a re-combination is the result—these points are elaborated with cumulative effect until we realize at last how little we are dealing with an independent unit, how much with a survival and re-organization of what seemed buried in the grave.

In the second place, we are invited to consider more external influences—schools and schoolmasters, neighbors, home, pecuniary circumstances, scenery, and, by-and-by, the religious and political atmosphere of the time. These also we are assured have played their part in making the individual what he is. We can estimate these early influences in any particular case with but small imagination if we fail to see how powerfully they also have molded mind and character and in what subtle ways they have determined the course of the future life.

This twofold relation of the individual, first, to his parents, and second, to his circumstances, is not peculiar to human beings. These two factors are responsible for making all living organisms what they are. When a naturalist attempts to unfold the life-history of any animal, he proceeds precisely on these same lines. Biography is really a branch of Natural History; and the biographer who discusses his hero as the resultant of these two tendencies, follows the scientific method as rigidly as Mr. Darwin in studying "Animals and Plants under Domestication."

Mr. Darwin, following Weismann, long ago pointed out that there are two main factors in all Evolution—the nature of the organism and the nature of the conditions. We have chosen our illustration from the highest or human species in order to define the meaning of these factors in the clearest way; but it must be remembered that the development of man under these directive influences is essentially the same as that of any other organism in the hands of Nature. We are dealing therefore with universal Law. It will still further serve to complete the conception of the general principle if we now substitute for the casual phrases by which the factors have been described the more accurate terminology of Science. Thus what Biography describes as parental influences, Biology would speak of as Heredity; and all that is involved in the second factor—the action of external circumstances and surroundings—the naturalist would include under the single term Environment. These two, Heredity and Environment, are the master-influences of the organic world. These have made all of us what we are. These forces are still ceaselessly playing upon all our lives. And he who truly understands these influences; he who has decided how much to allow to each; he who can regulate new forces as they arise, or adjust them to the old, so directing them as at one moment to make them co-operate, at another to counteract one another, understands the rationale of personal development. To seize continuously the opportunity of more and more perfect adjustment to better and higher conditions, to balance some inward evil with some purer influence acting from without, in a word to make our Environment at the same time that it is making us—these are the secrets of a well-ordered and successful life.

In the spiritual world, also, the subtle influences which form and transform the soul are Heredity and Environment. And here especially where all is invisible, where much that we feel to be real is yet so ill-defined, it becomes of vital practical moment to clarify the atmosphere as far as possible with conceptions borrowed from the natural life. Few things are less understood than the conditions of the spiritual life. The distressing incompetence of which most of us are conscious in trying to work out our spiritual experience is due perhaps less to the diseased will which we commonly blame for it than to imperfect knowledge of the right conditions. It does not occur to us how natural the spiritual is. We still strive for some strange transcendent thing; we seek to promote life by methods as unnatural as they prove unsuccessful; and only the utter incomprehensibility of the whole region prevents us seeing fully—what we already half-suspect—how completely we are missing the road. Living in the spiritual world, nevertheless, is just as simple as living in the natural world; and it is the same kind of simplicity. It is the same kind of simplicity for it is the same kind of world—there are not two kinds of worlds. The conditions of life in the one are the conditions of life in the other. And till these conditions are sensibly grasped, as the conditions of all life, it is impossible that the personal effort after the highest life should be other than a blind struggle carried on in fruitless sorrow and humiliation.

Of these two universal factors, Heredity and Environment, it is unnecessary to balance the relative importance here. The main influence, unquestionably, must be assigned to the former. In practice, however, and for an obvious reason, we are chiefly concerned with the latter. What Heredity has to do for us is determined outside ourselves. No man can select his own parents. But every man to some extent can choose his own Environment. His relation to it, however largely determined by Heredity in the first instance, is always open to alteration. And so great is his control over Environment and so radical its influence over him, that he can so direct it as either to undo, modify, perpetuate or intensify the earlier hereditary influences within certain limits. But the aspects of Environment which we have now to consider do not involve us in questions of such complexity. In what high and mystical sense, also, Heredity applies to the spiritual organism we need not just now inquire. In the simpler relations of the more external factor we shall find a large and fruitful field for study.

The Influence of Environment may be investigated in two main aspects. First, one might discuss the modern and very interesting question as to the power of Environment to induce what is known to recent science as Variation. A change in the surroundings of any animal, it is now well-known, can so react upon it as to cause it to change. By the attempt, conscious or unconscious, to adjust itself to the new conditions, a true physiological change is gradually wrought within the organism. Hunter, for example, in a classical experiment, so changed the Environment of a sea-gull by keeping it in captivity that it could only secure a grain diet. The effect was to modify the stomach of the bird, normally adapted to a fish diet, until in time it came to resemble in structure the gizzard of an ordinary grain-feeder such as the pigeon. Holmgren again reversed this experiment by feeding pigeons for a lengthened period on a meat-diet, with the result that the gizzard became transformed into the carnivorous stomach. Mr. Alfred Russel Wallace mentions the case of a Brazilian parrot which changes its color from green to red or yellow when fed on the fat of certain fishes. Not only changes of food, however, but changes of climate and of temperature, changes in surrounding organisms, in the case of marine animals even changes of pressure, of ocean currents, of light, and of many other circumstances, are known to exert a powerful modifying influence upon living organisms. These relations are still being worked out in many directions, but the influence of Environment as a prime factor in Variation is now a recognized doctrine of science.

Even the popular mind has been struck with the curious adaptation of nearly all animals to their habitat, for example in the matter of color. The sandy hue of the sole and flounder, the white of the polar bear with its suggestion of Arctic snows, the stripes of the Bengal tiger—as if the actual reeds of its native jungle had nature-printed themselves on its hide; these, and a hundred others which will occur to everyone, are marked instances of adaptation to Environment induced, by Natural Selection or otherwise, for the purpose, obviously in these cases at least, of protection.

To continue the investigation of the modifying action of Environment into the moral and spiritual spheres, would be to open a fascinating and suggestive inquiry. One might show how the moral man is acted upon and changed continuously by the influences, secret and open, of his surroundings, by the tone of society, by the company he keeps, by his occupation, by the books he reads, by Nature, by all, in short, that constitutes the habitual atmosphere of his thoughts and the little world of his daily choice. Or one might go deeper still and prove how the spiritual life also is modified from outside sources— its health or disease, its growth or decay, all its changes for better or for worse being determined by the varying and successive circumstances in which the religious habits are cultivated. But we must rather transfer our attention to a second aspect of Environment, not perhaps so fascinating but yet more important.

So much of the modern discussion of Environment revolves round the mere question of Variation that one is apt to overlook a previous question. Environment as a factor in life is not exhausted when we have realized its modifying influence. Its significance is scarcely touched. The great function of Environment is not to modify but to sustain. In sustaining life, it is true, it modifies. But the latter influence is incidental, the former essential. Our Environment is that in which we live and move and have our being. Without it we should neither live nor move nor have any being. In the organism lies the principle of life; in the Environment are the conditions of life. Without the fulfillment of these conditions, which are wholly supplied by Environment, there can be no life. An organism in itself is but a part; Nature is its complement. Alone, cut off from its surroundings, it is not. Alone, cut off from my surroundings, I am not— physically I am not. I am, only as I am sustained. I continue only as I receive. My Environment may modify me, but it has first to keep me. And all the time its secret transforming power is indirectly molding body and mind, it is directly active in the more open task of ministering to my myriad wants and from hour to hour sustaining life itself.

To understand the sustaining influence of Environment in the animal world, one has only to recall what the biologist terms the extrinsic or subsidiary conditions of vitality. Every living thing normally requires for its development an Environment containing air, light, heat, and water. In addition to these, if vitality is to be prolonged for any length of time, and if it is to be accompanied with growth and the expenditure of energy, there must be a constant supply of food. When we simply remember how indispensable food is to growth and work, and when we further bear in mind that the food-supply is solely contributed by the Environment, we shall realize at once the meaning and the truth of the proposition that without Environment there can be no life. Seventy per cent at least of the human body is made of pure water, the rest of gases and earths. These have all come from Environment. Through the secret pores of the skin two pounds of water are exhaled daily from every healthy adult. The supply is kept up by Environment. The Environment is really an unappropriated part of ourselves. Definite portions are continuously abstracted from it and added to the organism. And so long as the organism continues to grow, act, think, speak, work, or perform any other function demanding a supply of energy, there is a constant, simultaneous, and proportionate drain upon its surroundings.

This is a truth in the physical, and therefore in the spiritual, world of so great importance that we shall not mis-spend time if we follow it, for further confirmation, into another department of nature. Its significance in Biology is self-evident; let us appeal to Chemistry.

When a piece of coal is thrown on the fire, we say that it will radiate into the room a certain quantity of heat. This heat, in the popular conception, is supposed to reside in the coal and to be set free during the process of combustion. In reality, however, the heat energy is only in part contained in the coal. It is contained just as truly in the coal's Environment—that is to say, in the oxygen of the air. The atoms of carbon which compose the coal have a powerful affinity for the oxygen of the air. Whenever they are made to approach within a certain distance of one another, by the initial application of heat, they rush together with inconceivable velocity. The heat which appears at this moment, comes neither from the carbon alone, nor from the oxygen alone. These two substances are really inconsumable, and continue to exist, after they meet in a combined form, as carbonic acid gas. The heat is due to the energy developed by the chemical embrace, the precipitate rushing together of the molecules of carbon and the molecules of oxygen. It comes, therefore, partly from the coal and partly from the Environment. Coal alone never could produce heat, neither alone could Environment. The two are mutually dependent. And although in nearly all the arts we credit everything to the substance which we can weigh and handle, it is certain that in most cases the larger debt is due to an invisible Environment.

This is one of those great commonplaces which slip out of general reckoning by reason of their very largeness and simplicity. How profound, nevertheless, are the issues which hang on this elementary truth, we shall discover immediately. Nothing in this age is more needed in every department of knowledge than the rejuvenescence of the commonplace. In the spiritual world especially, he will be wise who courts acquaintance with the most ordinary and transparent facts of Nature; and in laying the foundations for a religious life he will make no unworthy beginning who carries with him an impressive sense of so obvious a truth as that without Environment there can be no life.

For what does this amount to in the spiritual world? Is it not merely the scientific re-statement of the reiterated aphorism of Christ, "Without Me ye can do nothing"? There is in the spiritual organism a principle of life; but that is not self-existent. It requires a second factor, a something in which to live and move and have its being, an Environment. Without this it cannot live or move or have any being. Without Environment the soul is as the carbon without the oxygen, as the fish without the water, as the animal frame without the extrinsic conditions of vitality.

And what is the spiritual Environment? It is God. Without this, therefore, there is no life, no thought, no energy nothing—"without Me ye can do nothing."

The cardinal error in the religious life is to attempt to live without an Environment. Spiritual experience occupies itself, not too much, but too exclusively, with one factor—the soul. We delight in dissecting this much tortured faculty, from time to time, in search of a certain something which we call our faith—forgetting that faith is but an attitude, an empty hand for grasping an environing Presence. And when we feel the need of a power by which to overcome the world, how often do we not seek to generate it within ourslves by some forced process, some fresh girding of the will, some strained activity which only leaves the soul in further exhaustion? To examine ourselves is good; but useless unless we also examine Environment.

To bewail our weakness is right, but not remedial. The cause must be investigated as well as the result. And yet, because we never see the other half of the problem, our failures even fail to instruct us. After each new collapse we begin our life anew, but on the old conditions; and the attempt ends as usual in the repetition—in the circumstances the inevitable repetition—of the old disaster. Not that at times we do not obtain glimpses of the true state of the case. After seasons of much discouragement, with the sore sense upon us of our abject feebleness, we do confer with ourselves, insisting for the thousandth time, "My soul, wait thou only upon God." But, the lesson is soon forgotten. The strength supplied we speedily credit to our own achievement; and even the temporary success is mistaken for a symptom of improved inward vitality. Once more we go on living without an Environment. And once more, after days of wasting without repairing, of spending without replenishing, we begin to perish with hunger, only returning to God again, as a last resort, when we have reached starvation point.

Now why do we do this? Why do we seek to breathe without an atmosphere, to drink without a well? Why this unscientific attempt to sustain life for weeks at a time without an Environment? It is because we have never truly seen the necessity for an Environment. We have not been working with a principle. We are told to "wait only upon God," but we do not know why. It has never been as clear to us that without God the soul will die as that without food the body will perish. In short, we have never comprehended the doctrine of the Persistence of Force. Instead of being content to transform energy we have tried to create it.

The Law of Nature here is as clear as Science can make it. In the words of Mr. Herbert Spencer, "It is a corollary from that primordial truth which, as we have seen, underlies all other truths, that whatever amount of power an organism expends in any shape is the correlate and equivalent of a power that was taken into it from without." We are dealing here with a simple question of dynamics. Whatever energy the soul expends must first be "taken into it from without." We are not Creators, but creatures; God is our refuge *and strength*. Communion with God, therefore, is a scientific necessity; and nothing will more help the defeated spirit which is struggling in the wreck of its religious life than a common-sense hold of this plain biological principle that without Environment he can do nothing. What he wants is not an occasional view, but a principle—a basal principle like this, broad as the universe, solid as nature. In the natural world we act upon this law unconsciously. We absorb heat, breathe air, draw on Environment all but automatically for meat and drink, for the nourishment of the senses, for mental stimulus, for all that, penetrating us from without, can prolong, enrich, and elevate life. But in the spiritual world we have all this to learn. We are new creatures, and even the bare living has to be acquired.

Now the great point in learning to live is to live naturally. As closely as possible we must follow the broad, clear lines of the natural life. And there are three things especially which it is necessary for us to keep continually in view. The first is that the organism contains within itself only one-half of what is essential to life; the second is that the other half is contained in the Environment; the third, that the condition of receptivity is simple union between the organism and the Environment.

Translated into the language of religion these propositions yield, and place on a scientific basis, truths of immense practical interest. To say, first, that the organism contains within itself only one-half of what is essential to life, is to repeat the evangelical confession, so worn and yet so true to universal experience, of the utter helplessness of man. Who has not come to the conclusion that he is but a part, a fraction of some larger whole? Who does not miss at every turn of his life an absent God? That man is but a part, he knows, for there is room in him for more. That God is the other part, he feels, because at times He satisfies his need. Who does not tremble often under that sicklier symptom of his incompleteness, his want of spiritual energy, his helplessness with sin? But now he understands both—the void in his life, the powerlessness of his will. He understands that, like all other energy, spiritual power is contained in Environment. He finds here at last the true root of all human frailty, emptiness, nothingness, sin. This is why "without Me ye can do nothing." Powerlessness is the normal state not only of this but of every organism—of every organism apart from its Environment.

The entire dependence of the soul upon God is not an exceptional mystery, nor is man's helplessness an arbitrary and unprecedented phenomenon. It is the law of all Nature. The spiritual man is not taxed beyond the natural. He is not purposely handicapped by singular limitations or unusual incapacities. God has not designedly made the religious life as hard as possible. The arrangements for the spiritual life are the same as for the natural life. When in their hours of unbelief men challenge their Creator for placing the obstacle of human frailty in the way of their highest development, their protest is against the order of nature. They object to the sun for being the source of energy and not the engine, to the carbonic acid being in the air and not in the plant. They would equip each organism with a personal atmosphere, each brain with a private store of energy; they would grow corn in the interior of the body, and make bread by a special apparatus in the digestive organs. They must, in short, have the creature transformed into a Creator. The organism must either depend on his environment, or be self-sufficient. But who will not rather approve the arrangement by which man in his creatural life may have unbroken access to an Infinite Power? What soul will seek to remain self-luminous when it knows that "The Lord God is a Sun"? Who will not willingly exchange his shallow vessel for Christ's well of living water? Even if the organism, launched into being like a ship putting out to sea, possessed a full equipment, its little store must soon come to an end. But in contact with a large and bounteous Environment its supply is limitless. In every direction its resources are infinite.

There is a modern school which protests against the doctrine of man's inability as the heartless fiction of a past theology. While some forms of that dogma, to any one who knows man, are incapable of defence, there are others which, to any one who knows Nature, are incapable of denial. Those who oppose it, in their jealousy for humanity, credit the organism with the properties of Environment. All true theology, on the other hand, has remained loyal to at least the root-idea in this truth. The New Testament is nowhere more impressive than where it insists on the fact of man's dependence. In its view the first step in religion is for man to feel his helplessness. Christ's first beatitude is to the poor in spirit. The condition of entrance into the spiritual kingdom is to possess the child-spirit—that state of mind combining at once the profoundest helplessness with the most artless feeling of dependence. Substantially the same idea underlies the countless passages in which Christ affirms that He has not come to call the righteous, but sinners to repentance. And in that farewell discourse into which the Great Teacher poured the most burning convictions of His life, He gives to this doctrine an ever increasing emphasis. No words could be more solemn or arresting than the sentence in the last great allegory devoted to this theme, "As the branch cannot bear fruit of itself except it abide in the vine, no more can ye except ye abide in Me." The word here, it will be observed again, is *cannot*. It is the imperative of natural law. Fruit-bearing without Christ is not an improbability, but an impossibility. As well expect the natural fruit to flourish without air and heat, without soil and sunshine. How thoroughly also Paul grasped this truth is apparent from a hundred pregnant passages in which he echoes his Master's teaching. To him life was hid with Christ in God. And that he embraced this not as a theory but as an experimental truth we gather from his constant confession, "When I am weak, then am I strong."

This leads by a natural transition to the second of the three points we are seeking to illustrate. We have seen that the organism contains within itself only one half of what is essential to life. We have next to observe, as the complement of this, how the second half is contained in the Environment.

One result of the due apprehension of our personal helplessness will be that we shall no longer waste our time over the impossible task of manufacturing energy for ourselves. Our science will bring to an abrupt end the long series of severe experiments in which we have indulged in the hope of finding a perpetual motion. And having decided upon this once for all, our first step in seeking a more satisfactory state of things must be to find a new source of energy. Following Nature, only one course is open to us. We must refer to Environment. The natural life owes all to Environment, so must the spiritual. Now the Environment of the spiritual life is God. As Nature therefore forms the complement of the natural life, God is the complement of the spiritual.

The proof of this? That Nature is not more natural to my body than God is to my soul. Every animal and plant has its own Environment. And the further one inquires into the relations of the one to the other, the more one sees the marvellous intricacy and beauty of the adjustments. These wonderful adaptations of each organism to its surroundings—of the fish to the water, of the eagle to the air, of the insect to the forest-bed; and of each part of every organism—the fish's swim-bladder, the eagle's eye, the insect's breathing tubes—which the old argument from design brought home to us with such enthusiasm, inspire us still with a sense of the boundless resource and skill of Nature in perfecting her arrangements for each single life. Down to the last detail the world is made for what is in it; and by whatever process things are as they are, all organisms find in surrounding Nature the ample complement of themselves. Man, too, finds in his Environment provision for all capacities, scope for the exercise of every faculty, room for the indulgence of each appetite, a just supply for every want. So the spiritual man at the apex of the pyramid of life finds in the vaster range of his Environment a provision, as much higher, it is true, as he is higher, but as delicately adjusted to his varying needs. And all this is supplied to him just as the lower organisms are ministered to by the lower environment, in the same simple ways, in the same constant sequence, as appropriately and as lavishly. We fail to praise the ceaseless ministry of the great inanimate world around us only because its kindness is unobtrusive. Nature is always noiseless. All her greatest gifts are given in secret. And we forget how truly every good and perfect gift comes from without, and from above, because no pause in her changeless beneficence teaches us the sad lessons of deprivation.

It is not a strange thing, then, for the soul to find its life in God. This is its native air. God as the Environment of the soul has been from the remotest age the doctrine of all the deepest thinkers in religion. How profoundly Hebrew poetry is saturated with this high thought will appear when we try to conceive of it with this left out. True poetry is only science in another form. And long before it was possible for religion to give scientific expression to its greatest truths, men of insight uttered themselves in psalms which could not have been truer to Nature had the most modern light controlled the inspiration. "As the hart panteth after the water-brooks, so panteth my soul after Thee, O God." What fine sense of analogy of the natural and the spiritual does not underlie these words. As the hart after its Environment, so man after his; as the water-brooks are fitly designed to meet the natural wants, so fitly does God implement the spiritual need of man. It will be noticed that in the Hebrew poets the longing for God never strikes one as morbid, or unnatural to the men who uttered it. It is as natural to them to long for God as for the swallow to seek her nest. Throughout all their images no suspicion rises within us that they are exaggerating. We feel how truly they are reading themselves, their deepest selves. No false note occurs in all their aspiration. There is no weariness even in their ceaseless sighing, except the lover's weariness for the absent—if they would fly away, it is only to be at rest. Men who have no soul can only wonder at this. Men who have a soul, but with little faith, can only envy it. How joyous a thing it was to the Hebrews to seek their God! How artlessly they call upon Him to entertain them in His pavilion, to cover them with His feathers, to hide them in His secret place, to hold them in the hollow of His hand or stretch around them the everlasting arms! These men were true children of Nature. As the humming-bird among its own palm-trees, as the ephemera in the sunshine of a summer evening, so they lived their joyous lives. And even the full share of the sadder experiences of life which came to all of them but drove them the further into the Secret Place, and led them with more consecration to make, as they expressed it, "the Lord their portion." All that has been said since from Marcus Aurelius to Swedenborg, from Augustine to Schleiermacher of a besetting God as the final complement of humanity is but a repetition of the Hebrew poets' faith. And even the New Testament has nothing higher to offer man than this. The psalmist's "God is our refuge and strength" is only the earlier form, less defined, less practicable, but not less noble, of Christ's "Come unto Me, and I will give you rest."

There is a brief phrase of Paul's which defines the relation with almost scientific accuracy—"Ye are complete in Him." In this is summed up the whole of the Bible anthropology—the completeness of man in God, his incompleteness apart from God.

If it be asked, In what is man incomplete, or In what does God complete him? the question is a wide one. But it may serve to show at least the direction in which the Divine Environment forms the complement of human life if we ask ourselves once more what it is in life that needs complementing. And to this question we receive the significant answer that it is in the higher departments alone, or mainly, that the incompleteness of our life appears. The lower departments of Nature are already complete enough. The world itself is about as good a world as might be. It has been long in the making, its furniture is all in, its laws are in perfect working order; and although wise men at various times have suggested improvements, there is on the whole a tolerably unanimous vote of confidence in things as they exist. The Divine Environment has little more to do for this planet so far as we can see, and so far as the existing gencration is concerned. Then the lower organic life of the world is also so far complete. God, through Evolution or otherwise, may still have finishing touches to add here and there, but already it is "all very good." It is difficult to conceive anything better of its kind than a lily or a cedar, an ant or an ant-eater. These organisms, so far as we can judge, lack nothing. It might be said of them, "they are complete in Nature." Of man also, of man the animal, it may be affirmed that his Environment satisfies him. He has food and drink, and good food and good drink. And there is in him no purely animal want which is not really provided for, and that apparently in the happiest possible way.

But the moment we pass beyond the mere animal life we begin to come upon an incompleteness. The symptoms at first are slight, and betray themselves only an an unexplained restlessness or a dull sense of want. Then the feverishness increases, becomes more defined, and passes slowly into abiding pain. To some come darker moments when the unrest deepens into a mental agony of which all the other woes of earth are mockeries—moments when the forsaken soul can only cry in terror for the Living God. Up to a point the natural Environment supplies man's wants, beyond that it only derides him. How much in man lies beyond that point? Very much—almost all, all that makes man man. The first suspicion of the terrible truth—so for the time let us call it—wakens with the dawn of the intellectual life. It is a solemn moment when the slow-moving mind reaches, at length, the verge of its mental horizon, and, looking over, sees nothing more. Its straining makes the abyss but more profound. Its cry comes back without an echo. Where is the Environment to complete this rational soul? Men either find one—One—or spend the rest of their days in trying to shut their eyes. The alternatives of the intellectual life are Christianity or Agnosticism. The Agnostic is right when he trumpets his incompleteness. He who is not complete in Him must be forever incomplete. Still more grave becomes man's case when he begins further to explore his moral and social nature. The problems of the heart and conscience are infinitely more perplexing than those of the intellect. Has love no future? Has right no triumph? Is the unfinished self to remain unfinished? Again, the alternatives are two, Christianity or Pessimism. But when we ascend the further height of the religious nature, the crisis comes. There, without Environment, the darkness is unutterable. So maddening now becomes the mystery that men are compelled to construct an Environment for themselves. No Environment here is unthinkable. An altar of some sort men must have—God, or Nature, or Law. But the anguish of Atheism is only a negative proof of man's incompleteness. A witness more overwhelming is the prayer of the Christian. What a very strange thing, is it not, for man to pray? It is the symbol at once of his littleness and of his greatness. Here the sense of imperfection, controlled and silenced in the narrower reaches of his being, becomes audible. Now he must utter himself. The sense of need is so real, and the sense of Environment, that he calls out to it, addressing it articulately, and imploring it to satisfy his need. Surely there is nothing more touching in Nature than this? Man could never so expose himself, so break through all constraint, except from a dire necessity. It is the suddenness and unpremeditatedness of Prayer that gives it a unique value as an apologetic.

Man has three questions to put to his Environment, three symbols of his incompleteness. They come from three different centers of his being. The first is the question of the intellect, What is Truth? The natural Environment answers, "Increase of Knowledge increaseth Sorrow," and "much study is a Weariness." Christ replies, "Learn of Me, and ye shall find Rest." Contrast the world's word "Weariness" with Christ's word "Rest." No other teacher since the world began has ever associated "learn" with "Rest." Learn of me, says the philosopher, and you shall find Restlessness. Learn of Me, says Christ, and ye shall find Rest. Thought, which the godless man has cursed, that eternally starved yet ever living specter, finds at last its imperishable glory; Thought is complete in Him. The second question is sent up from the moral nature, Who will show us any good? And again we have a contrast: the world's verdict, "There is none that doeth good, no, not one"; and Christ's, "There is none good but God only." And, finally, there is the lonely cry of the spirit, most pathetic and most deep of all, Where is he whom my soul seeketh? And the yearning is met as before, "I looked on my right hand, and beheld, but there was no man that would know me; refuge failed me, no man cared for my soul. I cried unto Thee, O Lord: I said, Thou art my refuge and my portion in the land of the living."

Are these the directions in which men in these days are seeking to complete their lives? The completion of Life is just now a supreme question. It is important to observe how it is being answered. If we ask Science or Philosophy they will refer us to Evolution. The struggle for Life, they assure us, is steadily eliminating imperfect forms, and as the fittest continue to survive we shall have a gradual perfecting of being. That is to say, that completeness is to be sought for in the organism—we are to be complete in Nature and in ourselves. To Evolution, certainly, all men will look for a further perfecting of Life. But it must be an Evolution which includes all the factors. Civilization, it may be said, will deal with the second factor. It will improve the Environment step by step as it improves the organism, or the organism as it improves the Environment. This is well, and it will perfect Life up to a point. But beyond that it cannot carry us. As the possibilities of the natural Life become more defined, its impossibilities will become the more appalling. The most perfect civilization would leave the best part of us still incomplete. Men will have to give up the experiment of attempting to live in half an Environment. Half an Environment will give but half a Life. Half an

Environment? He whose correspondences are with this world alone has only a thousandth part, a fraction, the mere rim and shade of an Environment, and only the fraction of a Life. How long will it take Science to believe its own creed, that the material universe we see around us is only a fragment of the universe we do not see? The very retention of the phrase "Material Universe," we are told, is the confession of our unbelief and ignorance; since "matter is the less important half of the material of the physical universe."

The thing to be aimed at is not an organism self-contained and self-sufficient, however high in the scale of being, but an organism complete in the whole Environment. It is open to any one to aim at a self-sufficient Life, but he will find no encouragement in Nature. The Life of the Body may complete itself in the physical world; that is its legitimate Environment. The Life of the senses, high and low, may perfect itself in Nature. Even the Life of thought may find a large complement in surrounding things. But the higher thought, and the conscience, and the religious Life, can only perfect themselves in God. To make the influence of Environment stop with the natural world is to doom the spiritual nature to death. For the soul, like the body, can never perfect itself in isolation. The law for both is to be complete in the appropriate Environment. And the perfection to be sought in the spiritual world is a perfection of relation, a perfect adjustment of that which is becoming perfect to that which is perfect.

The third problem, now simplified to a point, finally presents itself. Where do organism and Environment meet? How does that which is becoming perfect avail itself of its perfecting Environment? And the answer is, just as in Nature. The condition is simple receptivity. And yet this is perhaps the least simple of all conditions. It is so simple that we will not act upon it. But there is no other condition. Christ has condensed the whole truth into one memorable sentence, "As the branch cannot bear fruit of itself except it abide in the vine, no more can ye except ye abide in Me." And on the positive side, "He that abideth in Me the same bringeth forth much fruit."

❦

Chapter IX. Semi-Parasitism

Parasites are the paupers of Nature. They are forms of life which will not take the trouble to find their own food, but borrow or steal it from the more industrious. So deep-rooted is this tendency in Nature, that plants may become parasitic—it is an acquired habit—as well as animals; and both are found in every state of beggary, some doing a little for themselves, while others, more abject, refuse even to prepare their own food.

There are certain plants—the Dodder, for instance—which begin life with the best intentions, strike true roots into the soil, and really appear as if they meant to be independent for life. But after supporting themselves for a brief period they fix curious sucking discs into the stem and branches of adjacent plants. And after a little experimenting, the epiphyte finally ceases to do anything for its own support, thenceforth drawing all its supplies ready-made from the sap of its host. In this parasitic state it has no need for organs of nutrition of its own, and Nature therefore takes them away. Henceforth, to the botanist, the adult Dodder presents the degraded spectacle of a plant without a root, without a twig, without a leaf, and having a stem so useless as to be inadequate to bear its own weight.

In the Mistletoe the parasitic habit has reached a stage in some respects lower still. It has persisted in the downward course for so many generations that the young forms even have acquired the habit and usually begin life at once as parasites. The Mistletoe berries, which contain the seed of the future plant, are developed specially to minister to this degeneracy, for they glue themselves to the branches of some neighboring oak or apple, and there the young Mistletoe starts as a dependent from the first. . . .

Why does the naturalist think hardly of the parasites? Why does he speak of them as degraded, and despise them as the most ignoble creatures in Nature? What more can an animal do than eat, drink, and die tomorrow? If under the fostering care and protection of a higher organism it can eat better, drink more easily, live more merrily, and die, perhaps, not till the day after, why should it not do so? Is parasitism, after all, not a somewhat clever ruse? Is it not an ingenious way of securing the benefits of life while evading its responsibilities? And although this mode of livelihood is selfish, and possibly undignified, can it be said that it is immoral?

The naturalist's reply to this is brief. Parasitism, he will say, is one of the gravest crimes in Nature. It is a breach of the law of Evolution. Thou shalt evolve, thou shalt develop all thy faculties to the full, thou shalt attain to the highest conceivable perfection of thy race—and so perfect thy race—this is the first and greatest commandment of Nature. But the parasite has no thought for its race, or for perfection in any shape or form. It wants two things—food and shelter. How it gets them is of no moment. Each member lives exclusively on its own account, an isolated, indolent, selfish, and backsliding life.

The remarkable thing is that Nature permits the community to be taxed in this way apparently without protest. For the parasite is a consumer pure and simple. And the "perfect Economy of Nature" is surely for once at fault when it encourages species numbered by thousands which produce nothing for their own or for the general good, but live, and live luxuriously, at the expense of others?

Now when we look into the matter, we very soon perceive that instead of secretly countenancing this ingenious device by which parasitic animals and plants evade the great law of the Struggle for Life, Nature sets her face most sternly against it. And, instead of allowing the transgressors to slip through her fingers, as one might at first suppose, she visits upon them the most severe and terrible penalties. The parasite, she argues, not only injures itself, but wrongs others. It disobeys the fundamental law of its own being, and taxes the innocent to contribute to its disgrace. So that if Nature is just, if Nature has an avenging hand, if she holds one vial of wrath more full and bitter than another, it shall surely be poured out upon those who are guilty of this double sin. Let us see what form this punishment takes.

Observant visitors to the sea-side, or let us say to an aquarium, are familiar with those curious little creatures known as Hermit-crabs. The peculiarity of the Hermits is that they take up their abode in the cast-off shell of some other animal, not unusually the whelk; and here, like Diogenes in his tub, the creature lives a solitary, but by no means an inactive life.

The *Pagurus* (Hermit Crab), however, is not a parasite. And yet although in no sense of the word a parasite, this way of inhabiting throughout life a house built by another animal approaches so closely the parasitic habit, that we shall find it instructive as a preliminary illustration, to consider the effect of this free-house policy on the occupant. There is no doubt, to begin with, that, as has been already indicated, the habit is an acquired one. In its general anatomy the Hermit is essentially a crab. Now the crab is an animal which, from the nature of its environment, has to lead a somewhat rough and perilous life. Its days are spent among jagged rocks and boulders. Dashed about by every wave, attacked on every side by monsters of the deep, the crustacean has to protect itself by developing a strong and serviceable coat of mail.

How best to protect themselves has been the problem to which the whole crab family have addressed themselves; and, in considering the matter, the ancestors of the Hermit-crab hit on the happy device of re-utilizing the habitations of the molluscs which lay around them in plenty, well-built, and ready for immediate occupation. For generations and generations accordingly, the Hermit-crab has ceased to exercise itself upon questions of safety, and dwells in its little shell as proudly and securely as if its second-hand house were a fortress erected especially for its private use.

Wherein, then, has the Hermit suffered for this cheap, but real solution of a practical difficulty? Whether its laziness costs it any moral qualms, or whether its cleverness becomes to it a source of congratulation, we do not know; but judged from the appearance the animal makes under the searching gaze of the zoologist, its expedient is certainly not one to be commended. To the eye of Science its sin is written in the plainest characters on its very organization. It has suffered in its own anatomical structure just by as much as it has borrowed from an external source. Instead of being a perfect crustacean it has allowed certain important parts of its body to deteriorate. And several vital organs are partially or wholly atrophied.

Its sphere of life also is now seriously limited; and by a cheap expedient to secure safety, it has fatally lost its independence. It is plain from its anatomy that the Hermit-crab was not always a Hermit-crab. It was meant for higher things. Its ancestors doubtless were more or less perfect crustaceans, though what exact stage of development was reached before the hermit habit became fixed in the species we cannot tell. But from the moment the creature took to relying on an external source, it began to fall. It slowly lost in its own person all that it now draws from external aid.

As an important item in the day's work, namely, the securing of safety and shelter, was now guaranteed to it, one of the chief inducements to a life of high and vigilant effort was at the same time withdrawn. A number of functions, in fact, struck work. The whole of the parts, therefore, of the complex organism which ministered to these functions, from the lack of exercise, or total disuse, became gradually feeble; and ultimately, by the stern law that an unused organ must suffer a slow but inevitable atrophy, the creature not only lost all power of motion in these parts, but lost the parts themselves, and otherwise sank into a relatively degenerate condition.

Every normal crustacean, on the other hand, has the abdominal region of the body covered by a thick chitinous shell. In the Hermits this is represented only by a thin and delicate membrane—of which the sorry figure the creature cuts when drawn from its foreign hiding-place is sufficient evidence. Any one who now examines further this half-naked and woe-begone object, will perceive also that the fourth and fifth pair of limbs are either so small and wasted as to be quite useless or altogether rudimentary; and, although certainly the additional development of the extremity of the tail into an organ for holding on to its extemporized retreat may be regarded as a slight compensation, it is clear from the whole structure of the animal that it has allowed itself to undergo severe Degeneration.

In dealing with the Hermit-crab, in short, we are dealing with a case of physiological backsliding. That the creature has lost anything by this process from a practical point of view is not now argued. It might fairly be shown, as already indicated, that its freedom is impaired by its cumbrous eko-skeleton, and that, in contrast with other crabs, who lead a free and roving life, its independence generally is greatly limited. But from the physiological standpoint, there is no question that the Hermit tribe have neither discharged their responsibilities to Nature nor to themselves. If the end of life is merely to escape death, and serve themselves, possibly they have done well; but if it is to attain an ever increasing perfection, then they are backsliders indeed.

A zoologist's verdict would be that by this act they have forfeited to some extent their place in the animal scale. An animal is classed as low or high according as it is adapted to less or more complex conditions of life. This is the true standpoint from which to judge all living organisms. Were perfection merely a matter of continual eating and drinking, the Amoeba—the lowest known organism—might take rank with the highest, Man, for the one nourishes itself and saves its skin almost as completely as the other. But judged by the higher standard of Complexity, that is, by greater or lesser adaptation to more or less complex conditions, the gulf between them is infinite.

We have now received a preliminary idea, although not from the study of a true parasite, of the essential principles involved in parasitism. And we may proceed to point out the correlative in the moral and spiritual spheres. We confine ourselves for the present to one point. The difference between the Hermit-crab and a true parasite is, that the former has acquired a semi-parasitic habit only with reference to safety. It may be that the Hermit devours as a preliminary the accommodating mollusc whose tenement it covets; but it would become a real parasite only on the supposition that the whelk was of such size as to keep providing for it throughout life, and that the external and internal organs of the crab should disappear, while it lived henceforth, by simple imbibation, upon the elaborated juices of its host. All the mollusc provides, however, for the crustacean in this instance is safety, and, accordingly in the meantime we limit our application to this. The true parasite presents us with an organism so much more degraded in all its parts, that its lessons may well be reserved until we have paved the way to understand the deeper bearings of the subject.

The spiritual principle to be illustrated in the meantime stands thus: *Any principle which secures the safety of the individual without personal effort or the vital exercise of faculty is disastrous to moral character.* We do not begin by attempting to define words. Were we to define truly what is meant by safety or salvation, we should be spared further elaboration, and the law would stand out as a sententious common-place. But we have to deal with the ideas of safety as these are popularly held, and the chief purpose at this stage is to expose what may be called the Parasitic Doctrine of Salvation. The phases of religious experience about to be described may be unknown to many. It remains for those who are familiar with the religious conceptions of the masses to determine whether or not we are wasting words.

What is meant by the Parasitic Doctrine of Salvation one may, perhaps, best explain by sketching two of its leading types. The first is the doctrine of the Church of Rome; the second, that represented by the narrower Evangelical Religion. *We take these religions, however, not in their ideal form, with which possibly we should have little quarrel, but in their practical working, or in the form in which they are held especially by the rank and file of those who belong respectively to these communions.* For the strength or weakness of any religious system is best judged from the form in which it presents itself to, and influences the common mind.

No more perfect or more sad example of semi-parasitism exists than in the case of those illiterate thousands who, scattered everywhere throughout the habitable globe, swell the lower ranks of the Church of Rome. Had an organization been specially designed, indeed, to induce the parasitic habit in the souls of men, nothing better fitted to its disastrous end could be established than the system of Roman Catholicism. Roman Catholicism offers to the masses a a molluscan shell. They have simply to shelter themselves within its pale, and they are "safe." But what is this "safe"? It is an external safety—the safety of an institution. It is a salvation recommended to men by all that appeals to the motives in most common use with the vulgar and the superstitious, but which has as little vital connection with the individual soul as the dead whelk's shell with the living Hermit. Salvation is a relation at once vital, personal, and spiritual. This is mechanical and purely external. And this is of course the final secret of its marvelous success and world-wide power. A cheap religion is the desideratum of the human heart; and an assurance of salvation at the smallest possible cost forms the tempting bait held out to a conscience-stricken world by the Romish Church. Thousands, therefore, who have never been taught to use their faculties in "working out their own salvation," thousands who will not exercise themselves religiously, and who yet cannot be without the exercises of religion, intrust themselves in idle faith to that venerable house of refuge which for centuries has stood between God and man. A Church which has harbored generations of the elect, whose archives enshrine the names of saints whose foundations are consecrated with martyrs' blood—shall it not afford a sure asylum still for any soul which would make its peace with God? So, as the Hermit into the molluscan shell, creeps the poor soul within the pale of Rome, seeking, like Adam in the garden, to hide its nakedness from God.

Why does the true lover of men restrain not his lips in warning his fellows against this and all other priestly religions? It is not because he fails to see the prodigious energy of the Papal See, or to appreciate the many noble types of Christian manhood nurtured within its pale. *Nor is it because its teachers are often corrupt and its system of doctrine inadequate as a representation of the Truth—charges which have to be made more or less against all religions.* But it is because it ministers falsely to the deepest need of man, reduces the end of religion to selfishness, and offers safety without spirituality. *That these, theoretically, are its pretensions, we do not affirm; but that its practical working is to induce in man, and in its worst forms, the parasitic habit, is testified by results.* No one who has studied the re-

ligion of the Continent upon the spot, has failed to be impressed with
the appalling spectacle of tens of thousands of unregenerate men
sheltering themselves, as they conceive it for Eternity, behind the
Sacraments of Rome.

There is no stronger evidence of the inborn parasitic tendency in
man in things religious than the absolute complacency with which
even cultured men will hand over their eternal interests to the care
of a Church. We can never dismiss from memory the sadness with
which we once listened to the confession of a certain foreign professor: "I used to be concerned about religion," he said in substance,
"but religion is a great subject. I was very busy; there was little time
to settle it for myself. A Protestant, my attention was called to the
Roman Catholic religion. It suited my case. And instead of dabbling
in religion for myself I put myself in its hands. Once a year," he
concluded, "I go to mass." These were the words of one whose work
will live in the history of his country, one, too, who knew all about
parasitism. Yet, though he thought it not, this is parasitism in its
worst and most degrading form. Nor, in spite of its intellectual, not
to say moral sin, is this an extreme or exceptional case. It is a case,
which is being duplicated every day in our own country, only here
the confession is expressed with a candor which is rare in company
with actions betraying so signally the want of it.

The form of parasitism exhibited by a certain section of the narrower Evangelical school is altogether different from that of the
Church of Rome. The parasite in this case seeks its shelter, not in a
Church, but in a Doctrine or a Creed. *Let it be observed again that
we are not dealing with the Evangelical Religion, but only with one
of its parasitic forms*—a form which will at once be recognized by
all who know the popular Protestantism of this country. We confine
ourselves also at present to that form which finds its encouragement
in a single doctrine, that doctrine being the Doctrine of the Atonement—let us say, rather, a perverted form of this central truth.

The perverted Doctrine of the Atonement, which tends to beget
the parasitic habit, may be defined in a single sentence—it is very
much because it can be defined in a single sentence that it is a per-

version. Let us state it in a concrete form. It is put to the individual in the following syllogism: "You believe Christ died for sinners; you are a sinner; therefore Christ died for you; *and hence you are saved.*" Now what is this but another species of molluscan shell? Could any trap for a benighted soul be more ingeniously planned? It is not a superstition that is appealed to this time; it is reason. The agitated soul is invited to creep into the convolutions of a syllogism, and entrench itself behind a Doctrine more venerable even than the Church. But words are mere chitine. Doctrines may have no more vital contact with the soul than priest or sacrament, no further influence on life and character than stone and lime. And yet the apostles of parasitism pick a blackguard from the streets, pass him through this plausible formula, and turn him out a convert in the space of as many minutes as it takes to tell it.

The zeal of these men, assuredly, is not to be questioned: their instincts are right, and their work is often not in vain. It is possible, too, up to a certain point, to defend this Salvation by Formula. Are these not the very words of Scripture? Did not Christ Himself say, "It is finished"? And is it not written, "By grace are ye saved through faith," "Not of works, lest any man should boast," and "He that believeth on the Son hath everlasting life"? To which, however, one might also answer in the words of Scripture, "The Devils also believe," and "Except a man be born again he cannot see the Kingdom of God." But without seeming to make text refute text, let us ask rather what the supposed convert possesses at the end of the process. That Christ saves sinners, even blackguards from the streets, is a great fact; and that the simple words of the street evangelist do sometimes bring this home to man with convincing power is also a fact. But in ordinary circumstances, when the inquirer's mind is rapidly urged through the various stages of the above piece of logic, he is left to face the future and blot out the past with a formula of words.

To be sure these words may already convey a germ of truth, they may yet be filled in with a wealth of meaning and become a lifelong power. But we would state the case against Salvation by Formula with ignorant and unwarranted clemency did we for a moment convey the idea that this is always the actual result. The doctrine plays too well into the hands of the parasitic tendency to make it possible that in more than a minority of cases the result is anything but disastrous. And it is disastrous not in that, sooner or later, after losing half their lives, those who rely on the naked syllogism come to see their mistake, but in that thousands never come to see it at all. Are there not men who can prove to you and to the world, by the irresistible logic of texts, that they are saved, whom you know to be not only unworthy of the Kingdom of God—which we all are—but absolutely incapable of entering it? The condition of membership in the Kingdom of God is well known; who fulfill this condition and who do not, is not well known. And yet the moral test, in spite of the difficulty of its applications, will always, and rightly, be preferred by the world to the theological. Nevertheless, in spite of the world's verdict, the parasite is content. He is "safe." Years ago his mind worked through a certain chain of phrases in which the words "believe" and "saved" were the conspicuous terms. And from that moment, by all Scriptures, by all logic, and by all theology, his future was guaranteed. He took out, in short, an insurance policy, by which he was infallibly secured eternal life at death. This is not a matter to make light of. We wish we were caricaturing instead of representing things as they are. But we carry with us all who intimately know the spiritual condition of the Narrow Church in asserting that in some cases at least its members have nothing more to show for their religion than a formula, a syllogism, a cant phrase or an experience of some kind which happened long ago, and which men told them at the time was called Salvation. Need we proceed to formulate objections to the parasitism of Evangelicism? Between it and the Religion of the Church of Rome there is an affinity as real as it is unsuspected. For one thing these religions are spiritually disastrous as well as theologically erroneous in propagating a false conception of Christianity. The fundamental idea alike of the extreme Roman Catholic and extreme Evangelical Religions is Escape. Man's chief end is to "get off." And all factors in religion, the highest and most sacred, are degraded to this level. God, for example, is a Great Lawyer, Or

He is the Almighty Enemy; it is from Him we have to "get off." And Jesus Christ is the One who gets us off—a theological figure who contrives so to adjust matters federally that the way is clear. The Church in the one instance is a kind of conveyancing office where the transaction is duly concluded, each party accepting the other's terms; in the other case, a species of sheep-pen where the flock awaits impatiently and indolently the final consummation. Generally, the means are mistaken for the end, and the opening-up of the possibility of spiritual growth becomes the signal to stop growing.

Second, these being cheap religions, are inevitably accompanied by a cheap life. Safety being guaranteed from the first, there remains nothing else to be done. The mechanical way in which the transaction is effected, leaves the soul without stimulus, and the character remains untouched by the moral aspects of the sacrifice of Christ. He who is unjust is unjust still; he who is unholy is unholy still. Thus the whole scheme ministers to the Degeneration of Organs. For here, again, by just as much as the organism borrows mechanically from an external source, by so much exactly does it lose in its own organization. Whatever rest is provided by Christianity for the children of God, it is certainly never contemplated that it should supersede personal effort. And any rest which ministers to indifference is immoral and unreal—it makes parasites and not men. Just because God worketh in him, as the evidence and triumph of it, the true child of God works out his own salvation—works it out having really received it—not as a light thing, a superfluous labor, but with fear and trembling as a resonable and indispensable service.

If it be asked, then, shall the parasite be saved or shall he not, the answer is that the idea of salvation conveyed by the question makes a reply all but hopeless. But if by salvation is meant, a trusting in Christ *in order to likeness to Christ*, in order to that *holiness* without which no man shall see the Lord, the reply is that the parasite's hope is absolutely vain. So far from ministering to growth, parasitism ministers to decay. So far from ministering to holiness, that is to *wholeness*, parasitism ministers to exactly the opposite. One by one the spiritual faculties droop and die, one by one from lack of exercise the muscles of the soul grow weak and flaccid, one by one the moral activities cease. So from him that hath not, is taken away that which he hath, and after a few years of parasitism there is nothing left to save.

If our meaning up to this point has been sufficiently obscure to make the objection now possible that this protest against Parasitism is opposed to the doctrines of Free Grace, we cannot hope in a closing sentence to free the argument from a suspicion so ill-judged. The adjustment between Faith and Works does not fall within our province now. Salvation truly is the free gift of God, but he who really knows how much this means knows—and just because it means so much—how much of consequent action it involves. With the central doctrines of grace the whole scientific argument is in too wonderful harmony to be found wanting here. The natural life, not less than the eternal, is the gift of God. But life in either case is the beginning of growth and not the end of grace. To pause where we should begin, to retrograde when we should advance, to seek a mechanical security that we may cover inertia and find a wholesale salvation in which there is no personal sanctification—this is Parasitism.

Chapter X. Parasitism

Nature never provides for man's wants in any direction, bodily, mental, or spiritual, in such a form as that he can simply accept her gifts automatically. She puts all the mechanical powers at his disposal —but he must make his lever. She gives him corn but he must grind it. She elaborates coal, but he must dig for it. Corn is perfect, all the products of Nature are perfect, but he has everything to do to them before he can use them. So with truth; it is perfect, infallible. But he cannot use it as it stands. He must work, think, separate, dissolve, absorb, digest; and most of these he must do for himself and within himself. If it be replied that this is exactly what theology does, we answer it is exactly what it does not do. It simply does what the greengrocer does when he arranges his apples and plumbs in his shop-window. He may tell me a Magnum Bonum from a Victoria, or a Baldwin from a Newtown Pippin. But he does not help me to eat it.

His information is useful, and for scientific horticulture essential. Should a skeptical pomologist deny that there was such a thing as a Baldwin, or mistake it for a Newtown Pippin, we should be glad to refer to him; but if we were hungry, and an orchard were handy, we should not trouble. Truth in the Bible is an orchard rather than a museum. Dogmatism will be very valuable to us when scientific necessity makes us go to the museum. Criticism will be very useful in seeing that only fruit-bearers grow in the orchard. But truth in the doctrinal form is not natural, proper, assimilable food for the soul of man.

The final chapter of Natural Law in the Spiritual World, *"Classification," is really a discussion of Evolution, and the unity toward which it tends, and to the final triumph of continuity, Christianity, which discerns the end through the means and calls it Redemption. This section . . . sums up the thesis of his book, pulls together the main points of the other chapters, and leaves the individual Christian with knowledge of the Christian way of Salvation.*

❦

The tests for Life are of two kinds. It is remarkable that one of them was proposed, in the spiritual sphere, by Christ. Foreseeing the difficulty of determining the characters and functions of rudimentary organisms, He suggested that the point be decided by a further evolution. Time for development was to be allowed, during which the marks of Life, if any, would become more pronounced, while in the meantime judgment was to be suspended. "Let both grow together," He said, "until the harvest." This is a thoroughly scientific test. Obviously, however, it cannot assist us for the present —except in the way of enforcing extreme caution in attempting any classification at all.

The second test is at least not so manifestly impracticable. It is to apply the ordinary methods by which biology attempts to distinguish the organic from the inorganic. The characteristics of Life, according to Physiology, are four in number—Assimilation, Waste, Reproduction, and Spontaneous Action. If an organism is found to exercise these functions, it is said to be alive. Now these tests, in a spiritual sense, might fairly be applied to the spiritual man. The experiment would be a delicate one. It might not be open to every one to attempt it. This is a scientific question; and the experiment would have to be conducted under proper conditions and by competent persons. But even on the first statement it will be plain to all who are familiar with spiritual diagnosis that the experiment could be made, and especially on oneself, with some hope of success. . . . We are merely showing, at the moment, that the question "How do I know that I am alive" is not, in the spiritual sphere, incapable of solution. One might, nevertheless, single out some distinctively spiritual function and ask himself if he consciously discharged it. The discharging of that function is, upon biological principles, equivalent to being alive, and therefore the subject of the experiment could certainly come to some conclusion as to his place on a biological scale. The real significance of his actions on the moral scale might be less easy to determine, but he could at least tell where he stood as tested by the standard of life—he would know whether he was living or dead. After all, the best test of Life is just *living*. And living consists, as we have formerly seen, in corresponding with Environments. Those therefore who find within themselves, and regularly exercise, the faculties for corresponding with the Divine Environment, may be said to live the Spiritual Life. . . .

But if man's place among the Kingdoms is determined by his functions, a careful estimate of his life in itself and in its reaction upon surrounding lives, ought at once to betray his real position. No matter what may be the moral uprightness of his life, the honorableness of his career, or the orthodoxy of his creed, if he exercises the function of loving the world, that defines his world—he belongs to the Organic Kingdom. He cannot in that case belong to the higher Kingdom. "If any man love the world, the love of the Father is not in him." After all, it is by the general bent of a man's life, by his heart-impulses and secret desires, his spontaneous actions and abiding motives, that his generation is declared.

The exclusiveness of Christianity, separation from the world, uncompromising allegiance to the Kingdom of God, entire surrender of body, soul, and spirit to Christ—these are truths which rise into prominence from time to time, become the watchword of insignificant parties, rouse the church to attention and the world to opposition, and die down ultimately for want of lives to live them. The few enthusiasts who distinguish in these requirements the essential conditions of entrance into the Kingdom of Christ are overpowered by the weight of numbers, who see nothing more in Christianity than a mild religiousness, and who demand nothing more in themselves or in their fellow Christians than the participation in a conventional worship, the acceptance of traditional beliefs, and the living of an honest life. Yet nothing is more certain than that the enthusiasts are right. Any impartial survey . . . of the claims of Christ and of the nature of His society, will convince any one who cares to make the inquiry of the outstanding difference between the system of Christianity in the original contemplation and its representations in modern life. Christianity marks the advent of what is simply a new Kingdom. Its distinctions from the Kingdom below it are fundamental. It demands from its members activities and responses of an altogether novel order. It is, in the conception of its Founder, a Kingdom for which all its adherents must henceforth exclusively live and work, and which opens its gates alone upon those who, having counted the cost, are prepared to follow it if need be to the death. The surrender Christ demanded was absolute. Every aspirant for membership must seek first the Kingdom of God. And in order to enforce the demand of allegiance, or rather with an unconsciousness which contains the finest evidence for its justice, He even assumed the title of King—a claim which in other circumstances, and were these not the symbols of a higher royalty, seems so strangely foreign to one who is meek and lowly in heart.

But this imperious claim of a Kingdom upon its members is not peculiar to Christianity. It is the law in all departments of Nature that every organism must live for its Kingdom. And in defining living for the higher Kingdom as the condition of living in it, Christ enunciates a principle which all Nature has prepared us to expect. Every province has its peculiar exactions, every Kingdom levies upon its subjects the tax of an exclusive obedience, and punishes disloyalty always with death. It was the neglect of this principle—that every organism must live for its Kingdom if it is to live in it—which first slowly depopulated the spiritual world. The example of its Founder ceased to find imitators, and the consecration of His early followers came to be regarded as a superfluous enthusiasm. And it is this same misconception of the fundamental principle of all Kingdoms that has deprived modern Christianity of its vitality. The failure to regard the exclusive claims of Christ as more than accidental, rhetorical, or ideal; the failure to discern the essential difference between His Kingdom and all other systems based on the lines of natural religion, and therefore merely Organic; in a word, the general neglect of the claims of Christ as the Founder of a new and higher Kingdom—these have taken the very heart from the religion of Christ and left its evangel without power to impress or bless the world. Until even religious men see the uniqueness of Christ's society, until they acknowledge to the full extent its claim to be nothing less than a new Kingdom, they will continue the hopeless attempt to live for two Kingdoms at once. And hence the value of a more explicit Classification. For probably the most of the difficulties of trying to live the Christian life arise from attempting to half-live it. . . .

This is the final triumph of Continuity, the heart secret of Creation, the unspoken prophecy of Christianity. To Science, defining it as a working principle, this mighty process of amelioration is simply *Evolution*. To Christianity, discerning the end through the means, it is Redemption. . . .

Natural Law made its mark upon the entire religious world. One who heard it read first as a young man and remembered it vividly as an old man said, "It was a book so strange, so new in every respect, that we all loved to hear it, and could hardly hear too much. It was not a book of sermons, and yet it was tremendous preaching. It was not a religious book in the ordinary sense, and yet how full of religion; a deeply spiritual book, and yet as fascinating as a novel. How much it has done for the religious thinking and for the religious speech of the world. How reasonable it made religion, how simple and terrible its processes."[1]

1 Ralph Connor.

For those who want to read more, copies of Natural Law can be found in countless editions and formats in secondhand bookstores, on the shelves of homes which go back to the early nineteen hundreds, and in many public libraries.

"The Ascent of Man"

*H*ENRY DRUMMOND'S Lowell Lectures in Boston in April, 1893, were of such tremendous public interest that speculators bought up whole blocks of tickets for the series and sold them at fabulous prices. Everyone was curious to see and hear the famous author of Natural Law. For everyone who got in, ten were turned away. Drummond was forced to repeat each lecture the following day to satisfy the demand. A year later, after rather hasty revision because of the threat of a premature unofficial edition in America, the lectures were published in book form under the title The Ascent of Man.

In Natural Law Drummond had attempted to carry physical processes into the region of the moral and spiritual; in The Ascent he attempted the opposite task of showing the ethical at work in regions of life generally supposed to be given over to purely physical laws. He succeeded in exhibiting among the lower stages of the evolution of life bases and opportunities suitable for the action of moral feelings and for the formation of moral habits.

Whereas Darwin placed the major accent on the struggle for life, Drummond added what he considered a neglected emphasis, the struggle for the life of others. Nature had in it two factors, the self—survival of the fittest, and the other—the preservation of offspring. Drummond maintained and attempted to show that from the very beginning of life, selfishness and altruism were working side by side.

In this book he said he was presenting a history, not an argument—
self-ism and other-ism, the Prodigal Son and the Good Samaritan in
scientific language. Drummond believed that evolution was "God's
way of doing things"—"first the blade, then the ear, after that the
full corn in the ear."

Because of his forthright acceptance of evolution and Biblical
criticism, Drummond barely escaped persecution by the Free
Church, which had already dealt so drastically with W. Robertson
Smith. No less than twelve "overtures" (motions or petitions) were
brought before the General Assembly in May, 1895, shortly after
Drummond was stricken by the onset of the disease which proved to
be fatal. All of these overtures were based on The Ascent of Man.
He was ably defended by his brilliant friends, James Stalker and
Marcus Dods, and the charges were dismissed.

In the "Preface" Drummond confesses that evolution is assumed
as a working hypothesis throughout. He traces the development of
the individual during the earliest stages of his evolution, and his rise
as far as family life. He begins with the first principle of evolution—
the struggle for life. He ends with another great principle as a factor
in evolution—the struggle for the life of others. In his chapters on
"The struggle for the Life of Others," "The Evolution of the
Mother," and "The Evolution of the Father," Drummond makes
his own particular contribution to the teachings of evolution. In
these chapters he traces the dawn and development of altruism, unselfishness, duty, and the rudiments of a sense of righteousness. The
headings of his other chapters indicate the contents of each: "The
Ascent of the Body"; "The Scaffolding Left in the Body"; "The
Arrest of the Body"; "The Dawn of the Mind"; and "The Evolution
of Language."

In an extended introductory chapter Drummond sketches his
attitude toward evolution and the need for recognizing the great
principle of "The Struggle for the Life of Others." He claims that
evolution is "The Story of Creation as told by those who know it
best." He alleges that the danger in applying evolution as a method is
that it may not be carried far enough. If nature is the garment of God,

it is woven without seam throughout; if a revelation of God, it is the same yesterday, today, and forever; if the expression of His will, there is no variableness nor shadow of turning.

In a final chapter, "Involution," Drummond seeks to show an essential identity between Christianity and evolution. Both are methods of creation; both have for their object the making of more perfect living beings; both work through love. "Evolution and duty have the same author, the same end, the same spirit. There is no rivalry between these processes. Duty struck into the evolutionary process with no noise nor shock; it upset nothing of all that had been done; it took all the natural foundations precisely as it found them; it carried on the building by slow and gradual modification; and, through processes governed by rational laws, it put the finishing touches to The Ascent of Man."

Had Henry Drummond lived to follow out the hints contained in this last chapter, he had it in him to do the work of an evangelist to the scientific and cultured classes (many of whom he did reach) for which the great work he had already done would have seemed but a preparation. Part of the last chapter is quoted, not only because of these "hints" but for the summing up he gives to his entire theme.

❦

... The miracle of Evolution is not the process, but the product. Beside the wonder of the result, the problem of the process is a mere curiosity of Science. For what is the product? It is not mountain and valley, sky and sea, flower and star, this glorious and beautiful world in which Man's body finds its home. It is not the god-like gift of Mind nor the ordered cosmos where it finds so noble an exercise for its illimitable powers. It is that which of all other things in the universe commends itself, with increasing sureness as time goes on, to the reason and to the heart of Humanity—Love. Love is the final result of Evolution. That is what stands out in Nature as the supreme creation. Evolution is not progress in matter. Matter cannot progress. It is a progress in spirit, in that which is limitless, in that which is at once most human, most rational, and most divine. Whatever controversy rages as to the factor of Evolution, whatever mystery enshrouds its steps, no doubt exists of its goal. The great landmarks we have passed, and we are not yet half-way up the Ascent, each separately and all together have declared the course of Nature to be a rational course, and its end a moral end. At the furthest limit of time, in protoplasm itself, we saw start forth the two great currents which, by their action and reaction, as Selfishness and Unselfishness, were to supply in ever accentuating clearness the conditions of the moral life. Following their movements upward through the organic kingdom, we watched the results which each achieve—always high, and always waxing higher; and though what we called evil dogged each step with sinister and sometimes staggering malevolence, the balance when struck, was always good upon the whole. Then came the last great act of the organic process, the act which finally revealed to teleology its hitherto obscured end, the organization of the Mammalia, the Kingdom of the Mothers. So full of ethical possibility is this single creation that one might stake the character of evolution upon the Mammalia alone. On the biological side, as we have seen, the evolution of the Mammalia means the Evolution of Mothers; on the sociological side, the Evolution of the Family; and on the moral side, the Evolution of Love. How are we to characterize a process which ripened fruits like these? That the very animal kingom had for its end and crown a class of animals who owe their name, their place, and their whole existence to Altruism; that through these Mothers society has been furnished with an institution for generating, concentrating, purifying and re-distributing Love in all its enduring forms; that the perfecting of Love is thus not an incident in Nature, but everywhere the largest part of her task, begun with the first beginnings of life, and continuously developing quantitatively and qualitatively to the close—all this has been read into Nature by our own imaginings, or it is the revelation of a purpose of benevolence and a God whose name is Love. The skeptic, we are sometimes reminded, has presented crucial difficulties to the theist founded on the doctrine of Evolution. Here is a problem which the theist may leave with the skeptic. That that which has emerged has the qualities it has, that even the Mammalia should have emerged, that that class should stand related to the life of Man in the way it does, that Man has lived because he loved, and that he lives to love—these, on any theory but one, are insoluble problems. . . .

Up to this time no word has been spoken to reconcile Christianity with Evolution, or Evolution with Christianity. And why? Because the two are one. What is Evolution? A method of creation. What is its object? To make more perfect living beings. What is Christianity? A method of creation. What is its object? To make more perfect living beings. Through what does Evolution work? Through Love. Through what does Christianity work? Through Love. . . .

No man can run up the natural lines of Evolution without coming to Christianity in this way. But science has to deal with facts and with all facts, and the facts and processes which have received the name of Christian are the continuations of the scientific order, as much the successors of these facts and the continuations of these processes—due allowances being made for the differences in the planes, and for the new factors which appear with each new plane—as the facts and processes of biology are of those of the mineral world. We land here, not from choice, but from necessity. Christianity—it is not said [of] any particular form of Christianity—but Christianity, is the Further Evolution. . . .

The Ascent of Man and of Society is bound up henceforth with the conflict, the intensification, and the diffusion of the Struggle for the Life of Others. This is the Further Evolution, the page of history that lies before us, the closing act of the drama of Man. . . . The further Evolution must go on, the Higher Kingdom come—first the blade, where we are today; then the ear, where we shall be tomorrow; then the full corn in the ear, which awaits our children's children, and which we live to hasten.

Once again we have found the "poetry" of Drummond's science and the "suggestiveness" of his religion and have faced up to words that have not yet outrun their meaning.

Part III

HIS METHODS

1

"Spiritual Diagnosis"

*T*HE doctrines of the Christian religion are being re-examined with relentless thoroughness today. The trend of thinking is theological. The religious intellectuals of our century want solid foundations to stand on concerning the meaning of existence. Two world wars, the frightening possibilities of scientific advance, the frenzied pursuit of pagan ideologies, and the earnest efforts to unify Christendom have pushed men's thinking into deeper channels than those provided by the liberalism of the early years of our century. This swing away from the mere ethical emphasis of the Christian religion and the presentation of Jesus Christ as a good man and teacher, has resulted in such marked trends as neo-orthodoxy (with God's judgment and man's impotence to the fore), existentialism (stemming mainly from Kierkegaard, with many secular distortions, seeking to give an adequate underlying meaning to human existence), and re-statements of essential orthodoxy by many different individuals and groups, especially in the area of ecumenical relations—such as the World Council of Churches' Commission on "Faith and Order," and its statements on "Grace" and "The Nature of the Church."

The emphasis upon Jesus as Lord and Savior, as Redeemer and Reconciler, as God Himself, more nearly reveals the power of the Gospel found in the New Testament. There must be sound doctrine promulgated (to combat the Jesus-a-Good-Man heresy)—that man on his own is impotent, that only God can save him from himself, that God's gift of free will enables him to choose God's way to life or his own way to death, that Life beyond life is oneness with God and His will for man. But also to the fore, as a major emphasis, must come the necessity for conversion, a change of attitude and action in keeping with His will, and an understanding of the modern scientific approach to the Bible which enhances rather than destroys its usefulness. Such a conversion and such a knowledge of the Bible eliminates the fears of Drummond's day and provides a creative instrument for keeping man straight concerning the choices before him—self-destruction, or Redemption through Jesus Christ.

Theologians must continue to formulate statements of faith according to the truth revealed to them. But unless Christ becomes a living reality at the center of men's lives, unless the Gospel comes home personally to men by confronting them with the Person of Christ, unless men's lives are changed by Him, the formulated creedal statements of theologians, important as they are, cannot re-structure a man's faith. It is at this point Henry Drummond made his contribution. He bridged the gap between faith and practice; he led men to a re-thinking of Christianity and the acceptance of the results of that thinking in concrete terms of application. He faced men with the challenge of a Christ centered life in such a way they could not escape it. He did not ignore theology but emphasized living out the doctrine.

The Free Church had settled down to a theological stuffiness which stifled the living Spirit of Christ. The reality, freedom and life-changing power of the Gospel were blocked off from the ignorant, sinful and fettered lives that looked up but were not fed. Drummond realized that the mere preaching of sermons was not enough, that the majority of hearers were unaffected, that the preacher ought to come down and acquaint himself with the condition of his hearers one by one. Just as a doctor examines the cases in a hospital individually before pronouncing his diagnosis and prescribes the treatment, so the chief business of the Christian ministry should be thought of as clinical and not homiletical or theological. If one in physical pain should consult a doctor, certainly one with a sense of guilt should consult a minister.

So Henry Drummond presented his method of "spiritual diagnosis." The method was not new. It was used by Jesus. The pages of the New Testament are filled with examples. Our Lord called His disciples one by one; He dealt with sin, disease and misery case by case; His disciples learned their method from Him and, like Philip the Evangelist, Peter and Paul, and the rest, approached individuals as the Holy Spirit guided them. They were always ready to give specific answers to such questions as "What must I do to be saved, to find eternal life, to overcome temptation, to forsake sin, to settle unbelief, to cure my disease?" Their method was simple and practical, clear and immediate. The Church continued to produce men who were evangelists and who spent their lives going about and speaking the "good news" to all who would hear.

Henry Drummond was not the first one to recapture Jesus' method of one-by-one, but he did enunciate afresh to a bewildered generation the amazing truth of the Gospel and its power for making life new and different. This Gospel Henry Drummond presented as immediately believable and accessible. "Darwin's Origin of Species had come into the theological world like a plough into an ant-hill." Everywhere those who were thus rudely awakened from their old comfort and unthinking repose had swarmed forth angry and confused—and frightened. They forgot, for the moment, the Gospel injunction "the truth shall make you free." They also forgot that the main purpose of the Christian Church was to lead men to repentance and to new lives in Christ.

Henry Drummond, who knew his science, also knew His Gospel, and brought forth at a critical time a technique for fulfilling the Church's primary task "to preach the gospel to every creature . . ." and to see that our Lord's command "repent ye" led to changed lives. The timing was perfect. His presentation to the Theological Society that evening in November, 1873, of his paper "Spiritual Diagnosis," stirred those who heard to the possibilities of this "new" method; Moody's Great Mission began within the month and pulled many of these same young men into its tremendous sweep through Scotland; and the principles and methods, purely theoretical as laid down in Drummond's paper, were given a thorough and severe testing. Henry's long hours of thought and concern over the subject were not wasted, for the theories stood the test of application and "Spiritual Diagnosis" became a classic which marked the beginning of the modern movement of scientific, personal evangelism. Drummond never needed to revise the basic theories of this essay. It is not out-of-date but is still a valuable guide for those who are not yet experts in the technique of personal evangelism. The core of Henry Drummond's teaching on how to exercise the God-given power of the Christian religion to witness and to win is given in "Spiritual Diagnosis—An Argument for Placing the Study of the Soul on a Scientific Basis."

The study of the soul in health and disease ought to be as much an object of scientific study and training as the health and diseases of the body.

It has long been one of the favorite axioms of Apologetics, that a Christian life is the best argument for Christianity. . . . A free-thinker may go very far without meeting an argument to throw him back upon his own inner soul, but no one can live long, be he in high life or low life, without coming within the influence of a Christian man. . . .

Every atom in the universe can act on every other atom, but only through the atom next it. And if a man would act upon every other man, he can do so best by acting, one at a time, upon those beside him. . . .

But the capacity of acting upon individuals is now almost a lost art. It is hard to learn again. . . . Yet we must begin again, and begin far down. Christianity began with one. We have forgotten the simple way of the Founder of the greatest influence the world has ever seen —how He ran away from cities, how He shirked mobs, how He lagged behind the rest at Samaria to have a quiet talk with one woman at a well, how He stole away from crowds and entered into the house of one Syro-Phoenician woman. . . . In small groups of twos and threes He collected the early Church around Him. One by one the disciples were called—and there were only twelve in all. We all know well enough how to move the masses; we know how to draw a crowd around us, but to attract the units—that is the hard matter. . . . To draw souls one by one, to buttonhole them and steal from them the secret of their lives, to talk them clean out of themselves, . . . this is the spiritual science which is so difficult to acquire and so hard to practice. . . .

Of the three elements, body, mind, and soul, which make up a responsible human being, two only have been hitherto treated as fit subjects for scientific inquiry. . . . But the half is not accounted for. We wish . . . a spiritual psychology to tell us of the unseen realities of the soul. . . . It is an extraordinary and momentous fact that by far the most important factor in human life has been up to this time all but altogether ignored by the thinking world. . . . If the mind is large enough and varied enough to make a philosophy of mind possible, is the soul such a trifling part of man that it is not worth while seeking to frame a science of it—a science of it which men can learn, and which can be a guide and help in practice to all who feel an interest in the deepest thing in human life? It is no use to say there is no special soul—that there is a strange never-comprehended essence, half emotion, half affection, half reason, half unearthliness. . . . But this is the mere concealment of ignorance in mystery. There is a soul, and there is a spiritual life. . . .

Are we content to let this great spiritual life work silently around us without attempting to know more about it, analyze it, to make it more accessible to us and us to it? Are we to regard it as some weird element, unapproachable, mysterious, unstable, incomprehensible in its essence? There is, it is true, an element about it which keeps us at our distance from it; but as its groundwork is human, may we not see the points where it touches the human, the changes it effects, the hindrances to the changes, and the wonderful complexity of action and interaction which it originates? Are there materials here for a philosophy, and is it lawful to reduce it to a science? Can there, in short, be a *science of spirituality?*

... The facts of physical science lie in the order of the natural, and they are finite. The facts of spiritual science, if we may call it so, lie in the order of the supernatural, and they are infinite. They are pervaded by an element which no man can fathom. ... We look in a man's soul for that which we saw there yesterday, but the unseen influence has swept across the heart, and the spiritual scenery is changed. The man himself is the same, his passions unaltered in their strength, his foibles unchanged in their weakness, but the furniture of the soul has been moved, and the spiritual machinery goes on upon a new and suddenly developed principle. Here, then, our investigations are stopped at the outset. Dare we approach no nearer? Often we would fain do so. Often we are placed in such circumstances that plainly we must do so. A friend is in trouble, we are in trouble. But how are we to proceed? What guide have we in ministering to a soul diseased?

Is there no guide-book upon the subject, no chart or table of the logical history of the spiritual life, no chair of Spiritual Diagnosis? ... It is a dangerous thing to put forms and processes which exist only in the logical imagination into the hands of the inquirer. But when these works (writings of men who knew and practiced the science of the soul) are put into the hands of the Christian teacher or minister, their utility is beyond all praise. He, as spiritual adviser, should be thoroughly acquainted with the principles of conversion. He should know [them] as a physician his pharmacopoeia. He should know every phase of the human soul, in health and disease, in the fulness of joy and the blackness of despair. . . . The scheme of salvation, as we are accustomed to call it, should be ever clearly defined in his consciousness. The lower stages, the period of transition, its solemnity, its despairs, its glimmering light, its growing faith; and the Christian life begun, the laborious working out in fear and trembling, the slavish scrupulosity, still the fearfulness of fall, still remorse, more faith, more hope; and last of all the higher spiritual life, the realization of freedom, the disappearance of the slavish scrupulosity, the pervasion of the whole life with God. . . .

Let now any think that such knowledge is easily attained; nor have many attained it. The men to whom you or I would go if spiritual darkness spread across our souls, who are they? How few have penetration enough to diagnose our case, to observe our least apparent symptoms, to get out of us what we had resolved not to tell them, to see through and through us the evil and the good. Plenty there are to preach to us, but who will interview us, and anatomize us, and lay us bare to God's eye and our own? . . . To take [a person] by himself; to feel his pulse alone, and give him one particular earnest word—the only word that would do—all to himself—this is the simple feat which [we] look in vain for men to perform. . . . [God] hath appointed us to be our brother's keeper, nor will He do for my brother what could be done by me. We cannot expect the Spirit's help to teach us what only laziness and personal indifference hinder us from learning; and to despise a power which He gave us capacities to possess is not the way to show that we trust Him who gave it. . . .

This study of the Soul . . . is a difficult study. It is difficult, because the Soul as far transcends the mind in complexity and in variety as the mind the body. The Soul is an infinitely large subject—an infinitely deep and mysterious subject. . . .

Every man is a problem to every other man—much more every spiritual man. It is hard to know a man's brain, and harder to know his feelings; but the hardest of all is to know his religious convictions. It is hard to know the deepest that a man has. . . . The difficulty of analyzing our neighbor's character arises from the fact that every man is in reality a *threefold* man. When two persons are in conversation, there are really six persons in conversation. . . . Suppose that John and Tom are in conversation, there are *three Johns* and *three Toms*, who are accounted for in this way: Three Johns—the real John, known only to his Maker; John's ideal John, John as he thinks himself, never the real John, and often very unlike him; Tom's ideal of John, John as Tom thinks him, never the real John, nor John's John, but often unlike either. Three Toms—The real Tom, Tom's ideal Tom, John's ideal Tom.

In this way when I talk to another it is not me that he hears talking, but his ideal of me; nor do I talk to him as he defines himself, but to my ideal of him. Now that ideal will, without almost inconceivable care and penetration on my part, be quite differnt also from his real self as God only knows him, so that instead of speaking to his real soul, I may possibly be speaking to his ideal of his own soul, or more likely to my ideal of it.

From this it will be seen at a glance that the power of soul analysis is a hard thing to possess oneself of. It requires intense discrimination and knowledge of human nature—much and deep study of human life and character. The man with whom you speak being made up of two ideals—his own and yours, and one real—God's, it is one of the hardest possible tasks to abandon your ideal of him and get to know the real—God's. Then, having known it, so far as possible to man, there remains the greatest difficulty of all—to introduce him to himself. You have created a new man for him, and he will not recognize him at first. He can see no resemblance to his ideal self; the new creature is not such a lovely picture as he would like to own; the lines are harshly drawn, and there is little grace and no poetry in it. But he must be told that none of us is what he seems; and if he would deal faithfully with himself, he must try to see himself differently from what he seems. Then he must be led with much delicacy to make a little introspection of himself; and with the mirror lifted to his own soul you read off together some of the indications which are defining themselves vaguely upon its surface. Even in social and domestic circles the difficulty of performing this apparently simple operation upon human nature is so keenly felt that scarce one friend will be found with a friendship true enough to perform it to another. And in religious matters it will be at once conceded that the complexity of the difficulties increases the problem a hundredfold.

There is a danger, however, . . . in exaggerating these difficulties; and . . . the further objection . . . that, by attaching so much importance to the human power, we take away the one great element in salvation—its Divine freeness through the grace of God.

Is not religion for the poor and illiterate, is not the way easy to find? Thank God it is so! So little can man do to enlighten it. But he can do something, and he ought to do more. . . . Not for himself does man live. Every action of every man has an ancestry and a posterity— an ancestry and a posterity in other lives. . . . How do you explain that most wonderful phenomenon . . . *the silence of God?* God keeping silence! And man doubting and sinning and repenting all alone, and groping blindfold after truth, and losing his way and working out his salvation with painful trembling and fear! It is an unfathomable mystery; but may it not be, in small part, just for this that, on the one hand, God offers man the glory and honor of sharing His work; and on the other, that He wishes human souls to be graven with the marks of other human souls in all their free and infinite variety? God is a God of variety. No two leaves are the same, no two sand grains, no two souls. And as the universe would be but a poor affair if every leaf were the counterpart of the oak leaf or the birch, so would the spiritual world present but a sorry spectacle if we were all duplicates of John Calvin. Therefore has God made room for individual action in the building up of His Kingdom upon earth; and therefore it is not a presumption but a duty for every man to be molding and making the souls around him, to be perfecting and guiding his own faculties for this great work.

The great danger in doing this work, next to doing it without any education for it, is to overdo it. In dealing with a case which is once put into our hands we are apt to consider it too much of a professional and personal matter. Our influence has become too conscious. We have found what a powerful thing it may become, and we seek a "reputation for influence." Thus our pride is smitten if success does not at once crown our efforts, and we attempt to second them by unlawful means. We assume the didactic when we should simply be attractive or suggestive. We encourage the favorable and forget to notice an unfavorable symptom. . . . And, finally, we assume too much upon ourselves, forgetting that we are but fellow-workers together with God, and by taking too officious an interest, the individual, making nothing of it, is apt to throw the responsibility of non-success upon us, and so spoil not only our whole influence with others, but his own chance of being bettered in the future by others. . . .

We do wish a scientific treatment of the subject; and if there is anything to sadden and humble in the contemplation of the religious work of the day, it is the thought of the crude and slipshod treatment of one of the most sacred subjects in the religious life.

We are not ignoring the power of God in conversion by not speaking of it. You say He can work with the roughest tools even on the finest of marbles. Without denying it, He would not polish diamonds on grindstones if he could get lapidaries to do it better. It won't do to talk religiously, or complacently, or *blasphemously* of trusting in Him when we are too lazy to qualify ourselves for being worth the using in His service. Don't fear that we shall become too acute at diagnosing and prescribing for souls, and so take the matter out of God's hands.

And now . . . as to the great subject of the training and exercise of the power of spiritual discernment, what is it possible for us to say? . . . .

[The great men of religion] were most of them wanting in that delicacy of handling which makes analysis effective instead of insulting; . . . they were quite destitute of the foremost quality which distinguishes the successful diagnosist—respect, veneration even, for the soul of another. A man may be ever so gross and vulgar, but when you come to deal with the deepest that is in him, he becomes sensitive and feminine. Brusqueness and an impolite familiarity may do very well when dealing with his brains, but without tenderness and courtesy you can only approach his heart to shock it. The whole of etiquette is founded on respect; and by far the highest and tenderest etiquette is the etiquette of soul and soul.

To know and remember the surpassing dignity of the human soul —for its own sake, for its great God-like elements, for its immortality, above all for His sake who made it and gave Himself for it—this is the first axiom to be remembered. . . .

We must try to be . . . "a man that knows men in the street, at their work, human nature in its shirt-sleeves—who makes bargains with deacons instead of talking over texts with them, and a man who has found out that there are plenty of praying rogues and swearing saints in the world."

. . . If any man develop this faculty of reading others, of reading them in order to profit by them, he will never be without practice. Men do not say much about these things, but the amount of spiritual longing in the world at the present moment is absolutely incredible. No one can ever even faintly appreciate the intense spiritual unrest which seethes around him; but one who has tried to discern, who has begun by private experiment, by looking into himself, by taking observations upon the people near him and known to him, has witnessed a spectacle sufficient to call for the loudest and most emphatic action. . . . I have but vaguely hinted at this subject; I venture to think it a question of vital interest, giving life a mission, giving a new and burning interest even to the most commonplace surroundings, and opening up a field for life-long study and effort.

In this pioneering essay Drummond advanced a thesis which became the outline for a workable method of personal evangelism. His insistence that the regular work of the pulpit should be supplemented by constant dealing with individuals about their spiritual state changed the very nature of the pastoral ministry. In maintaining that the mere preaching of sermons leaves the majority of hearers unaffected, and that the preacher should come down from the pulpit and acquaint himself with the conditions of his hearers one by one, as a doctor examines his cases in a hospital, Drummond revolutionized the ineffective ivory tower approach, common in his day and ours. By the application of his thesis (with its immediate and thorough testing in the Great Mission) he proved his point that this clinical approach was the chief business of the Christian ministry.

Henry Drummond believed in personal dealing more and more, and in the inadequacy of mere preaching. He popularized such terms as "diagnosis" and "clinical" which led men to explore psychological methods of soul therapeutics more thoroughly. Such studies as James' The Varieties of Religious Experience, Begbies' Twice-Born Men, Walters' Soul Surgery, Shoemaker's Twice-Born Ministers, Zahniser's The Soul Doctor, Jones' Social Law in the Spiritual World tell part of the story. Drummond made the clinical treatment of sin something like a literal process, a case history, not something theoretical. Although there have been many distortions and abuses of this method by shallow and unconsecrated men who were not of Drummond's spiritual stature, it still remains the best technique of personal evangelism.

It was Henry Drummond who inspired such great evangelicals as Bishop Stephen C. Neill, who, in the Drummond tradition, said to a group of clergy and laity at a great convention: "In your journey back to your parishes, you must ask if God gives you some responsibility to be of service to Him—and what strange things have happened to me in my personal experience of journeys (all over the world)! That doesn't mean we have to be the fusty kind of Evangelicals or get involved in other people's affairs. It does mean we should be sensitive, watchful, always ready to speak that word God gives us when we look around at the desperate need of men and women, the urgent tragic need of men and women." For example, if one were reading this book in public, on some journey perhaps, and an inquiry was made, "Who is Henry Drummond?"—one could tell what has been discovered so far and continue as the inquirer gives opportunity and as God leads.

Ian Maclaren, one of Drummond's close friends, may have had him in mind as he wrote the story "Beside the Bonnie Briar Bush," where he contrasted the theological wisdom of the young minister with the wiser wisdom of the old elder in the words spoken by the latter—"Speak a good word for the Lord Jesus."

Dwight L. Moody urged men to do personal work—"Jump in and try it; go at it; you will make mistakes enough to keep you humble."

Henry Drummond heeded this injunction and found miracles of redemption unfolding before his eyes, following some word from God through him, and under his touch.

2

The Inquiry Room

*S*INCE the theory of clinical diagnosis and treatment enunciated by Drummond in "Spiritual Diagnosis" was tested and proven correct in the inquiry room of the Great Mission, we need to examine this method more closely.

Just before Chicago was destroyed by flames in 1871 Mr. Moody had dismissed a congregation, telling them to go home and think what they would do with Christ. He never met them again. He regarded this as one of the greatest mistakes of his life, and he determined never to repeat it. From that time on he laid great stress on the after-meeting, which took place at the close of an evangelistic address, in which he tried to bring individual souls to an immediate decision as to the great issues he had just brought before them.

"Personal dealing is of the most vital importance," said Mr. Moody in discussing the inquiry room and its uses. "No one can tell how many souls have been lost through lack of following up the preaching of the Gospel by personal work. It is deplorable how few church members are qualified to deal with inquirers. And yet that is the very work in which they ought to aid the pastor most efficiently. People are not usually converted under the preaching of a minister. It is in the inquiry meeting that they are most likely to be brought to Christ.

"Some people can't see the use of the inquiry meetings; they think they are something new, and that we haven't any authority for them.

234

But they are no innovation. We read about them all through the Bible. When John the Baptist was preaching, he was interrupted. It would be a good thing if people would interrupt the minister now and then in the middle of some metaphysical sermon and ask what he means. The only way to make sure that people understand what he is talking about is to let them ask questions. I don't know what some men who have got the whole thing written out would do if some one should get up and ask, 'What must I do to be saved?' Yet such questions would do more good than anything else you could have. They would wake up a spirit of inquiry.

"Some people say, 'All you want to do is to make the preaching so plain that plain people will understand it.' Well, Christ was a plain preacher, and yet he asked, 'Have ye understood all these things?' (St. Matthew 13:5.) He encouraged them to inquire. I think sometimes, when the minister is preaching over their heads, people would be greatly relieved if he would stop and ask whether they understood it. His very object is to make the Word of God clear. Christ was a plain preacher; but when He preached to Saul the man was only awakened. Christ could have convicted and converted him, but He honored a human agency, and sent Ananias to tell the word whereby he was to be saved. Philip was sent away into the desert to talk to one man in the chariot. We must have personal work—hand-to-hand work—if we are going to have results."[1]

It was first in face to face encounter in Moody's inquiry room—later in private talks almost everywhere—that Henry Drummond learned how to be a successful fisher of men. His voice, his eyes, his sympathy, his strength, his personal charm stirred men to hope and inspired their confidence, enabling them to trust him with their past.

A great deal of the work was painful. "Such tales of woe I've heard in Moody's inquiry room that I've felt I must go and change my very clothes after the contact." Yet he never flinched from the ordeal and found great joy in the participation in what he felt was the great need of the churches, to provide a place where men might fight to a finish

[1] The Life of Dwight L. Moody, by his son, William R. Moody (New York: Fleming H. Revell Company, 1900), pp. 488-93.

the battle against specific evils, to give an opportunity for spiritual cartharsis. Drummond maintained that no matter how helpful sermons were, they must be made specific. And he believed every minister should provide the opportunity for people to come to him after the service, by appointment, on the street, at a dinner or a meeting, or "by night," and have the age old desire, "Sir, we would see Jesus," satisfied. The inquiry room was simply a means of giving the "how" and the "why" of the Christian religion in small, personal doses, made to fit the individual's spiritual longing and unrest.

Today we need to pull aside the curtains of this innermost sanctuary of souls and try to recapture the techniques which still apply. These "anxious inquirers" apparently had their needs met and were sent on their way rejoicing. Drummond never said much about the actual dealing with individuals. He felt he must keep these "tales of woe" inviolate. But what we as Christians (both laity and clergy) need to know today is the method he used so successfully in the inquiry room, a technique to master and use in the form which fits each situation best—how to help people get out of their "slough of despond," out of the "bog and mire" of their doubts and sins.

A close study of "Spiritual Diagnosis" will reveal the principles which became his stock-in-trade, will furnish the clues to the way Drummond carried through his belief in "the recoverableness of man at his worst." A rough outline of his method follows.[2]

His first task was to win a man's confidence, which he did through his message, his very person and attitude, and to establish close harmonious relations with him. Since no two persons were alike the approach varied with the individual before him. Each experience added to his knowledge of human nature, developed his spirit of apprehension and discernment, and gave him quicker access to the soul of another.

This led inevitably to a man pouring out his heart to him in private confession. He unlocked men's hearts and learned the worst about them. He probed as a doctor to find the real block, the real difficulty

[2] The five headings or stages are taken from Soul Surgery, Chap. II. "The Principle of Personal Evangelism."

or infection, the last little stronghold unyielded to God. He was supremely tactful in dealing with individuals. Tenderness and courtesy, founded on respect, were essential in dealing with souls laid bare before him. He always sought for the festering sore of moral degradation more earnestly than the frequent substitute of "intellectual" difficulties. Drummond sought to uncover that one definite sin with which the secret history of the individual was woven through and through, which he preferred to Christ and found so hard to give up. It frequently took drastic measures to get all the poison out. John R. Mott once said, out of his experience in dealing with sinful persons in the Drummond tradition, "It is awfully hard to deal honestly with sin in one's effort to be tactful and sympathetic, but a surgeon is not friendly if he fails to put in the knife and remove the cause of the malady."

First win the confidence, second hear the confession, and third strive to bring the man to a point of conviction. Most of those who sought Drummond in the inquiry room were already convicted and were ready to do what was necessary to begin a new life on a different basis from the old. Drummond sought to show men the wonder of their real selves in Christ. He was always "convincing men of righteousness," showing them how much they had missed of the "unsearchable riches of Christ." He led each man to the conviction that only as he appropriated fully God's great gift of life could he be truly his real self.

The next step was conversion. Drummond brought men into a new relationship with Christ; thousands changed the direction of their lives under his influence during this brief time with him in the inquiry room. The success of Drummond in leading men to make this decision depended in large measure on his ability to translate the basic facts of Christian faith into simple language—into the man's own language—with complete freedom from religious clichés, superficiality, "pat" answers, and "a holier than thou" attitude. Because Christ was real to Drummond he made Him real to others. Just here was and is the crux of all evangelistic success—the reality of Christ. Unless and until Christ comes alive in a man's life, no man will want to tell others or can tell others to win them, regardless of his knowledge of "techniques." Drummond possessed many natural gifts and had tremendous power over the lives of others; but everyone, as he finally gives his life to Christ, can tell the story as far as he has learned it, ever growing in effectiveness. To accept Christ and begin living life for Him—this is conversion and the climax of all personal evangelistic work.

The hardest part of all was the conservation of the progress made and a continuation of the process so well begun. The aftermath, the long and difficult road ahead, was all-important. The first blush of enthusiasm would fade. Therefore here was a need for developing a continuous prayer life and fellowship with others going along the same way of life. Drummond made this clear one evening to a group in these words:

"I cannot guarantee that the stars will shine brighter when you leave this hall to-night, or that when you wake to-morrow a new world will open before you. But I do guarantee that Christ will keep that which is committed to Him. He will keep His promise, and you will find something real and dependable to rely on and to lead you away from documental evidence to Him who speaks in your hearts at this moment. Gentlemen, He will be your leader, He will be your guide, He will be your highest ideal. He has asked you for your life, and He will make you, just as you are, at this moment His—entirely His."

Fundamentally, the inquiry-room technique, under Moody, was simply an opportunity to make concrete and vocal a decision to be a fully committed Christian and to get a few of the more important problems straightened out. The brief moment in the after-session was only a beginning. It was the chance to confirm and make public to another the inner decision which had already been made. The most important part of the work was the follow-up, the continuing contact at definite times and places, a growing practice and fellowship in the new way of life.

Sample of an attempt to apply this technique today:

FOR AN AFTER-SERMON INQUIRY

(Those who wish to pursue further any part of the sermon, concerning clarification, personal problems, implications, techniques, and the like.)

Name ....

Address ....

Telephone number—Home.....Business......

Would like to see the Pastor (state the most convenient time for you) Day......Hour.......

Place....................................

(Note: The Pastor will call Sunday evening to confirm this date or, if this is not convenient, check here and call him Monday morning ☐ .)

3

Beyond Moody

*T*HE methods Henry Drummond learned under Moody were refined and reshaped especially for the student work at the Edinburgh Oddfellows Hall meetings. He made good use of the inquiry-room technique. A student (Ralph Connor) describes one of these after-meetings. "When his address was over he stood looking at us out of those marvelous eyes of his with a kind of yearning look, and then in the frankest . . . manner, he invited any man who would like to have a little private conversation with him on the matter to step into the side room. By some strange tact of his own, he gave us the feeling that it would be a perfectly natural . . . and manly thing for anyone to go and speak to him about that Friend. Leaving this invitation with the meeting Drummond passed into a side room. The singing went on, and here and there over the hall and from the gallery men got up and passed through the door through which Drummond had disappeared."

When asked at Northfield about this "after-meeting" Drummond replied: "We say the night is early, and there will be a half-hour or an hour of free talk, and that the men are invited to gather in knots all over the room and just talk over these things a little. Three or four men have their eye generally on a man, and they get into conversation with him. The hall is kept open an hour or so, and by the end of that time a good deal has been done. There is a great deal more done on the street. As a man goes away from the meeting somebody

walks with him to his lodgings. That is how our after-session works."
(This method has been developed in group dynamics today as "buzz
sessions.")

There was no excitement attached to these after-meetings but
many "anxious inquirers"—beset by doubt, fear, dishonesty, frustration, cursing, gambling, sex—were guided to peace. The address
got the men to the point of knowing what to say so that only a few
moments were necessary for talking with Drummond and taking
their first step, making their initial decision. Usually those who were
waiting to see Drummond were engaged in conversation with another
student until their turn in the small side room. When Drummond
found the conversation needed to be prolonged he made a date
for seeing this man later in the evening or the next morning in St.
George's Square or arranged for a special trip back from Glasgow the
following Saturday. His rendezvous for talks and walks were famous,
and few could resist his appeal to come under the mastership of
Christ.

The conversations and the walk-talks were endless. To a numerous
number of students, through ten school terms, these evenings at the
Oddfellows Hall were the turning point of life; to countless others
the conversations with one or two, the private talk that followed on
the street or in the lodgings ("digs") left seeds which bore fruit in
many corners of the globe. Drummond was at his best in these con-
versational walks. His eyes, already trained to miss nothing, caught his
themes and illustrations from nature and people, and turned them to
good account as he walked and talked things through with some confused and guilt-ridden student. Some tree formation, a bird flashing
past, a flower; some incident on a street corner, the view from the
Castle Esplanade, a Punch and Judy show, a pile of trunks at Wa-
verly Station, the quiet and beauty of "The Meadows" and St.
George's Park—all he saw pertinent to the problem at hand was
woven into the conversation.

Unfortunately one must imagine what went on after these Sunday
evening meetings, but a sufficient number of anecdotes in extant letters and reminiscences make clear what actually took place. Since

most of the students lived across "The Meadows" there was always a chance for a brisk walk in the cold of winter, with a scarf around the neck, ending up in the student's "digs" where the conversation was finished under the flare of a gas jet in front of a smoky fire in the grate. One can still trace the many walkways Henry Drummond took with his "anxious inquirers" with whom he walked until a decision was made or a problem of mind or conscience was settled.

Since the follow-up and the continuous training and fellowship were so important for the newly started Christian, and since it took more than one walk or talk to settle the changed life into a new discipline and growth, many adjuncts to the Oddfellows Hall meetings were provided, and furnished further examples of Henry Drummond's methods in winning University men to the Christian way of life. Of course all the men were encouraged to belong to some church. In addition, Bible-reading and prayer-learning groups were formed and met regularly in some hospitable place—opened regularly were the homes of the Simpsons, the Whytes, the Barbours, the Charterises, the Dodses, and others. These gatherings, usually on Saturdays, of some twenty-five or thirty students and faculty members, consisted mainly of a lot of "free conversation" all intended to instruct and enrich the lives recently committed to Christ.

During the summer months Bible study and reading, and small prayer groups, went on without interruption by twos and threes in the students' rooms or larger groups in homes. Special gatherings were arranged for an uninterrupted period of several days at places like Bonskeid House, where the Barbours often invited groups. Then, of course, there were the holiday missions and the deputations to other universities. All of these activities deepened the students' personal knowledge of Christ and His way and improved their ability to bring others into personal relationship with the Lord Jesus Christ. Other outlets for the new life of zeal and service inspired by the Oddfellows Hall meetings were the "University Settlement" work and visiting hospitals, especially the Royal Infirmary where so many of the young medical students were at home.

Drummond raised up a great band of speakers and workers who

learned and practiced the methods of the new evangelism. The deep and abiding impression of such work formed indelibly the characters of students who carried this experience with them into their communities as professional men who were also Christians. That hall near "The Meadows" and those "walks" influenced these men all their lives long because they had listened to and heard the one who introduced them to Jesus Christ as Lord and Master.

A Note on Source Material

THERE are only two ways to find material on Henry Drummond. One is to try the library; the other is to haunt the secondhand bookshops. There are usually copies of various editions of his addresses, one or more of the many editions of *Natural Law*, and an occasional copy of one of his biographies to be found. (Try to find a copy of *The Life of Henry Drummond* by George Adam Smith or the title *Henry Drummond* in the Famous Scots Series by James Young Simpson.) But all the written sources have been out of print for a long time. That is, all except a few addresses, especially one. From the very beginning *The Greatest Thing in the World* has never been out of print in English and can be purchased in almost any bookstore. That is the main reason this volume was attempted —to restore the life and works, in part, of Henry Drummond and make them available to the average reader.

Every scrap of information which could be tracked down in Scotland was consulted, especially in Edinburgh, Glasgow, Stirling and Aberdeen, all the way from personal records and reminiscences to the full resources of several great libraries—New College, Edinburgh, Trinity College, Glasgow, University of Edinburgh and the National Library of Scotland.

A very special word of appreciation goes to the librarians of New College and Trinity College—the Rev. Messrs. Primrose and James Mackintosh; to the members of Henry Drummond's family as well as friends and admirers—especially his nephew J. Graham Drummond and the Earl and Marquis of Aberdeen; and to many others for their kindness, generosity and help given to a stranger in pursuit of the living spirit of Henry Drummond—a grandnephew H. J. H. Drummond, a grandniece Mrs. Donald Macrae, a niece Mrs. Irvine Robertson, a grandniece Mrs. Norah Walker, the widow of James Young Simpson—one of Drummond's biographers, the Vicar of the Henry Drummond Parish Church, Possilpark, the Rev. Keith Spence and many others, not least of whom was my wife who made this book possible and who helped greatly in selecting and editing the Drummond material.

Index

Finite, 175
"First," 57
Follower of Christ, 126
Fraternity, 94
Free Church College, 31, 33, 34, 47, 59
Free Church of Scotland, 22, 26-27, 33-34, 217, 222
Free Church Theological Society, 173
Free Grace, 210
Free St. Cuthbert's Church, 23
Free St. George's Church, 45
Friendship, 115, 157, 170
Frustration, 241
Further Evolution, 220

"Gaiety Club, The," 30, 51
Gambling, 241
Geikie, Professor Archibald, 23, 31, 36
General Assembly, The Free Church, 33, 39, 47, 217
Generosity, 163-64, 168
Gentleman, 165
Geology, 23, 32, 36, 75, 81, 118, 146
Giving, 165-66
Gladness, 150
Glenelm Lodge, 19-20
God, 69, 72, 77, 81, 110, 144, 157, 164, 169, 176, 188, 196, 222, 229
God's image, 95
Good Samaritan, 217
Good Temper, 163, 166
"Good-tidings," 150
Gordon, Frank (Ralph Connor), 30
Gospel, The, 147, 155, 159, 170, 173, 178-79, 181, 222-24
Grace, 116, 207, 222, 229
Great Mission, The, 25, 27-29, 45, 47, 53, 224, 231, 234
Greatest Need of the World, The, 110
Greatest Thing in the World, The, 53, 131, 160, 171, 245
Greyfriars' Church, 60
Grosvenor House, 47-49, 143, 160
Guilelessness, 163, 166
"Gum," 57

Hado House, 49, 61
Happiness, 92, 95, 164
Harvard, 50-51, 56, 118, 130

Heart, 196
Heaven, 95, 162
Heaviness, 150-52
Heredity, 183-84
Hodder & Stoughton, 38
Holiness, 163, 209
Holmes, Ralph W., 36
Holy Spirit, 69, 223
Holiday Missions, 46, 50
Humility, 137, 163-64
Humanity, 145-46, 150, 157, 173, 191, 218
Human nature, 228
Humble, 168

Ideal Life, The, 31, 86, 96
Ideals, 129, 146
Ideologies, 221
"Ill-Temper," 86, 88, 93
Image, 114, 117-18, 169, 175, 194
Imagination, 175, 177-78
Incarnation, The, 81, 176
Incompleteness, 196
Indulgences, 177
Infinity, 152, 175
Inquirer, 232
"Inquiry room," 27-28, 234-36, 239-40
Intellect, 175, 196, 237
"Involution," 218

Japan, 52
Jesus Christ, 171, 173, 221
Jones, Rufus M., 180, 232
Joy, 131, 132, 149-51
Junior League, 18-19
Justice, 176

Kierkegaard, 222
Kindness, 163, 168, 171
King's Park, 19-20
Kingdom of God, 136, 147-48, 156-57, 159, 208, 212

Law, 143, 156, 159, 162, 167, 176, 181, 183, 189, 196, 200
Law of causation, 70
Lamb, Charles, 21, 60, 128
Language, 119, 130, 237
Language of religion, 119

Pessimism, 196
Peter, 147, 162, 223
Phelps, William Lyon, 51
Philip the Evangelist, 223, 235
Philomathic Debating Society, 21
Philosopher, 197
Philosophy, 35, 41, 69, 141, 155, 159, 171, 174, 197
Pleasure, 164
Poetry, 193
Possilpark, 34-36, 47, 61-62, 96, 143
Possilpark Church, 86
Posterity, 229
Power, 161
Practice, 121, 124, 135, 167-68
Praise, 149
Prayer, 32, 70, 92, 115-16, 171, 196, 242
Prevention, 156
Pride, 135
"Prince, The," 22
Principle, 186
"Problem of Foreign Missions, The," 52
Procrastination, 146
Prodigal Son, The, 92, 217
"Professor," 42
Program of Christianity, The, 49, 131, 145, 149-50, 155
Progress, 218, 238
Propaganda, 159
Protestant, 206
Psychology, 225, 232
Purity, 176

Rationalism, 174
Reality, 237
Reason, 174-77, 207
Receptivity, 198
Reconciliation, 181, 222
Redeemer, 222
Redemption, 157, 170, 211, 214, 222, 233
Regeneration, 64, 69, 76, 101, 170
Relationship, 237
"Relationship theology," 142
Religion, 44, 64, 119, 125, 140, 144-45, 159, 167, 169-70, 174, 181, 206, 208, 229
Renfield Free Church, 35-36

Repentance, 224
Respect, 230
Rest, 131, 138, 142, 197
Restlessness, 132-33, 141
Revelation, 76-77, 173, 175
Revised Version, 167-68
Riego Street Mission, 23, 56
Right, 196
Righteousness, 127, 217
Robertson of Brighton, 21
Rocky Mountains, 36, 161
Roman Catholicism, 204, 206
Ross, David Morison, 30
Royal Infirmary, 242

Sacrifice, 169
Safe, 205
Salvation, 79, 170, 205, 208-11, 227, 229
Salvation by Formula, 207
Sanctification, 117, 143, 154
Sanctifying, 116, 126
Saul, 98, 235
Save, 145-47
Saved, 171, 207-8
Savior, 146, 149, 154, 222
Schleiermacher, 194
Science, 31-32, 36, 40, 66, 70, 72, 74, 77, 180-81, 183, 192, 198, 214, 218, 220, 224
Science and religion, 22, 31, 36-37, 52, 65-66
Science of spirituality, 226
Scientific authorities, 124
Scientific method, The, 68, 70-72, 77
Scientific spirit, The, 71
Scientific theology, 25, 69, 77, 80
Scriptures, 207-8
"Seek ye first the kingdom of God," 44, 57, 64, 127, 130
Self-denial, 165
Selfishness, 87, 94, 135, 144, 205, 216, 219
Self-restraint, 167
Semi-parasite, 201
Sensitive, 232
Sermons, 120
Serving, 166
Sex, 241
Shoemaker, Samuel M., 232

Set in Linotype Electra
Format by Katharine Sitterly
Manufactured by The Haddon Craftsmen, Inc.
Published by HARPER & BROTHERS, New York